Political Mourning

Heather Pool

Political Mourning

*Identity and Responsibility
in the Wake of Tragedy*

TEMPLE UNIVERSITY PRESS
Philadelphia • Rome • Tokyo

TEMPLE UNIVERSITY PRESS
Philadelphia, Pennsylvania 19122
tupress.temple.edu

A version of Chapter 2 appeared as "The Politics of Mourning: The Triangle Fire and
Political Belonging" in *Polity* 44, no. 2 (April 2012): 182–211. A version of Chapter 3
appeared as "Mourning Emmett Till" in *Law, Culture and the Humanities* 11, no. 3
(October 2015): 414–444.

Library of Congress Cataloging-in-Publication Data

Names: Pool, Heather N. author.
Title: Political mourning : identity and responsibility in the wake of tragedy /
  Heather Pool.
Description: Philadelphia : Temple University Press, 2021. | Includes bibliographical
  references and index. | Summary: "Political Mourning examines four case studies—the
  Triangle Fire, Emmett Till's murder, the attacks of September 11th, and the Black Lives
  Matter movement—to shed light on moments when everyday people died, when their
  deaths were the basis of calls for political change, and when such a change actually
  occurred"—Provided by publisher.
Identifiers: LCCN 2020038672 (print) | LCCN 2020038673 (ebook) | ISBN 9781439918920
  (cloth) | ISBN 9781439918937 (paperback) | ISBN 9781439918944 (pdf)
Subjects: LCSH: Till, Emmett, 1941–1955—Death and burial—Public opinion. | Triangle
  Shirtwaist Company—Fire, 1911—Public opinion. | September 11 Terrorist Attacks,
  2001—Public opinion. | Black lives matter movement—Public opinion. | Grief—Political
  aspects—United States. | Bereavement—Political aspects—United States. | Social
  problems—United States—Case studies.
Classification: LCC HN59.2 .P657 2021 (print) | LCC HN59.2 (ebook) |
  DDC 303.48/40973—dc23
LC record available at https://lccn.loc.gov/2020038672
LC ebook record available at https://lccn.loc.gov/2020038673

Printed in the United States of America

9 8 7 6 5 4 3 2 1

To Lisa, my partner in joy, sorrow,

and everything in between

Contents

Preface

Reading, writing, and thinking about death is hard. Witnessing it is even harder. Those of us who lived through and remember September 11, 2001, recall its profound impact even if we were thousands of miles away. Practically all of us remember where we were when we heard. Those of us close enough to experience the devastation of that day firsthand have a different set of memories. This topic—political mourning—grew out of my own experience on the streets of Lower Manhattan on September 11. I was living on the Jersey Shore and commuting to Lower Manhattan via NJ Transit; I had visited New York several times, but I was unfamiliar with the area around the World Trade Center. It was my eleventh day of work at a brand-new job. When a coworker came into our workspace a few minutes before 9:00 A.M. and said, "A plane hit the World Trade Center!" the handful of us already in the office went downstairs to see for ourselves.

The landing gear from the first plane was on the sidewalk in front of my building on Rector Street, just off the West Side Highway. A crowd from surrounding buildings gathered, and we all just stood there, gazing—almost mute—at the massive fire raging one hundred stories up, wondering how many were already dead, how many were trapped, and how the fire department would even begin to put the fire out. Emergency vehicles were starting to arrive, but it was oddly quiet as people gathered in groups, looking up, talking with the strangers or coworkers they found themselves next to.

Then the second plane flew low over our heads, so fast that the images in my memory are like low-speed film capturing a high-speed object: frame

1, the plane is far left; frame 2, the plane is directly in front of me, close enough that I can see each window, as I realize it is a commercial jet, filled with passengers; frame 3, the tail as it flew out of sight and into the tower. I don't remember if I or any of us spoke a word; all I could think was *no*. Chaos erupted on the street, as bystanders panicked and ran.

After the second plane disappeared, I went back upstairs to grab my things and head out. I thought about how much suffering was going to be rained down on whoever had coordinated this attack; one plane might be an accident, but two was a pattern. I had little doubt the American response would be swift and deadly. Immediately, the parallel struck me: those we would soon bomb would have this experience or worse. This feeling of threat was sadly common in the world; it was only unusual on this day by virtue of being located near the financial center of a powerful hegemon.

I gathered my things, ready to leave, but I was faced with a problem; I didn't know where to go. I had come into Manhattan on the PATH train, exiting into the station under the World Trade Center, and I had no idea how to get off the island. I ended up standing, unsure, at the intersection of Washington and Rector. The owner of a nearby bar saw me and asked if I needed to make a call, and I gratefully said yes. It didn't matter, of course; I couldn't get through. But I found a few coworkers, too, and as the bartender started pouring drinks and patrons started lighting cigarettes, we sat near the door watching the news as it replayed the planes smashing into the twin towers.

Then the lights went out. None of us knew, really, what was happening. I glimpsed a burly, red-haired man, fleeing as if for his life, as he burst through the doors into the dark bar; he was covered with white dust and bleeding from his arm. The bar owner yelled at us to get down and get away from the door; he seemed to have realized that a tower was collapsing and that we needed to move away from the entrance. My office manager told us to cover our faces with the cloth napkins on the tables, already set for lunch. Her first concern was smoke from fire, but the thickness in the air was not smoke. After a few seconds of chaos, everything went oddly still, the air heavy. Although most of us were unclear about what had just happened, the South Tower had collapsed.

We tried to exit the restaurant through the basement kitchen's stairs up into the alley, but something was blocking the exit. A handful of us left through the front door, into the gray, silent air. We walked into millions of pieces of shuffled paper in all directions, everything covered with a fine, itchy, heavy dust, filled with pulverized concrete and who knows what else. We could see only a few feet ahead of us; all sounds were muffled and near. We had entered the bar on a sunny, though terrible, day; we exited into gray twilight. There were very few people around. As we left the bar, we saw a handful of dazed firefighters walking toward the World Trade Center. The choking dust was everywhere, falling out of the sky and rising up with each step.

I was walking with my manager, Jennifer Siegel (soon to be Siegel-McNamara), whose fiancé, John, was a firefighter. She was worried out of her mind. We walked up Rector, past Trinity Church, and then down Broadway, soon reaching the Charging Bull at Bowling Green. There, the sky darkened again. We briefly took refuge in a glass-fronted lobby but quickly decided that was a bad idea. With tens of thousands others, we walked across the Brooklyn Bridge, aiming for the Brooklyn Borough Hall area, where Jen's friend worked. That person, of course, was long gone by the time we arrived. Two older, Middle Eastern men working in an office near Borough Hall asked if we needed anything. Dirty and thirsty, needing a bathroom, and desperately wanting to let family and friends know we were alive, we gratefully accepted their offer of assistance. These kind men provided shelter in their office for few minutes, cool water, and a sense of calm. I had been trying unsuccessfully to call my partner, Lisa, via cell phone since we left the bar, and I tried several more times on the landline. Still no luck. I finally remembered that I knew people outside the New York/New Jersey area; I called my parents in Oklahoma, immediately got through, and asked them to let Lisa know I was alive.

After resting a few minutes, we started walking to Jen's apartment in Bay Ridge. We arrived mid- to late afternoon, having been driven the last mile or so by a kind stranger who went out of his way to help us. Jen's fiancé had clearly left in a hurry, headed to the towers. I was able to contact a friend, Daniel Tanaka, who lived in Astoria. He had watched from 2 Lafayette, near City Hall, as the first tower fell, certain that I was dead. He had identification that got him through the numerous checkpoints and allowed him to use the BQE (a major freeway) as long as he was by himself. It took him about half an hour to get to me in Bay Ridge. It took us about two hours to return to the apartment he shared with Mary Dietsch, as we detoured around the many roadblocks around fire and police stations and hospitals.

It was only when we arrived at Dan and Mary's place that I learned both buildings had fallen, the Pentagon had been hit, and a fourth hijacked plane had gone down. I saw for the first time the images those watching from afar had seen dozens if not hundreds of times already—the wobble and collapse of the first tower, the pancaking explosions of both towers, the dust-covered firefighters, the smoking rubble of the Pentagon. In each picture of New York, I wondered if I would see myself. I tried to figure out where in Lower Manhattan the image was taken and whether I'd been nearby when the image was snapped.

That night, whisky in hand, we stood on the roof of their apartment building. Every tall building in sight had red aviation lights blinking, even with no commercial air traffic. We heard the occasional shriek of fighter jets or the thump of police helicopters; it was surreal not to hear flights leaving and landing at nearby LaGuardia. The city was unnaturally silent. Lower Manhattan glowed ominously.

I needed to get home. The PATH train from Penn Station was still running, so the next morning I took the subway to Penn Station and then boarded the train to Newark. You could tell who had been caught in the dust by looking at their shoes; if they had gray dust where the sole met the upper, they, too, had fled the World Trade Center area. It was a somber ride, with people talking quietly, looking at one another's shoes, briefly making eye contact and nodding, and then staring out the window again. A few minutes before we arrived at Newark, the conductor informed us that there was a bomb threat at Newark Penn Station and that we were to exit the train and immediately leave the station. I was done. Although I had intended to take the train all the way to our home in Bradley Beach, another hour and a half ride away, I walked out of the station until I saw a payphone and called friends—Matthew Schertz and Kelly Nash—in Montclair to come pick me up. I finally saw my partner, Lisa, at their apartment, more than twenty-four hours after the first plane flew into the tower.

Strangers went out of their way to help me several times on September 11, my friends went to great lengths to harbor me, and I was finally safe. I knew it should feel like a gift. But I couldn't really feel anything. I was thoroughly numb. It was unfathomable that this had happened. It was unfathomable that I had lived through it. It was like I had watched the whole thing on television, despite not having seen news coverage of the building collapses until it was almost dark. I've never remembered any day with such clarity, particularly small things, snapshot images of the mundane paired with the surreal: the landing gear on the sidewalk; a potato halfway through the french-fry cutter at the bar that morning, half whole and half in tidy rectangles; a baby stroller turned upside down on a Sōbe delivery van near the entrance to the Brooklyn Bridge; the walk across the Brooklyn Bridge on a glorious fall day with thousands of others fleeing destruction.

I stayed in our apartment on the Jersey Shore for the next two weeks. My workplace was in the red zone, being patrolled by soldiers with guns, so there was no place to go. There was also no TV to watch. All the broadcast towers had been on top of the World Trade Center, and we did not have cable, so we got exactly one local channel. I watched that one channel all day, read everything I could find about the events of the day in the *New York Times*, and tried to use logic to find my way through trauma.

It didn't work. Learning everything about *that day* did not explain why the United States reacted the way it eventually did. It didn't explain why Osama bin Laden bore such animus toward us. It didn't explain why nineteen hijackers were willing to act in such blatantly immoral ways. It didn't explain why so many New Yorkers didn't want to bomb Afghanistan, and then Iraq, back to the stone age. It didn't explain why so many outside New York wanted to. Considering only that day, I realized, could not answer the questions I had. That realization—though I doubt it was conscious—led me to study politics via political theory, because it was ideas about who we were, the history, and the institutions that already existed that shaped the aftermath of that day.

I was lucky—so lucky—to have survived physically unscathed. But the aftereffects of having been so close to ground zero lasted a long time. I tried therapy; when they asked me about my relationship with my father, I left and never went back. I tried drinking; that didn't work so well, either. Eventually, though, I found solace in study, in teaching, in thinking broadly about what it means to be a human in an unpredictable world. What can we do to decrease the likelihood of such horrific events happening again? When we see the effects of malicious acts or realize we are passively accepting injustice, what can we do to repair the world?

My hope is that this book—born of my own trauma but written in an attempt to broaden the frame—will give us tools to more justly and humanely respond to the next terrible but predictable death(s): to interrupt the state's sovereign mourning for its own power and return our focus to the human costs of imperial hubris; to see the suffering of children in cages on our southern border as our responsibility because mere luck put us on the northern edge of that border; to stop taking for granted the many unequal forms and types of deaths; and to understand that our responsibility to one another is the result of our interdependence. We humans owe one another more than nations let us see. From protecting women's bodily autonomy, to offering safe haven to refugees, to working for the safety of young queers, to providing high-quality end-of-life care to our elders, we have to do better. My hope is that this book can help us begin to do the politics of mourning more honestly and justly, working to enlarge our sense of responsibility and connection, responding to tragedy with humility rather than pride.

Acknowledgments

This project has been under construction for a very long time. It began as a dissertation in political science at the University of Washington (UW), steered by an impossibly good committee consisting of Jack "Chip" Turner as chair and rounded out by Michael McCann, Christine Di Stefano, and Naomi Murakawa. This project was a risk for both Chip and me; his encouragement has helped me find my voice as a scholar and a teacher. Chip's consistent nudges—every six months he has texted to ask, "Where is the book?"—ensured that I never gave up, even when it felt like a reasonable option. Christine Di Stefano was an outstanding mentor from the moment I arrived at UW. During my time there, she offered honest critique paired with deep mentorship, modeling intellectual rigor along with humane generosity. Michael McCann's ability to see and articulate complexity has indelibly shaped this project and its expression, and his encyclopedic knowledge has been helpful on many occasions. Naomi Murakawa graciously read multiple iterations, always pointing me toward productive avenues of revision. From early brainstorming sessions to final drafts of the dissertation, Naomi provided tremendous support for this project and for me. Additional faculty at the University of Washington made it a welcoming start to my professional life, including Jamie Mayerfeld, George Lovell, Peter May, and Nancy Hartsock (who, though she is no longer with us, was a truly inspiring teacher and mentor). I am particularly grateful for the research funds provided by the Peter May Graduate Research Grant in 2010, which allowed me to purchase several essential texts cited in this book. When I hear tales of woe from other doctoral candidates about their dissertation committees, I sheepishly admit that I had an amazing group of thinkers, scholars, and critics whose goal was to think with and push me. I actually enjoyed writing my dissertation! This project has tripled in size and morphed considerably since then, but many core insights grew out of conversations with my graduate school mentors.

Glenn Mackin, David Watkins, Jason Lambacher, Sooenn Park, Tim Deak, Jennifer Fredette, Deepa Bhandaru, Matthew Walton, Annie Menzel, Larry Cushnie, Allison Rank, James Chamberlain, Erin Adam-Mayo, and Kirstine Taylor were all in my political theory orbit and helped make classes and teaching more fun. Lots of other folks made the madness of grad school bearable, including Amanda Fulmer, Shauna Fisher, Sophia Wilson, Karam Dana, Betsy Cooper, and Katie Banks. The UW Political Science Department was a great place to land, and I thoroughly enjoyed the mix of smart and thoughtful humans who landed in that gorgeous, damp, and gray place with me.

Several scholars have helped me along the way with conversations, encouragement, new ideas, and critique. Simon Stow, Bonnie Honig, and Barbara Welke, in particular, have taken the time to talk with me or read drafts. Political theorists who regularly attend the Western Political Science Association's conference have listened to and helped improve practically every part of this book or have written on mourning and race in influential ways, including Andrew Dilts, Alexander Hirsch, David McIvor, and Sara Rushing. Susan Burgess and Renee Cramer were both invaluable mentors as I moved through the tenure process with this book still incomplete. Three dear friends from grad school—Allison Rank, Jennifer Fredette, and Kirstine Taylor—have generously read several drafts, offering insightful suggestions each time, in addition to forming a posse of powerful early-career scholars whose support and encouragement have been lifesaving.

Before arriving at UW, I learned how to learn at St. John's College in Santa Fe. I was definitely not the best student there, but I found a core group of friends who helped me take myself seriously: Paul Dunn, Kelly Nash, Mary Dietsch, Matthew Schertz, and Dan Tanaka. My family in New Mexico always provided a safe haven; Mark, Pauline, Carol, and Anna Wilder graciously opened their hearts and home to me. And Sally Dunn, my undergraduate mentor at St. John's, was the first person to push me to write more clearly and eschew clichés. Her friendship remains one of the best things to come out of my four years at St. John's.

Denison University, my professional home, has been generous in all the right ways. The administration granted sufficient pre- and post-tenure leave for me to complete this book, as well as more than sufficient professional development funds. The senior political science majors in my 2015 seminar "The Politics of Memory, Trauma, and Mourning" and my 2017 seminar "What Does It Mean to Be White?" all pushed me to think harder and more clearly about my assumptions and claims.

I am so grateful to Aaron Javsicas, editor in chief of Temple University Press, for his patience (much patience!) and his belief in this book from the beginning. I am so pleased that my first book has come into the world under Aaron's thoughtful guidance.

The blind reviewers of Chapter 2 as it appeared in *Polity* and Chapter 3 as it appeared in *Law, Culture, and the Humanities* pushed me early in the writing process to more productively frame my central questions. The two anonymous reviewers for the book proposal helped me begin to bring the pieces of the manuscript closer together. But I owe a great debt to the final reviewer, whose generosity and critical prods helped push me to close gaps and forge new connections. This person was thinking *with* me even as they were pushing me to make claims clearer. So many generous reviewers and colleagues have helped me improve this manuscript; of course, any and all errors that remain are my own.

While my family of birth may not always understand what I am doing or why, they have always wanted the best for me. For teaching me to ask questions, to work hard, and to do whatever I thought I was big enough to, I am grateful to my parents, William and Harriet Pool. I thank them both for a lifetime of support and love. That is true, too, of my dear sisters—Laurie Crawford, Dawna Blue, and Michelle Buchanan—whose encouragement and support through all aspects of my life I could not do without. My father died at the end of 2020, and the pandemic prevented me from attending his interment. While I study political mourning, I cannot comprehend how to adequately mourn him.

Most of all, I am grateful to the younger versions of Lisa Clarke and Heather Pool for sticking together. The only reason this book exists is because Lisa believes in me. After having a master's thesis rejected in the early 2000s, I had given up on being an academic and was working at a job I loathed. One night, while we were sitting on our stoop on Staten Island, Lisa reminded me that when we met—when I was in grad school the first time around—I was happy. As I hemmed and hawed about how hard it would be to get a job, she reminded me that the chance of success was worth the risk of failure. Two days after that conversation, I started studying for the GRE. Two months later, I submitted four applications to Ph.D. programs. Several years, careers, cars, and addresses later, I continue to wonder at my good fortune for having found a partner who is convinced I am smarter, kinder, and wiser than I actually am. Lisa's family—Mary and Deirdre Clarke in

New York, as well as the many aunts, uncles, and cousins in the United States and Ireland—have wrapped their arms around me in ways I could not have imagined twenty years ago. As I was beginning to think about mourning as a political concept, Jim Clarke was ending his life. Being with Lisa and her family as they mourned his loss helped move me to think more deeply about mourning.

Political Mourning

Introduction

The Rise of Black Lives Matter

In early 2012, George Zimmerman, a Hispanic twenty-eight-year-old, shot Trayvon Martin, a black seventeen-year-old. Martin had been staying in Sanford, Florida, at his father's fiancée's home. After calling the police on the evening of February 26 and being advised to let the police handle it, Zimmerman—part of the local neighborhood watch—chased Martin. There was a violent encounter between them, and Zimmerman shot Martin. When the police arrived seconds later, Martin was face down on the grass and unresponsive.

The local prosecutor initially declined to press charges; Zimmerman's weapon was legal and registered, and Florida is a "stand your ground" state that made self-defense in the face of grave bodily harm not a crime. For about a week and a half, the story remained a local one. When Martin's family hired an attorney and began to call for further investigation into his death, the story went national in mid-March. State Attorney Angela Corey issued a probable cause arrest warrant in April 2012, charging Zimmerman with second-degree murder. Zimmerman's trial began in June 2013 and concluded in July with a verdict of not guilty.[1]

Shortly thereafter, in response to the failure of law to hold Zimmerman accountable for Martin's death, Black Lives Matter (BLM) coalesced as a local movement. The movement became national in scope and visibility after a white police officer shot and killed a young African American, Mike Brown, in the summer of 2014 in Ferguson, Missouri. Black people—often unarmed—have disproportionately been killed by police (e.g., Tamir Rice, Freddie Gray, Eric Garner, and Philando Castile, among others). BLM seeks to make visible the disparate numbers of violent black deaths, whether committed by white citizens or by police officers, but it focuses particularly on police/state violence against black bodies.

The claim embodied in the name Black Lives Matter is both simple and profound. A movement at once contemporary but part of a long lineage of radical black thought (as argued by Chris Lebron[2]), it asserts what should be fundamental in a democratic polity—that all lives *should* matter. But this normative, inclusive aspiration has been obstructed by our racially exclusive democracy: what Joel Olson calls "white democracy."[3] The phrase "All Lives Matter" quickly arose in response as a pushback against the particularized effort to attend to the disproportionate effects of police violence on *black* lives.[4] The events that led to the formation and emergence of BLM illuminate a series of important questions about the relationship between death and politics. What leads us to respond politically to the deaths of some citizens and not others? What can we learn about how mourning and politics are related if we consider the context and details of particular cases alongside the aspirational and normative claims of democratic theory? In general, what are the possibilities and limitations of mobilizing mourning to call for and ground political change?

While BLM is the most contemporary example of such a movement or political response to the deaths of everyday people, BLM is not the first American movement that sought to transform mourning into political change; nor will it be the last. At watershed moments throughout American political history, deaths of everyday people have mobilized the living to call for political change, and that change nudged the polity closer to our democratic aspirations. But not all mournable moments move us toward justice or democratic inclusion; some lead us toward injustice or exclusion. Calls for change that draw on death as their justification can lead to varied results, ranging from targeted, state-sponsored vengeance to expansions of the boundaries of belonging to include formerly rejected persons as part of the nation. The inability to state with certainty, in advance, the outcome of any mournable moment is why this book is necessary. For example, as I finish writing this paragraph in May 2020, it is impossible to know whether the United States or other countries will respond to the coronavirus pandemic of 2020 with a sense of shared fate that moves us to increase the social safety net or with a turn toward a more individualistic free-for-all. This book examines four mournable moments (with brief reflections on the current pandemic in the Afterword) with the hope of identifying the outlines of a process of democratic mourning. While private mourning is a universal experience, the political mourning analyzed here is different. Political mourning occurs when political actors—citizens or elites—invoke the deaths of every-day citizens to argue for political change.

Why Do Some Deaths Matter Politically?

Black Lives Matter is one of many examples of a particular death or series of deaths moving the political needle. But one might argue that the goals and actions of the movement inspired a white backlash that has led to the installation of a new vision of Americanness in the form of President Donald Trump. Surely that was not the intention of the organizers—citizens who demanded institutional and political change to eradicate the disproportionate killing of black men by police. And yet that is what happened. So *how* did this happen?

To more fully explain how particular deaths shape political outcomes, I focus on how political identity and political responsibility intersect. For now, however, I simply want to highlight that there is a relationship between these two concepts. If we perceive a harm to those we identify as belonging to a political "us," we are more likely to respond to that harm and to mourn the losses of those we perceive as "ours."

There are numerous examples of this disparity in contemporary politics. One recent set of examples of this juxtaposition were terrorist attacks in Paris and Beirut in 2015. On November 12, 2015, a double suicide bombing occurred in a Beirut shopping district at a busy hour, killing 43 people. The next day, a coordinated series of attacks ripped through Paris as individuals opened fire in a stadium and concert venue and then spilled out into the streets, randomly killing those found there. These attacks killed 130 people. The Islamic State (ISIS) claimed responsibility for both attacks. But the world responded very differently to the events in Beirut than it did to the events in Paris. Anne Barnard, in the *New York Times*, offered a synopsis of the different responses to these attacks by those around the world:

> Monuments around the world lit up in the colors of the French flag; presidential speeches touted the need to defend "shared values"; Facebook offered users a one-click option to overlay their profile pictures with the French tricolor, a service not offered for the Lebanese flag. On Friday the social media giant even activated Safety Check, a feature usually reserved for natural disasters that lets people alert loved ones that they are unhurt; they had not activated it the day before for Beirut.[5]

One might argue that it was the mere number of individuals killed by the attacks that led to the different responses. And yet if that was the case,

Americans would have responded with more sympathy and concern to the earthquake in Haiti in 2010 (more than two hundred thousand deaths) than they did to Hurricane Katrina in 2005 (about two thousand deaths). Instead, it seems more plausible to suggest that the majority of Americans identify more strongly with residents of Paris and New Orleans than they do with residents of Beirut or Port-au-Prince. This stronger sense of identification with the residents of Paris and New Orleans leads to a more robust sense of responsibility for their well-being: its strongest expression is a sense that our fates are linked, while a weaker expression would be a sense that we owe some assistance.[6] It makes sense that Americans would respond more robustly to events within our own country. But if that is the case, why the outpouring of sympathy for Paris and not Beirut? The explanation, I suggest, is that conceptions of identity strongly affect our ability to register the losses of others as politically salient and thus as a site of responsibility, both within and across political borders. The majority of Americans identify more directly with (white) French citizens than with (nonwhite) Lebanese citizens and thus experience French losses as more our own.

In Chapter 1, I more fully explicate the political theoretical aspects of responsibility and identity that ground my claims. Let me here offer a brief sketch of why these concepts are central. I begin with identity. This account is consistent with Amartya Sen's and Martha Nussbaum's capabilities approach and assumes that a state should seek to enable flourishing and the good life for all its citizens.[7] It also assumes that equality is a central value of democracy. As David McIvor argues in *Mourning in America*, recognition of others *as citizens* (not subjects or mere denizens) in a shared democratic project requires that we attend to unequally borne losses and burdens.[8] Similarly, Juliet Hooker argues that political solidarity—"reciprocal relations of trust and obligation established between members of a political community that are necessary in order for long-term egalitarian political projects to flourish"—is crucial to democratic life, but has been obstructed by racial cleavages.[9] Clearly, in America today we do not yet live in a world where losses are randomly distributed. Some lives are accorded protection and safety, while other lives are more precarious (to use Judith Butler's language[10]). The divisions between protected and vulnerable often align with identity categories such as race, gender, nationality, sexuality, or disability. A central component of the case studies that follow is a consideration of how identity categories, with a particular focus on race, shape whose losses are visible and how the boundaries of who counts as part of the dominant "we" can be shifted after moments of loss. Thus, the first theoretical concept that weaves throughout this text is identity. How do political-identity categories shape the political response to moments of loss? Can we see changes in the construction of those categories after the loss and the political response?

When, how, and why do the borders between insider and outsider shift? I argue that moments of visible death are often moments of identity transformation in profoundly political ways, moments when the "we" in "We the People" may contract or expand. In the wake of tragic deaths, we often do identity differently.

In the United States, one of the central identity categories is race; this work is thus focused on how racial boundaries enabled political mourning and then shifted after these moments. All four case studies centrally consider constructions of racial identity as a core component of Americanness (though there is, to a lesser degree, some discussion of gender). Following critical race theorists, I am persuaded that white domination is a core feature of American political life at individual and institutional levels. As a result, the grievous harms and disproportionate deaths and losses of people of color rarely receive the attention paid to similar losses experienced by white people.[11] Black Lives Matter is an example of political pushback against this invisibility of the losses experienced by people of color. Furthermore, the taken-for-granted, often invisible suffering of everyday people— for example, workers in unsafe factories or young black men—may be exposed by visible, sudden, yet entirely predictable events. The events I consider here all involve some shift in identity categories; in some instances a formerly excluded racial group is now included in the category of American as a result of tragic events, while in other cases a formerly included group is excluded. In sum, identity categories (in this instance, racial categories) fundamentally shape the possibility and practices of political mourning after tragedies and can, in turn, be transformed by the responses to that mourning.

The second central concept is responsibility. In an ideal democracy, we bear and recognize responsibility to one another to ensure flourishing (or in the more standoffish version of liberal democracy, to ensure that all have an equal opportunity to flourish). In turn, we act with the conviction that others bear some similar responsibility toward us. We trust that the system is not rigged against us; if it is shown to be rigged against us, we turn to the law for redress afterward or to the political process to change future conditions. But the legal responsibility sought after a particular event is not the same as political responsibility; legal responsibility is necessary but not sufficient. When, after tragic events, law fails to locate and hold persons or entities accountable, those of us left behind are primed to articulate an expanded, more proactive sense of political responsibility for conditions in the future rather than one limited to redress for events in the past. That is, this new sense of responsibility is not limited to an individual's responsibility for the tragic event itself, but can be expanded to include responsibility for the conditions that enabled that event. Thus, the understanding of responsibility

I discuss is greater than law or legal responsibility; nonetheless, in the four case studies included here, law's failure plays a considerable role in illuminating failures of democratic politics and political institutions.

An example might help. The White Star Line did not include enough lifeboats on the RMS *Titanic* because the lifeboats cluttered the decks of the opulent ship and the builders were confident the ship was unsinkable. White Star acted according to law when it included fewer lifeboats and life jackets than necessary should the ship need to be wholly abandoned. After the *Titanic* sank on its maiden voyage, survivors or relatives of the dead sought damages but obtained the barest minimum of payments; the law sided with the haves rather than the have-nots.[12] White Star was not in any legal way responsible for the accident. However, political inquiries on both sides of the Atlantic determined that while human error (particularly focusing on the failure of the nearby *Californian* to come to the *Titanic*'s rescue) and corporate hubris certainly played a role in the tragedy, safety features such the lack of lifeboats and life jackets were the more fundamental factor. Thus, while White Star had complied with the law, the law itself was inadequate to ensure safety for all passengers; the problem was a *political* failure to enact law rather than a failure to enforce it. Thus, representatives in both the United Kingdom and the United States updated codes to ensure that passenger ships in the future should include enough lifeboats and life jackets for all passengers. Here, individual responsibility—conceived through individual legal guilt or corporate responsibility for damages—was shown to be inadequate in a political sense. Legislators were thus moved to expand responsibility not only to include violations of the law in the past but to take up collective responsibility for the law's present inadequacies by making new and better law that sought to ensure no such tragedy occurred in the future. They changed the laws because political responsibility—by creating laws that bound a political community—is prior to and more expansive than legal responsibility.

This work is grounded in political theory and thus pulls from some of the norms and literature that define this subfield. Drawing inspiration from Sheldon Wolin, I take political theory to include a shared set of questions, a shared and inherited vocabulary, and a tradition of inquiry that provides a rich historical trajectory while also focusing our inquiry on politics, dedicating us to "to becom[ing] wiser about political things."[13] Here, I offer an immersive overview of three historical events and one evolving contemporary example, viewed through the lens of a processual theory of political mourning, in an effort to show how these events generated particular meanings. Wolin argues that political theorists take facts seriously, but that when theorists add conceptual analysis to factual descriptions, they render "political facts significant."[14] New meanings or interpretations are generated through this marriage of empirical and theoretical analysis, as the concepts help us identify connections between seemingly disparate events. Wolin suggests that political theorists "draw connections between political phenomena; they impart some order to what might otherwise appear to be a hopeless chaos of activities; they mediate between us and the political world we seek to render intelligible; they create an area of determinate awareness and thus help to separate the relevant phenomena from the irrelevant."[15] Given the complicated contexts and aftermaths of a death, my hope is that the conceptual analysis of events I offer here helps separate relevant from irrelevant phenomena.

But as a piece of scholarship about *politics*, this work draws on a broad array of literatures that consider the significance of death in politics, ranging from American political development to trauma studies to sociology to policy work. As a result of this blend, fellow political theorists may find the political theory portions less than satisfying; political theory often focuses heavily on textual analysis and engagement. While that practice of interpretation is a valuable one, I have purposefully limited the kind of exegesis and extended textual analysis that often defines political theory to foreground how political theoretical concepts can help us make sense of political life. Thus, although this is a theoretically oriented work, it is grounded in the contexts and practices that shape particular events, seeking to bring together the tools of political theory with political practice. I trace how the concepts of identity and responsibility shape political mourning by looking in depth at the public responses to and political outcomes enabled by actual deaths. Individuals died, and their deaths were held up as justifications to call for specific kinds of political change. I believe that it is only by putting political theory and actual politics together that we can make sense of why there are different responses to similar events and how mourning can become politically significant.

At the end of the first chapter, I provide a processual theory of political mourning that seeks to trace how some deaths served as the basis for calls for political change. This process is then tracked through the examples that serve as the body of the work. The model of political mourning I lay out attends to both the creativity, freedom, and actions of individual agents and the glacial inertia of institutions and political processes, while including context as a crucial component of the story. For now, however, I offer this brief summary of the model that is more fully explained in the next chapter. First, there is a context—here, I am particularly focused on conceptions of identity and responsibility—that precedes the death event. Generally, there has been a public discussion of whether this group of people count as "us," whether they are "real" Americans. Without this larger context within which particular deaths occur, it is difficult if not impossible to understand the reactions of journalists, legislators, and citizens. Thus, to make sense of claims that any particular death is politically significant, we must attend to conditions prior to the event itself. Second, there is a highly visible death or deaths and a considerable public response. In general, the loss is widely known and receives considerable media attention. Third, agents—whether the bereaved or political elites, often both—elevate the deaths to mobilize support for specific, concrete, political change. These called-for political responses can be diverse. The third component, then, seeks to account for how individual actors—whether they are elites, loved ones, or activists—draw on a visible death to call for particular changes. Often, depending on whether the dead are seen *as citizens*, mourners are also calling on the wider polity to think differently about those who died, calling for us to see them as part of the "we" in "We the People." (To recall the example of Black Lives Matter, the call is for all Americans to *act as if black lives mattered*.) Fourth, the law tries but fails to hold any individual(s) responsible, exposing the impossibility of addressing political responsibility via legal means given a context of structural injustice or oppression. The fourth component, then, exposes how we conceptualize responsibility, demonstrates the incomplete nature of legal responsibility, and considers how and why collective political responsibility is assigned, rejected, or accepted. Fifth is an examination of whether political change has occurred. In the first three case studies examined in the book, some political change occurs; in the fourth, Black Lives Matter, I suggest that while a Deweyan public has formed, its demands have not yet become institutionalized (if anything, its demands have led to a considerable backlash against its stated goals).[16] To summarize, then, the five components of a process of political mourning are context, visibility, agents, responsibility, and political change.

I trace how this process plays out in four examples, which form the main body of this work. The first is the Triangle Fire of 1911; the second is Emmett Till's 1955 lynching; the third is the attacks of September 11, 2001; and the fourth is the ongoing struggle of the Black Lives Matter movement. These events occur in different places and eras, and the death count ranges from one to thousands. Further, the outcomes of the events differ radically. And yet in these examples, a similar process unfolds—contested identities, a highly visible deadly event that is widely publicized, agents calling for political change in the name of the dead, failed efforts to locate legal responsibility, and then political action. Identity and responsibility intersect in this process. We act in the names of those we identify with because we feel some sort of political responsibility toward them and ourselves—toward the body politic that enables the flourishing and protection of our own individual bodies.

To be clear, although the work presented here marries the empirical and the theoretical, I am not necessarily making causal claims. While I use events as my site of analysis, the analysis draws heavily from normative theory to highlight the possibilities and limitations of political mourning, with a focus on how various pieces fit in historical cases. Deaths can powerfully move us, but they can move us in undemocratic and unjust directions. What I seek to understand is how democratic mourning has been realized or short-circuited by the combination of context and actors, as well as conceptions of identity and responsibility. For example, a death that is not particularly unusual may become politically significant if it happens after a prior priming event. Likewise, a death that might be politically significant may be removed from the public domain when the loved ones of the deceased request privacy rather than acting in political ways. The murder of twenty-year-old Mollie Tibbetts in 2018 exemplifies both these traits. After Donald Trump's entry into the Republican field of presidential candidates in 2015 with the language of Mexicans as criminals, drug dealers, and rapists, Tibbetts's murder by a Mexican national without proper U.S. documentation led many Americans to call for further restrictions on immigration and increased punishment for those in the United States without proper documents. In this sense, a death that otherwise would be unremarkable *became* political by virtue of the context and prior events.[17] The response by Tibbetts's father, however, was a request to leave the family alone. He wrote, "Please leave us out of your debate. Allow us to grieve in privacy and with dignity."[18] The context made her death prime material for political mourning, but her father refused to use her death for political ends. The democratic end to which her death might have been effectively directed was gender-based violence rather than anti-immigrant xenophobia. But the commonality of young women being killed by young men makes it difficult for these deaths to serve as catalysts for political change.

As John Seery writes in *Political Theory for Mortals*, "Death figures importantly . . . in the canon of Western political thought."[19] This book takes that claim seriously, while also arguing that death figures importantly in actual politics, too. When we, as individuals, lose someone who matters to us, we are forced to pause and consider who we are after losing that person; we may reevaluate our purpose, our identity, our place in the world, and our values. While it is relatively easy to grasp this on a personal level, I argue here that political communities often engage in a similar kind of post-loss reflection about who we are and what we owe one another *politically*. I further argue that this reflection can enable political action that responds to the loss in explicitly political ways—sometimes in ways that newly recognize or expand the boundaries of our collective responsibility for justice and sometimes in ways that do not. It is the central claim of this book that the deaths of everyday citizens, at particular moments and in the wake of a contingent process by which these deaths are made political, can move the living to political action. These actions can extend beyond ethical or legal obligation by taking up new definitions of responsibility on the basis of re-shaped boundaries of belonging. Sometimes, though not often, these deaths can lead us to act not only politically but democratically and justly. Further, the book asserts that to more fully understand how we have acted in such ways in the past helps us imagine the possibilities and limitations of using death to motivate political action. My hope is that this book helps provide the tools necessary to approach mourning politically.

Making Mourning Political

Death and Politics

One of the main goals for this work is to locate the boundaries around the "political" in "political mourning." While there may be political aspects to all death and loss, death and loss are not imagined as always political in this work. Certainly, death and loss are universal experiences that affect every human; being human means being mortal. But to say that all death is political is to make "political" so broad as to be meaningless. In this, I take to heart Sheldon Wolin's exhortation to find the boundaries of the political, even if those boundaries are "created." In the introduction to *Politics and Vision*, Wolin writes:

> The ideas and categories that we use in political analysis are not of the same order as institutional "facts," nor are they "contained," so to speak, in the facts. They represent, instead, an added element, something created by the political theorist. Concepts like "power," "authority," "consent," and so forth are not real "things," although they are intended to point to some significant aspect about political things. Their function is to render political facts significant, either for purposes of analysis, criticism, or justification, or a combination of all three.[1]

I seek to render political change that occurs after the fact of the deaths of everyday people—change linked by citizens and policy makers to those deaths—politically significant in order to trace how conceptions of responsibility and identity shape our perception of losses, and how they might be transformed in the wake of those deaths. Importantly, I focus not on how states treat war dead or respond to the deaths of political leaders, because these are explicitly political already. Instead, this work focuses on moments when everyday citizens die—not soldiers or statesmen but citizens—and we pay attention. I am not arguing that only the instances I address are political or even that they are the best examples of political mourning; nor am I arguing that all mourning is political. To do so would blunt the edge of my general claim, which is that these instances of political mourning are sites where we can see political responsibility and political identities intersect, transform, and shift. As Bonnie Honig argues, the question is not whether we lament the dead; the question is how we lament their deaths.[2] (I would add to that the question of to what end we do so.) In line with Honig's urging to attend to the *politics* of lamentation rather than the politics of *lamentation*—to consider words and actions, the context in which these occur, and the various forms of power that crosscut and shape the reception of action or speech—I seek to consider how some deaths have mobilized actors to call for political change with a particular focus on how the mourning for these deaths has *become* political rather than remaining private or even public.[3]

Mourning—preceded by loss and, in all my cases, involving a body that arrests our attention—is a particularly rich site of inquiry because of the profoundly visceral encounter with the bodies that results from collective actions or inactions. To make all death political evacuates the force of analyzing the politically significant conditions that lead to some premature deaths becoming a part of the taken-for-granted status quo and therefore perceived as neutral or natural when instead they are the result of policy action or inaction. The purpose of this work is to suggest that we attend to the everyday premature deaths that currently recede into the background in our society with the goal of imagining a world in which each person has the opportunity to die a private death after having had the opportunity to live a full and complete life (such a life would involve political participation).

In general, I seek to accomplish for political mourning what Peter Verovšek tries to accomplish for the politics of memory. In "Collective Memory, Politics, and the Influence of the Past," Verovšek argues for a limited definition of "the politics of memory" with the goal of making cases comparable.[4] "The politics of memory" as a phrase appears more often than one might think within the contemporary scholarly universe. Verovšek provides an overview of various meanings of memory within some portion of this universe and concludes that there is little agreement among scholars who use the phrase regarding what, exactly, makes up a *politics* of memory. The result, then, is little comparability among cases. One may find a work in, say, anthropology or English that is subtitled "politics of memory" but find little about politics within its pages. Verovšek argues that those wishing to investigate the politics of memory should instead focus on the substantive content of collective memory expressed within the state as well as the interactive channels through which ideas about the past are conveyed, disputed, silenced, and negotiated in society as a whole. This narrower understanding of the politics of memory puts the focus on the channels and interactions through which collective memories pass on their way to the political center, and on how the narratives voiced within political institutions refract back out to the periphery.[5]

What Verovšek does for the politics of memory—limit it to instances where the political center and political institutions remain important parts of the analysis—is what I seek to do for the politics of mourning. This shifts the question from whether a particular death *is* political to instead ask *how it comes into politics*. Shifting perspective in this way helps us see the process by which taken-for-granted losses may come to serve as the ground to contest existing conditions; we may come to see these losses as unnecessary, as preventable, as unjust in ways that we simply did not before. When this shift occurs, it is more likely to generate claims of collective responsibility that in turn can lead to calls for democratically oriented state action to change the status quo moving forward.

A caveat before I begin is in order, however. Many different terms will appear—grief, trauma, and mourning, among others. While there are shades of difference between these terms, all of them refer to something lost: typically, a loss that causes a rupture in everyday life. Loss leads us—as individuals—"to feel sorrow, grief, or regret" when a loved one dies or departs, or when a cherished ideal moves beyond reach. But that same dictionary definition of mourning goes on to suggest other, more externally expressive acts.[6] I choose to focus on mourning because of this rich set of meanings, ranging from an individual's internal feeling (synonymous with grief) to external collective expressions (community burial rituals) and even up to political expressions (such as states honoring esteemed citizens or erecting war memorials for war dead). Thus, "mourning" can refer to feeling, experience, and action; for my purposes, this provokes a productive sense of ambiguity. Mourning is related to grief, trauma, and loss, but it is a more capacious concept that bridges individual, collective, and political expressions. This book focuses primarily on the latter: what *political* mourning is and why it matters.

That mourning can have political significance is tied to the fact that loss is a fundamental part of democratic political life. From a psychoanalytic perspective, Anne Norton and David McIvor suggest that the foundational experience of subject formation is the loss of a clear-cut sense of good and evil (where good is what I want and bad is what I do not).[7] This has political implications because it is in the process of subject formation that we learn to negotiate ambivalence and grapple with complications—both essential components of democratic life. From the perspective of democratic theory, Bonnie Honig, William Connolly, Simon Stow, Danielle Allen, and Melvin Rogers all point out that learning to lose well is one of the crucial components of democratic life in the sense that by playing the game, we agree that not everyone can win all the time.[8] For a democracy to function, democratic citizens must develop the skills to learn from losing—what Stow calls developing a tragic orientation to politics—wherein we are able to still see the humanity of those we have beaten in an election or even of those we have defeated in war.[9] Ideally, within a democratic polity, losses are distributed relatively equitably; if one group always wins and another always loses, then it begins to look less like a democracy.

Before articulating a more complete version of political mourning and the politics of mourning, I should first clarify how private mourning, public mourning, and political mourning differ. While the bulk of later chapters deal primarily with political mourning, it is necessary to first demonstrate that mourning—typically thought of as a private experience—can have political dimensions.

Private Mourning

I define mourning as an affective response to loss whose outward expressions signify one's place in a community projected backward and forward in time. Let me begin by parsing the various parts of this working definition. My general framework of mourning draws more heavily on the sociological formation, historical effects, and institutional responses to the deaths of everyday citizens, because these responses provide a richer discussion of the interrelation between individual and community, between political identity and responsibility, than do many psychoanalytic or therapeutic investigations of mourning.[10] However, there are certainly connections between psychoanalytic theory and politics. For example, David McIvor offers an analysis of "the democratic work of mourning" that combines the two fields, arguing that "the work of mourning . . . can be seen as a psychopolitical process" that includes both internal dimensions and external recognition.[11] While McIvor's work is invaluable, it is considerably more grounded in psychoanalysis than this work and is a complementary inquiry.

All mourning is preceded by loss. Loss comes first. But not all losses prompt mourning. To mourn a loss requires a certain amount of self-reflection, while the loss itself is somewhat objective. I am interested only in losses that cause mourning. In particular, given the subjective nature of the experience of loss, I focus on deaths as the easiest type of loss to analyze. Our response to loss is often deeply internal. Mourning is initially a feeling in response to a real or perceived loss. Mourning thus occurs at the intersection of an individual's private, internal world and the larger, social world that surrounds the person. Thus, while the experience of loss may be intensely personal, the internalized feelings of loss have social dimensions because we live in communities and develop individual identities within these communities. The loss of those with whom we are in community— with whom we share a remembered past, a present way of life, a projected future—deeply affects our individual worlds. As a result, mourning is one of the few spaces where we fully grasp the impact of others on us. Thus, while it is an internal feeling, it occurs because others are part of our lives.

However, mourning is not just an internalized feeling; it often motivates some external expressive action. Almost universally, there are customs surrounding expressions of mourning. Who mourns whom, the form and content of rituals that express the intensity of one's sorrow, the stories that will be told about the suffered loss—these maintain community boundaries, mores, and ideals. While internally experienced feelings of loss are grouped under a rubric of mourning, these feelings are often accompanied by specific, contextual, outward expressions of loss, which are also covered by the meaning of the term "mourning." These outward expressions are an effort to order the world in accordance with the perceived importance of the loss.[12] For example, a great and powerful man is mourned with a lavish funeral and lowered flags because he is part of a community of power, while a homeless woman who dies on the street is buried without ceremony in a potter's field. The different outward expressions of mourning are indicative of the recognition offered by the communities to which each belonged and are, by extension, an expression of their perceived worth to society. Do these different expressions reflect the intensity of feelings of loss experienced by those individuals left behind? No: surely the homeless woman's death elicits mourning among her family or friends. But without power, money, and public stature, her family and friends may not be able to publicly mourn her in a way they wish. To be mourned in public by friends, peers, family, and associates is an expression of the status of the deceased as well as of his or her membership in a community (or communities).

Mourning takes place in time. While it is experienced in the moment one is in, those feelings are projected into the past and future. Mourning involves a present loss, but we also mourn an irretrievable past and a future that must now be faced alone, without our beloved. The shared past, the lost object, and the possible futures we would like to have shared are all beyond reach. We are left only with the swirl of the present's confusion. Mourning is a psychic effort to square a lost past with a changed future even as we experience the onslaught of present grief.[13] Mourning lays bare hopes resting on what might have been and, in doing so, clarifies often-unstated assumptions about wished-for futures. Articulating these now-lost futures forces the mourner to come to terms with an utterly changed reality.

While mourning is often thought of as a privatizing state, however, this need not be the case. Judith Butler claims that mourning can serve as an entry point into rethinking a democratic way of life based on a collective recognition of bodily vulnerability. Since all bodies are vulnerable, loss serves as a reminder that although we must politically and legally strive to achieve autonomy and individuation, these goals are never fully attainable. We realize our universal vulnerability when losing a loved one, because we are temporarily "undone by each other," as the shared experiences and meanings that constitute each individual's self are lost when our co-experiencers die.[14] Those who mourn must begin a slow process of rebuilding a sense of self without their beloved. Such losses, Butler asserts, should make us question the stark independence of this experiencing "I." Butler argues that while "many people think that grief is privatizing, that it returns us to a solitary situation . . . I think it exposes the constitutive sociality of the self, a basis for thinking a political community of a complex order."[15] For Butler, this constitutive sociality and vulnerability, when properly attended to, can help us realize the depths of our interdependence. The hope Butler holds out is that this can have political effects, perhaps even that it *should* have political effects. The experience of a constitutive loss should lead us to a political ontology that takes vulnerability as a primary starting point. The effect, argues Butler, should be an egalitarian effort to reduce suffering and loss. However, as I note below, there is good reason to suggest that this connection between private loss and a shift toward egalitarian political action is not automatic; loss *may* lead to political engagement, but it may not.

Public Mourning

While mourning in public may have political significance, public mourning lacks the explicitly political calls for change that define political mourning. To be clear, my project is primarily concerned with mourning when it is used to call for *political* change. However, public mourning is a real phenomenon. We might conceive of public mourning as the public response to the death of a popular artist or musician (say, Prince or John Lennon) that the public admires or feels connected to. While public mourning takes the private rites of mourning public, it does not necessarily lead us to question the health, ideals, or potential future of a political community. As a result, while some, but certainly not all, public mourning is political, all political mourning is public. Thus mourning in public is a necessary but not suffi-cient condition for a loss to qualify as political mourning.

Political Mourning

If we conceive of mourning on an individual level as an affective state that has expressive results and involves conceptions of community belonging, shared interpretations of the past, and projections of a collective future, it is but a short step to considering mourning as a site where communal *political* identity is shaped. This work focuses on how race both shapes and can be transformed in moments of political mourning. While the same can be done for other identity categories, the focus of this work is on race.[16]

Political communities selectively mourn citizens. Not all citizens are given state funerals honoring those who died in service to the nation, and I do not argue that they should be.[17] However, there are losses that lead to explicitly political mourning. I define political mourning as an affective communal response to a loss that threatens (or is perceived to threaten) the historical narrative, present expression, or future possibility of the political community and/or the ideals that sustain that political community. Politi-cal mourning is expressed through (1) public, often explicitly political, dis-cussions of these ideals and (2) the political actions that directly respond to specific losses in an effort to incorporate the loss into a coherent narrative.[18]

While perhaps not as individually formative as the family or local com-munity into which we are born, the political community in which we live certainly forges affective bonds that are brought to the surface in scripted moments. The flag, the national anthem, or memorials for fallen soldiers prod these affective moments of shared identification. We share this nation; we belong to this idealized community; we are citizens with shared ideals. Once these identifications are made, the loss of the idealized nation, being expelled from or unrecognized by it, or a shift in the nation's ideals could be experienced as a loss that would prompt mourning. We form affective bonds with one another based on our shared membership in the imagined com-munity.[19] We develop solidarity with our fellow citizens, which is part of what makes democracy work. As Juliet Hooker argues, "Because democratic politics require consent, citizens must develop solidarity."[20]

These affective ties are deeply rooted in shared ideals that connect the past, the present, and the possibility of a shared future. When there is a threat (real or perceived) to the narrative coherence that binds these tempo-ral sites, our response is often to create a story that sutures the wound caused by the loss or changes the narrative so that coherence can be restored in the future.[21] The narrative may alter the shared history, it may reinterpret the event of loss itself, or it may project a new future. But for mourning to be political, it must include a visible effort to publicize the loss and identify how it threatens communal ideals of who we were, who we are, and who we wish to be. We are moved to respond in order to preserve a particular conception of what it means to belong to this group or to share this identity. In a putative democracy attuned to concepts like equality and fairness, when a loss is successfully framed as having been unequal and unfair, it may spark questions about what we as a political community may do to minimize similar losses in the future.

Return to the example of the great and important man above: imagine now that he is a president or legendary senator. Mourning his loss is one way a citizen can identify herself as a member of the political community. We all recall state funerals for slain or deceased leaders or the lying in state, repose, or honor of persons who died and who were nationally important figures.[22] These outward expressions of communal grief signify a widespread esteem for these figures based on their service to the nation. Events like these communalize the loss; they include citizens in an idealized community through expressions of affective ties and rituals of mourning. These events index the deceased's perceived value to the political community.

Such occasions also bring average citizens into a shared political community built partially on shared loss. A moment such as the loss of a great leader also casts our thoughts backward and forward in time. The individual's past service is honored in an effort to continue an idealized communal identity narrative that binds the present political community to a storied past, while his or her loss puts into doubt the envisioned shared future that a political community requires. We ask whether current leaders have the skills to captain the ship of state or to carry forward the political projects that bind us to our past. These kinds of losses play on chords similar to those found in the more individualized laments previously discussed.

I hope this example makes clear that mourning is frequently invested with explicitly political overtones that take up themes of collective identification, status, belonging, obligation, and political continuity. We can readily understand that when a political leader, soldier, or firefighter dies in service to the nation or community, we ought to honor their commitment to the community through expressions of collective loss; because they gave their lives in service to us, we should honor them in death. But as this book argues, there are times when the deaths of everyday people—persons who are not elites, are not famous, and do not die in service to the state—prompt similar affective responses, status evaluations, and efforts to forge a coherent historical narrative. When the deaths of everyday people are significant in number, tragedy, or sheer brutality—in short, when their deaths shock us into noticing them and are connected to calls for political change because we are responsible for the political conditions that led to their deaths—they are prime sites to investigate how mourning contests, creates, and transforms identity categories by prompting calls for political change.

One way to make sense of why the deaths of everyday citizens is an important site to consider political mourning is to recall the contours of John Dewey's publics.[23] Dewey argues that politics is the process of a public coming to know itself as a public (essentially coming to understand that each person is a member of a group that faces a shared problem) and then acting to address that problem. The challenge, however, is how to facilitate recognition of belonging to the group, and then motivate us to act to address the shared problem. Given these challenges, political mourning can help overcome several of the problems Dewey identifies as barriers to creative democracy: apathy, indirect effects, the problem of presentation, and the development of judgment.

First, political mourning helps overcome the problem of apathy or paralysis, which Dewey identifies as "an inability to identify one's self with particular issues. . . . Men feel they are caught in the sweep of forces too vast to understand or master. Thought is brought to a standstill and action paralyzed."[24] A loss such as the deaths of everyday people can focus other citizens on one instance, which can enable a sense of empowerment and specificity. Although the world as a whole may be too much to change, when we see a discrete instance of visible loss that might have been prevented, we might be able to come together to prevent another such loss in the future by making concrete, identifiable changes meant to ensure these deaths were not in vain.

Second, political mourning helps citizens realize the indirect effects of our failures to act. Dewey writes, "An inchoate public is capable of organization only when indirect consequences are perceived, and when it is possible to project agencies which order their occurrence. At present, many consequences are felt rather than perceived; they are suffered, but they cannot be said to be known, for they are not, by those who experience them, referred to their origins."[25] We might have a general sense that something is wrong, but until we recognize that we can collectively act to address the problem specifically, we do not. For example, while we may understand that workplaces are dangerous, that racism kills, or that terrorism is a threat, until we recognize that we, as a public, can regulate labor to prevent harm, eradicate bias in law and life, and act in ways that do not foster the nihilistic response of terrorist violence, we have no way of interpreting the indirect effects in a way that leads us to change collective conditions.

Third, moments of political mourning also directly respond to Dewey's problem of presentation. Dewey recognizes that it is difficult to break through the crust of people's habits to get them to see things in new ways;

this is why art can make a significant contribution to the development of organized publics.[26] In light of Dewey's insights, it is significant that all my examples rely heavily on images and have served as the basis of literary and visual works of art to communicate the importance of the loss and the urgent need to engage in structural change to address the correct cause. The shock of seeing or reading about the harms caused by our failure to act, particularly when paired with the law's inability or refusal to hold someone responsible, can help us realize that we must act politically. We must perceive and then act differently if we want to avoid similar outcomes in the future.

Finally, political mourning addresses one of the most pressing problems Dewey identifies with the formation of a public because it provides a space of inquiry in which we may develop judgment. Dewey writes that "the essential need . . . is the improvement of the methods and conditions of debate, discussion and persuasion. That is *the* problem of the public. We have asserted that this improvement depends essentially upon freeing and perfecting the processes of inquiry and of dissemination of their conditions."[27] Dewey points out that this inquiry need not be done by experts, but should instead be opened up to anyone with the judgment necessary to act on knowledge supplied by others about common concerns.

Considering Dewey's focus on mobilizing citizens out of apathy, widely visible losses that prompt discussions of responsibility can be seen as moments when publics are formed. In response to visible losses, citizens and political leaders often propose specific institutional reforms. Disasters that take the lives of average citizens lead to new processes meant to avoid or minimize similar disasters in the future. When the state responds to such events, it may do so in a more or less democratic way; as I argue in the final half of the book, the mourning taken up by the state can sometimes be used to expand the state's rather than the people's security and power. In the Deweyan framework, the focus ought always to be on the people, so that we understand the state as an expression of a problem-solving apparatus driven by the people's needs. As examples, airplane crashes increase air safety by improving design as well as oversight, mining disasters prompt new detection protocols or state-enforced safety measures (even if doing so increases costs for mine owners), and sinking ships lead state agencies to demand improved designs. While these processes or new institutions may not entirely succeed, the formal adoption of revised codes, regulations, or designs indicates new awareness and signals that these citizens' lives matter. Further, they signal that these are collective problems, which means that using collective power to solve them is acceptable. These instances help illustrate how specific losses can motivate political change. Yet some collective problems remain diffused or invisible to the majority so that even if a public emerges, it is not strong enough to gain the power needed to move the existing state—for example, when harm is isolated within a minority or disempowered population. The question, then, is whether the larger polity will see those losses as worthy of redress. As I discuss more fully later in this chapter and return to in the chapter on Black Lives Matter, to more fully flesh out Dewey's conception of a public, we must also attend to how race, as a salient political identity, complicates this democratic formation.

Making Mourning Political

A large body of literature—from disciplines as disparate as world literature to history to anthropology to psychology—links death and politics. Much of this literature simply assumes that the deaths or losses being considered are political. With some notable exceptions that attend to institutional politics (particularly within the discipline of history), many humanities-centric fields call mourning, death, or loss political without sufficient engagement with the practices of politics and political institutions to satisfy those of us who study politics. Many such works seem to have adopted the word "politics" to mean "widespread" or "collectively significant" rather than addressing how political institutions—courts, parliamentary bodies, police, and so on—have enabled the losses experienced and fundamentally shaped the responses to those losses.[28]

Butler, along with others working in a psychoanalytic paradigm, provides important insights into how the state's interest in holding the line between matters of private and public significance does not fully describe the human experience. And yet to posit a social self who is vulnerable and interdependent is not necessarily to posit a political self or political subjectivity. Some political theorists—Jenny Edkins and Wendy Brown, for instance—critique questionable assumptions about sovereignty that lead to harmful disavowals of dependence.[29] The social self as mourning subject is one who has been made aware of how much she depends on others for her sense of self. Thus, loss, mourning, and grief are expressions of our shared humanity as expressed through our vulnerability and fragility. Because these are ontological conditions, the assertion is that they have political significance. And yet there may be good reasons to demand more of the adjective "political." We may want to reserve that word for a more specific setting, more than merely "collective." In this, I follow Bonnie Honig's argument that we should attend not to the "politics of *lamentation*," but to the "*politics* of lamentation."[30] While the social self may (rightly) feel responsible, the response may remain in the realm of feeling sad rather than acting to change the conditions.

Bonnie Honig suggests that Judith Butler's attention to "mortalist humanism" prioritizes the equality of vulnerability and death rather than the agonistic space of democracy; attending too much to our shared mortal condition, Honig suggests, removes our focus from striving for equality in life.[31] In agreement with Honig's focus on seeking equality in life rather than death, this book suggests that those mourning the dead are doing so not because we are all equal in death, but to bring attention to lives cut prematurely short and—in the name of these dead—demanding change. That is, mourners who demand change do so because the dead were not equal in life *or* death. Rather than merely mourn the dead—which, as Honig so deftly points out, has the potential to reduce politics to ethics—the mourners I describe seek to change the future in order to equalize the odds of dying a good death after having lived a good life. Most of us hope for a good, full life, followed by a good, easy death. Yet many of our fellow citizens are denied both. Thus, while mobilizing in response to particular past deaths, the actors in the situations I discuss throughout this text use the deaths of everyday people to demand changes in the conditions of future *life*, thus satisfying Honig's concern to foreground and enable the agonistic democratic politics that Honig seeks to protect.

Simon Stow, in *American Mourning*, offers a way to bring Butler's emphasis on bodily vulnerability together with Honig's focus on agonistic democracy.[32] Stow suggests that a shared mortalist humanism is not natural but must be created; we must develop an orientation to life that accepts, even embraces, its pervasive tragic dimensions as a precursor to (rather than a replacement of) democratic politics. By developing a tragic orientation to life, Stow suggests that we can begin to generate the resilience and responsibility Honig prioritizes.[33] In essence, Stow suggests that while death and loss may be universal, recognizing this universality is a necessary foundation for democratic politics, but this recognition alone does not necessarily lead to democratic politics. Instead, Stow suggests that recognizing and acting on this universality is a political achievement rather than inevitable; it requires a tragic orientation to both life and politics. This book seeks to put Butler's emphasis on the political potential of the universal reality of death together with Honig's attention to its limitations as a *necessary* political trajectory. Thus, like Stow, I seek to attend to how death, while universal, requires actors and actual politics to achieve the agonistic democracy Honig emphasizes.

While historians often attend to how political communities respond to losses, one limitation of historical works is a too-tight focus on memorialization as a political outcome.[34] Thus, mourning and memory become essentially the same thing; to remember via memorialization is to mourn. Certainly, those a nation chooses to remember and those it chooses to forget are deeply political; the politics of memory is an important site of inquiry. But memorials tend to be static even when they draw particular mourners after the fact. To overgeneralize for the purposes of analytic clarity, memorials are generally one-offs in ways that legislation and policies are not; memorials are literally set in stone, even if their meaning shifts over time.[35] They often are state-centric as well, either supporting stories of sovereignty the state wishes to embody or challenging the reach of that sovereignty through resistance. To limit a politics of mourning to a study of memorials does not get at the larger question of how a political community bounds identity and responsibility through interactions shaped by institutions well into the future.[36]

Social scientists draw attention to power and institutions in ways that are helpful for this project. For example, in the introduction to *Trauma: A Social Theory*, Jeffrey Alexander writes:

> Cultural trauma occurs when members of a collectivity feel they have been subjected to a horrendous event that leaves indelible marks upon their group consciousness, marking their memories forever and changing their future identity in fundamental and irrevocable ways. . . . It is by constructing cultural traumas that social groups, national societies, and sometimes even entire civilizations not only cognitively identify the existence and source of human suffering but "take on board" some significant responsibility for it.[37]

Alexander goes on to write that "events do not, in and of themselves, create collective trauma. Events are not inherently traumatic. Trauma is a socially mediated attribution."[38] This is not to say that such events are not experienced as traumatic on an individual level. It is instead to say that many such events are not *labeled* as trauma or understood as such by a larger audience. What sets sociological work such as Alexander's apart is a focus on claim-making, carrier groups, audience, narrative creation, and institutional arenas as the components from which cultural trauma—and thus collective identity and responsibility—are shaped.[39] While Alexander takes a slightly broader approach than Verovšek, their aim is similar; while Alexander seeks to explain how trauma is *constructed* by groups as a foundation of their collective identity, Verovšek shows how the memory of an event *becomes* political.[40] Focusing not only on actors and context but also on institutions sets the social science articulations of trauma apart from many works in the humanities.

Within political science, political responses to the deaths of everyday citizens have been addressed from a policy perspective. To some extent, the events that lead to the politics of mourning I lay out in the final section of this chapter can be thought of as "focusing events" that, in public policy literature, draw our attention to a known but ignored problem.[41] According to John Kingdon, focusing events "focus attention on a problem that was already 'in the back of people's minds.'"[42] Policy scholars follow Kingdon's lead; for example, Peter May and Tom Birkland examine how policy can change after catastrophic events in their books *Recovering from Catastrophes* and *Lessons of Disaster*, respectively.[43] Birkland is particularly helpful in thinking through how events do or do not lead to policy changes. In Birkland's prior book, *After Disaster*, he recognizes that policy makers respond more forcefully to events that harm humans than to those that do not. Thus, a hurricane that makes landfall in a highly populated area is more likely to lead to policy change while one that makes landfall in uninhabited areas is less so.[44] (I would supplement that by noting that it also probably matters whether the hurricane made landfall in a wealthy or a poor, a white or a black community.) As a result, there is a distinction between *potential* focusing events and *actual* focusing events. As with all agenda-setting processes, "whether or how crises emerge depends upon the way in which they are interpreted by relevant actors, which determine whether those events become policy issues."[45]

But policy change is only at the end of the story I tell. Some losses, usually borne by those with lesser standing and who are not perceived as belonging within the polity, remain invisible or ignored, and so do not generate discussion in public or political forums. These losses become a part of the neutral, normal background; the fact that blacks die younger and poorer than whites or that lesbian, gay, bisexual, transgender, and queer (LGBTQ) teens disproportionately die of suicide or by violence remains invisible as a focusing event until some singular event captures the attention of a larger audience. Only then do those not directly affected begin to imagine the failure is not individual but institutional, such that transformation of the polity itself may be necessary. Policy studies helpfully illustrate how significant events shape political responses. But to more fully understand why some events and not others succeed in this, we must delve deeper into theoretical constructions of political identity and responsibility. My assumption is that both are elastic; they can shift and change as events unfold. Identity can expand to include those who had been excluded or contract to exclude those who had once been included. Similarly, the boundaries of our responsibility can expand or contract. It is important to attend to events that may trigger these shifts. My suggestion is that political mourning is a powerful site to examine these two important political concepts in tandem, but that to do so, we must look at audience, actors, and actions.

I am certainly not the first person to connect democracy and death in American political life within the field of political theory. Two recent works in political theory—David McIvor's *Mourning in America* and Simon Stow's *American Mourning*—address similar questions.[46] Both offer valuable insights and suggest that the combination of death, politics, and America is a fertile site of analysis. Like Stow and McIvor, I too focus on race as a central category of analysis. Yet they turn to different frameworks to analyze the connections between death, politics, and American identity: Stow to the Greeks and McIvor to psychoanalytic strands of analysis.[47] McIvor focuses on psychoanalysis and identifies the Kleinian depressive position with a democratic orientation to mourning. Identifying loss as the heart of identity formation, the depressive position is the result of maturation, experience, and learning to see the world as complicated and filled with ambivalence. This is quite helpful in thinking through the limitations and possibilities of mourning. But it does not necessarily shed light on how particular political contexts and agents shape the larger collective response to death. McIvor's insightful overview of the depressive position as maturation provides a normatively good orientation to democratic mourning.

Similarly, Stow's typology of mourning—ranging from romantic to vengeful to nostalgic to tragic—suggests that we can cultivate a "democratically productive tragic mourning" that is imbued by ambivalence and "questioning in its style, structure, and effect."[48] His analysis of the various ways mourning can support or interfere with democratic life are helpful to show how mourning can lead to undesirable, undemocratic outcomes. I am persuaded by Stow that at the heart of democracy is a willingness to see our fellow citizens—as well as our fellow humans from other countries—as worthy of respect. For Stow, that willingness extends to include fellow humans who do terrible things, such as Osama bin Laden.

Taken together, Stow and McIvor demonstrate that political mourning can appear in democratically and undemocratically oriented ways. These two authors make a convincing case that there are more and less normatively desirable ways to engage in political mourning, to such an extent that it is worthwhile to map their insights onto more examples. This book differs, though, in that I have identified a process that runs through both democratically and undemocratically oriented examples of political mourning. It also shows that it is more than a general orientation toward democracy that shapes outcomes; it is a combination of context, elites, and everyday people. What sets this book apart is a detailed focus on three historical events and one contemporary movement to trace a process of political mourning, drawing on works in political theory, American political development, and social movement theory, as well as scholarship in history, trauma studies, and media studies.

The bulk of the book is made up of deep dives into moments when everyday people died and their deaths served to justify calls for political action: the Triangle Fire in New York in 1911, the lynching of Emmett Till in 1955, the events of September 11, and the contemporary Movement for

Black Lives. Given the dissimilarities in time and place, numbers of bodies, and types of deaths, it is striking that a similar process unfolds. Articulating this process enables us, as analysts of and witnesses to contemporary mournable moments, to be better equipped to understand the available positions and objections open to those who mourn, as well as giving us the tools to effectively intervene by asking the right questions in the wake of tragedies. Identifying various frames put forward by political elites as well as by those whose loved ones have perished enables us to more effectively advocate for collective and political responsibility rather than relying on the law as our sole mechanism of accountability. Additionally, it provides a means to redirect our attention to shared political values of democratic equality and justice rather than to wallow in endless grief and the dangerous, blind rage that can follow loss. In short, the process of political mourning I offer here traces how grief can be turned into politics and what that might enable and obstruct.

Identity and the Borders of Belonging

The question of who counts as a citizen has long exercised the imagination of political thinkers.[49] Some political theorists have considered this question of identity via psychoanalytic theory. Anne Norton and David McIvor, in particular, argue via Melanie Klein's object relations theory that learning to navigate loss is a foundational part of coming into subjectivity at both the individual and the collective level.[50] As a result, though Klein does not extend her insights into politics, both Norton and McIvor persuasively argue that doing so gives us a deeper understanding of how self and citizen are related. Decidedly less psychoanalytic in focus, William Connolly has argued that political identity is always grounded in difference; the goal for democratic citizens and politics is not to eradicate difference, but to engage across differences without demonizing those perceived as other.[51] These have all contributed significantly to my own thinking, and I owe them a scholarly debt. However, this work is less guided by the psychoanalytic work on identity formation than it is by the formation of political identity categories in law and practice.

Scholars working on identity within American political development and history have noted that American citizenship is at best an incomplete and at worst an incoherent category; this is particularly evident regarding race. For example, Rogers Smith argues that the meaning of citizenship draws on multiple traditions, while Elizabeth Cohen argues that we need more than a single category to describe different forms of citizenship.[52] Smith and Cohen point out that the ideals defining us and the ability to realize the rights and responsibilities of citizenship have always been contested, shifting, even contradictory in impulse. In a similar vein, historian Barbara Young Welke argues that while we can identify a single category of citizenship in the nineteenth century, it is defined by the exclusion of women, nonwhites, and the disabled.[53] Judith Shklar argues that American citizenship is defined not by participation but by standing: the rights to vote and work that were long denied to white women and all people of color.[54] Smith, Cohen, Welke, and Shklar all highlight the tension between the myth of equality and the persistent practices by which some groups are consistently excluded. Race, in all these works, is a central category of exclusion from the status, rights, responsibilities, and identity of full citizenship. This project takes these arguments seriously by investigating moments when the borders of belonging shift—while these categories are generally stable, there are moments when who counts as a citizen expands or contracts. Race is often at the center of that story. As discussed in the Introduction, this book focuses primarily on how race as a political identity is shaped, bounded, and transformed; as a result, the examples all consider the significance of racial categories in shaping whose deaths matter.

Yet to make sense of how stories affect our lived world, we must attend not only to discursive power but also to how identity stories have substantively shaped our lives. In *How Americans Make Race*, Clarissa Rile Hayward argues that to focus primarily on discursive aspects of stories and narratives of identity does not adequately explain how *political* spaces of racial inclusion or exclusion are reproduced in the future, long after the stories told about identity have changed.[55] As a result, we must consider not just the origin of stories about identity but how those identity stories become objectified and institutionalized and thus shape our lived world. Once identity narratives have been institutionalized, they become taken for granted and thus more difficult to challenge.

As an example, consider Hayward's argument about the identity narrative of "Americans as a home-owning people."[56] This story connects responsible citizenship to home ownership. When developers were trying to use this story to secure public funding for housing developments, they relied on racial identity categories to determine who was fit to receive credit to purchase a home (whites) and who was not (blacks and other racial minorities). Once this story was institutionalized during the Great Depression through federal intervention into the housing market and its future secured through federally backed low-interest loans (made available in white suburbs where redlining and restrictive covenants ensured the exclusion of people of color), white suburbs marked by single-family homes and mortgages were favorably contrasted with black urban spaces dominated by multiple family dwellings and rents. These spaces then came to define whiteness and blackness, while the active role of the state in creating those spaces was obscured through time.

And yet to people living in white and black spaces, it is clear that these spaces are defined in part by who inhabits them; they are black or white spaces.

Hayward's careful tracing of how stories about race turn into institutions that reflect those stories, which in turn shape future spaces, is a crucial component of my understanding of identity. While *stories* about who we are undoubtedly matter, to make sense of how those stories (and the identities shaped by them) are projected into the future, we must also attend to how those stories are *institutionalized*. This is why political action is the last component in political mourning—not only has there been a shift in our understanding of who "we" are, but there has also been some institutional response that serves to materialize a commitment to a particular set of citizens. Because whiteness has so often been a central component of what it means to be a "real American," tracing how race shapes political mourning is essential to the inquiry. Recall Dewey's analysis of a public forming the institutions of state. If we consider that state to have been defined by the collective problems of whites (often about how to effectively control blacks), even if a self-aware black public forms, for its interests to be institutionalized would require a profound reimagining of the purpose and functions of a formerly white-defined state.

However, those on the margins are not wholly without resources. In *Reflections on Political Identity*, Anne Norton considers the centrality of the liminal figure to collective identity. She writes, "The existence of the liminal indicates the presence of difference. . . . Liminars . . . are between identities. In politics, they are between allegiances."[57] The frontiersman, for example, stood between the poles of whites and native people; white by birth but taking up the practices and norms of natives, frontiersmen were partially accepted by both communities but fully accepted by neither. Liminars are both like and unlike us, which leads us to be frightened by them; there is a triadic quality to this relationship, because liminars fall somewhere in between "us" and "them." When we focus only on the otherness of the liminar, collapsing the triad into a dyad, we reject liminars as wholly foreign, leading to fear, rejection, expulsion, or violence. And yet by virtue of being excluded from the exercise of power, liminars may "transform weakness into strength" by asserting a dedication to ideals that existing institutional structures have not upheld.[58] Resistance is thus possible, even powerful, when liminars mobilize their status as excluded from purportedly universal democratic ideals to call for change.

Consider, for example, just a few liminars in American political history who, though excluded from full citizenship, asserted American ideals to demand the nation live up to them: William Apess argued that Chief Powhatan was a better example of true Christianity than the Puritans. Elizabeth Cady Stanton's "Address at Seneca Falls" explicitly linked the ideal of equality laid out in the Declaration to the exclusion of women by the same government. Frederick Douglass's "What to the Slave Is the Fourth of July" powerfully exposes the hypocrisy of a holiday celebrating freedom in a state that sanctioned slavery. These liminars call attention to the gap between our aspirations toward democratic equality and the substantive inequality built into our political institutions, making sense of why mourners who take their grief public can generate powerful calls for political change. When people who have experienced loss (in particular, a loss enabled by politically accepted conditions of inequality) take their grief public, the audience (their democratic fellow citizens) has two options: admit that aspirations toward democratic equality are mere rhetoric or do democracy better. The mourners may assert full citizenship that has not yet been realized, and in the best-case scenario, they motivate others—particularly those in positions of power—to act on their behalf. Liminars, then, can mobilize their sameness to demonstrate the absurdity of their exclusion from benefits that are supposedly available to all.

Because liminality is fluid, Norton writes that "liminars become most active and powerful when they recognize not only their common experience of exploitation and subordination but also the formal resemblance of that experience to the experience of liminal groups in other structural relations."[59] By linking their subordination to the subordination of others, liminars can generate broad demands for change; they can begin to form a Deweyan public who both feels and perceives a shared problem. Sometimes, they are even able to recruit members of the dominating group into their ranks as activists. To coalesce into such groups that identify oppression across identity groups, however, is rare.

Rarer still is for these moments to turn into political movements that become potent political forces. In *Political Process and the Development of Black Insurgency, 1930–1970*, Doug McAdam argues that to make sense of the civil rights movement's rise, we must first account for the context, shaped by broad socioeconomic processes. Within a given context, to understand why a movement coalesces, we must consider the "indigenous organizational strength" (resources it has and can develop, via structure, leadership, and membership, as well as material and economic resources); "expanding political opportunities" (accounting for new actors, institutions, available resources, or momentous events); and "cognitive liberation" (when an oppressed group believes it can realize its aims).[60] While I am not arguing that all the instances I draw on here rise to the level of social movements in McAdam's sense (though Black Lives Matter clearly does), the process I lay out is similar. A broad context, marked by contested identities and exclusion from the polity, is the starting point. Organizational strength is analogous to political actors who make calls for particular changes in the wake of tragic events; these actors generally are backed by social and cultural networks that bear witness to their loss and serve as supportive, sympathetic fellow mourners. The event itself serves to expand political opportunities by grabbing the public's attention. The horror of a sudden event generates sustained interest in ways that quotidian "exploitation and subordination" (to use Norton's phrase) does not.[61] Political opportunity structures shift in the wake of terrible losses—what had been taken for granted is now up for debate. Political actors seize this moment to employ their loss in support of calls for political change; they come to realize that this is the moment to press their demands. Not only does it seem possible to attain their desired ends; those who are left mourning may feel they have nothing left to lose. Having experienced grief and loss, they may find that failing to honor their loved ones' memories by calling for structural change is more painful than seeking change and failing. What McAdam calls cognitive liberation, then, may in these examples be understood as the conviction that failing to act is worse than acting and failing.

Political identity is fluid, contested, and powerful. Those excluded (in the United States, primarily people of color) seek inclusion; those already included (whites) usually resist those efforts. And yet there are moments when those included yield to demands of the excluded and expand the borders of belonging to cover them. Mournable moments present a democratic polity with an opportunity to reevaluate and lessen the gap between ideals and reality—moments when we recognize and embrace a political, collective responsibility to do better by our fellow citizens. But this is not always what occurs. Sometimes, the gap is widened because the excluded are seen as a threat to whom we bear no responsibility. This relationship between identity and responsibility thus requires a more explicit consideration of what political responsibility entails.

Responsibility

How we conceptualize and institutionalize collective responsibility is a crucial part of any political community. To whom does the collective owe what? From Thomas Hobbes's seventeenth-century founding of the social contract tradition, a social contractarian state has been understood to owe protection to its citizens. However, as shown above, groups are often excluded from that equal protection on the basis of ascriptive identities. The question, then, is how democratic political communities come to recognize and take up collective responsibility or refuse it. As the borders of identity shift, the depth or breadth of our responsibilities to one another do too.

As recent works on responsibility in political theory suggest, political responsibility cannot be reduced to legal responsibility or guilt; rather, responsibility must be understood in a more specifically political sense. This shift requires a deeper, more collective understanding of responsibility than legal guilt or moral accounting.[62] The latter are necessary, but not sufficient to fully flesh out a *political* responsibility. Moral accounting, as Shalini Satkunanandan suggests, leads to a kind of debtor's view of responsibility, where we can know what is owed in advance. Similarly, Chad Lavin and Iris Marion Young argue that understanding responsibility via a legal framework alone narrows our focus to actors rather than institutions or context. Thus, as the title of Iris Marion Young's final book—*Responsibility for Justice*—suggests, we must come to realize that our political responsibility for justice extends to context and institutions as well.

Reconsiderations of political responsibility in the wake of widely visible deaths is a critical component of political mourning. Before a death can spark calls for political change, it has to be made clear that the more individualized story of responsibility that typically holds cannot account for the events just witnessed. Broadening the account of responsibility often occurs precisely because law is either incapable or framed as incapable of providing redress—the law finds individual agents not guilty, or the state bypasses legal remedies altogether. In the examples in the following chapters, how mourners, observing citizens, and elites conceptualize and attribute responsibility fundamentally shapes the kind of political change that results.

My suggestion, then, is that when our responsibility is expanded—when we realize that we, as a democratic polity, are collectively responsible for shaping the conditions of our lives and thus providing the possibility (or impossibility) of a good life for any one of us—political mourning may transform the landscape so that citizens are made more or less free from arbitrary constraints as a result of their race, gender, class, disability, or sexuality. Thus, political responsibility and the possibilities of freedom from structural constraints are inextricably linked. The greater the sense of political responsibility to secure just conditions of everyday life for all, the greater the possibility of freedom within any given individual's life.

The issue, though, is how to generate and make good on the promise of political responsibility when it is so tempting to fall back on a moral or legal framework. In *Burdens of Political Responsibility*, Jade Schiff asks how the responsiveness that precedes and enables responsibility can be generated, because "responsiveness is prior to the assumption of responsibility for suffering."[63] As a result,

> before we can begin to discharge our responsibilities—however we conceive of them—we need to be able to acknowledge and experience connections between our activities and others' suffering. We need [to] not just understand those connections intellectually or

theoretically, but be attuned to them in practice, to experience in various ways the burdens of our responsibilities.[64]

Schiff notes that dominant narratives of responsibility as moral or legal generally disable the responsiveness that precedes responsibility; this is the condition of "ordinary politics." During such times, narratives of responsibility work well enough that they are unquestioned by the majority. Ordinary politics, however, are undone by extraordinary moments of crisis or rupture "that can engender profound disorientation" because they "disturb our sense of ourselves and the world, and draw attention to both through that very disturbance."[65] When Schiff writes "our responsibilities—however we conceive of them," she suggests an important prerequisite to taking up responsibility: an affective orientation that recognizes the suffering of others as our responsibility. This is crucial to the larger argument of this book— that ordinary politics works against a broader articulation of responsibility, and that moments of rupture or crisis can illuminate the poverty of that account and enable us to understand responsibility in a more political, more capacious way. Moments of rupture can help us see how unjust structures result from our misunderstood responsibility.

The limited, legal understanding of responsibility is called a liability model by Lavin, the blame or fault model by Young, and debt justice by Satkunanandan. These theorists are making important claims about the deeply political nature of law. That is, they are critical legal theorists challenging the role of law as a legitimator of inequality. This is significant. If law fails to adequately assign responsibility (in part because its institutions have been constructed in too narrow a field for this more complex articulation of responsibility), the situation can invoke a sense of disruption or disturbance that can generate the kind of responsiveness that Schiff theorizes or the conversion experience Satkunanandan describes. Thus, moments of legal failure—always combinations of human agency and structural constraints—are moments when responsibility of this broader kind can be more clearly seen. These moments of legal failure make clear that law and legal frameworks are embedded within and the result of what Antonio Vázquez-Arroyo calls "predicaments of power."[66] Law is not out there, above politics; it is part of the story of responsibility that works to delimit the reach of responsibility to punishment and reward after the fact or to commitments specified and chosen in advance rather than to political responsibility for a shared future. While each of the authors addressed here critiques the legal sphere through a series of examples, my larger project seeks to trace more precisely how particular legal failures—when no *one* can be held responsible—can become narratives that open us up to Schiff's responsiveness. However, unlike Schiff's subtle and perceptive reading of novels and philosophy, this book seeks to uncover those moments in historical, political events. The law is a powerful site of legitimacy narratives, and thus when it is shown incapable of assigning responsibility in a satisfactory way, the legitimacy of law (and possibly of politics more broadly) is called into question.

Political responsibility is greater than legality, morality, ethics, or law. Thus, we must imagine and locate political responsibility on its own terms, not as a subset of morality. Our understanding of responsibility, then, is integrally connected to our understanding of the purpose and reach of politics. This is why Vázquez-Arroyo argues for a social-democratic articulation of citizenship rather than a liberal-democratic one; for responsibility to be meaningful, citizens must share in political power through participation rather than more abstract representation.[67] Here we see the connection between identity—those who count as citizens—and responsibility most clearly; we tend to see and respond to the suffering or needs of those we see as one of us while remaining oblivious to the suffering or needs of those who are not. And yet in moments that expose the distance between ideals and reality, our sense of responsibility—like the borders of belonging—can expand or contract.

A Process Model of Political Mourning

Part of what sets this book apart is a focus on how mourning *becomes* political by examining several instances where death served as the justification for political calls for change. This requires in-depth considerations of actual political processes. Put differently, what are the contours, as well as the possibilities and limitations, of what I call political mourning? To borrow a phrase from Rogers Smith, I conceive of political mourning as a moment "through which conceptions of political membership, allegiance, and identity are formed and transformed."[68] Moments of political mourning reveal how political identity and responsibility are conceptualized and, importantly, how they play out in specifically *political* rather than private, cultural, or historical ways. Smith urges researchers to immerse themselves in the historical moment under discussion in order to understand how political processes are shaped by identity claims, which in turn shape the possibility of future political processes and identity claims. Similarly, Kerwin Lee Klein advises scholars to consider the *political effects* of identity-making processes or memory-consolidating moments rather than focus on the tensions between interests and identity or between memory and history.[69] Because mourning helps shape institutions and ideas that affect all our lives, the political processes that follow moments of loss deserve inquiry.

Some may argue that this work isolates mourning as a variable. To be clear, this is not my purpose. After most deaths like the ones I describe in what follows, people mourn in public. But most of these do not lead to political change. Thus, it is not the mourning per se that is the catalyst; in that sense, the argument does not focus on mourning in isolation. Rather, the focus is on moments when *mourning becomes political*: that is, when highly visible deaths provoke mourners to gather up prior instances and harms into one very visible event that comes to stand in for a host of similar problems and helps those not affected begin to *see* the loss differently.[70] In that sense, these moments may be extraordinary in that they gain visibility, but they are certainly not isolated or isolatable. Often, previous such deaths elicited no larger collective response. Thus, it becomes clear that agency—the agency of mourners and political actors—is a central part of the story I tell below. Mourning *becomes* political through a process, and while that process is shaped by a context, it is also driven by people who make decisions and act in public. There are times when highly visible deaths can make everyday violence visible and the body politic responds. The question, then, is why and how any particular mournable event reaches the political agenda, opens up questions of responsibility, and leads to political action advocating for change. Mourning is not an isolated variable; it is instead a process. Mourning that becomes political occurs within a context where identities are contested, focuses on a highly visible event, leads to debates about the extent of our political responsibility, involves actors, and leads to political change. The focus on process suggests that these events are not isolated but instead occur within larger contexts that shape the construction of political identity and thus responsibility; as the title of this chapter suggests, the political mourning I consider occurs when these events *become* political.

This approach takes social movement literature seriously. The works of scholars such as Doug McAdam, Francesca Polletta, and Keeanga-Yamahtta Taylor demonstrate how social movements build solidarity and motivate action.[71] While these works are important, they have a slightly different focus from my own. McAdam and Polletta, in particular, do deep archival work and interviews to provide a more complete picture of how and why social movements rise and sustain participation. While there are aspects of movement building in this work, my focus is not necessarily how movements build, though that ends up being part of the story of political mourning; it is instead on how events are used to mobilize calls for change. Sometimes these events serve as foundational moments in a movement's birth, but often it is not the mourners themselves who become leaders in the movements. Similarly, movement participants may refer to a moment of political mourning as one reason why they joined movements, but the event itself is not likely why they chose to stay. Thus, while social movement scholarship shows up regularly in the following pages, this is not necessarily a work on social movements (though it owes that literature a great debt).

But why focus on mourning the bodies of everyday people rather than those of soldiers or political leaders? Beginning with the ancients and continuing through recent works, political theorists have asserted a link between death and political practice.[72] The widespread collective remembrance of the deaths of political leaders and soldiers demonstrates that the mourning following the loss of political leaders or soldiers always bears political meaning. But there are times when other bodies—the bodies of average citizens—focus our collective political hopes and fears; these bodies, and the wider political response to them, clarify who has standing within the polity. When everyday citizens are collectively mourned, their bodies provide a means to reenvision the political past and present while enabling us to project a different political future, one where such deaths are made less likely. This is different than attending to how we remember war dead; excellent scholarship in memorialization studies captures the significance of war dead to political communities.[73] Similarly, when political leaders die or are assassinated, it surely affects the nation's understanding of itself and its future; think of how Abraham Lincoln's death radically shifted the aftermath of the Civil War or how Yitzhak Rabin's assassination made the Oslo Peace Accords less likely to be implemented. Unlike these instances, my focus is how the deaths of everyday citizens may play a role in fostering political change. These deaths, when they reveal a collective problem that we knew but did not name, can help a Deweyan public form to demand an institutional response from the state. In this sense, a particular death can reveal a common, shared problem that needs to be addressed.

Political mourning is related to but different from the politics of memory and collective memory.[74] For one, mourning occurs closer in time to the actual loss than in the literature on the politics of memory. That is, before a loss can be remembered, commemorated, or historicized, it must be experienced. Mourning, then, links a loss to the later memory of it. But the politics of mourning I lay out here need not leave any physical marker of its significance and may not be widely remembered to be significant. The significance of the politics of mourning lies in its *political effects* in terms of institutional change and/or of the consolidation or dissolution of belonging within the polity, as well as the contraction or expansion of our collective responsibility. Memorials and other visible commemorations thus need not be central. While the mourning may disappear from memory, the institutional response to that event then becomes the norm going forward; it shapes the future.

Similarly, the politics of mourning differs from collective identity or cultural trauma. Political mourning helps illuminate an important moment when collective identification is consolidated;[75] it is a singularly powerful moment within a larger arc of collective identification that deserves study in and of itself. Similarly, while political mourning may be related to the large-scale traumas investigated by the cultural trauma literature,[76] mourning may be unable to address the full scope of larger cultural traumas. Instead, it is a more human-sized representation of those larger traumas. It presents political collectives with a concrete event that may enable them to see the effects of trauma in new ways.

I have used the language of political mourning to argue that there are times when loss and death have explicitly political meanings that contribute to calls for political change. I now shift from a discussion of why we might think of mourning as political to an overview of the politics of mourning. That is, even if we assume that mourning can become political, how would we know? I argue that there are five components of a process of political mourning: context, visibility, actors, responsibility, and political change.

First, context is crucial. Thus, the mourning I trace after key events is often preceded by contests over who counts as one of us: contests over the *borders of political identity*. In this work, the main identity category under investigation is race. Who are we? Who is not one of us? Who deserves full citizenship, and who does not? Whose rights or security is the state organized to protect? Given how difficult it is for the politically and socially marginalized—those Elizabeth Cohen calls semi-citizens or Anne Norton calls liminars[77]—to gain recognition of and redress for the disproportionate losses they experience (e.g., premature deaths or substandard education and housing), the political identities of those who become the objects of political mourning must have already been contested. Without a previous, widely visible political challenge to the given borders of belonging, a tragic event will more easily be interpreted as a sad, singular, unavoidable tragedy rather than the manifestation of a deeper problem that must be addressed via structural changes. As Dewey argues in *The Public and Its Problems*, our tendency is to focus on events rather than conditions, but a prior debate over us-ness can illuminate conditions that preceded the event. When preceded by a more explicitly political challenge that makes injustice visible but fails to resolve its effects, a loss is better able to gain traction. This is a complex business, however. If a tragic death cannot be connected to a prior political contest over belonging, it may not adequately serve to generate political mourning. It may then be perceived as an individual flaw—as the individual's responsibility or fault—rather than a political issue.

Second, *loss and mourning must be widely visible*, particularly to those outside the affected community. A great variety of deaths attract our attention; they vary in number, publicness, brutality, senselessness, and other ways. The politics of mourning, however, depends on people taking their grief public. It depends on making a private loss symbolic of some larger problem that collective politics has failed to address. Some who have lost loved ones are unwilling to do this. As a result, their loved ones may rest in peace but not become the basis of a politics of mourning. Others immediately contact the media and political leaders in an effort to call attention to their loss, generally with the hopes that other such deaths may be avoided in the future. Rather than quietly accepting a loss, these mourners frame their story in a way that invites people into their loss and thus multiplies its affective impact.

Visibility is perhaps the most daunting obstacle to mobilizing a politics of mourning, because gaining the attention of those not directly affected is a considerable challenge. This is made easier if a prior, explicitly political challenge about the contours of membership or belonging has attained widespread visibility but failed to attain institutional change. Making mourning visible often draws criticism from those whose privilege rests on the institutional arrangements that enabled the loss. In these moments, those opposed to particular called-for changes resort to condemning the politicization of mourning.[78] To overcome this challenge, mourners who take their grief public must carefully walk the line between making their mourning visible and making it too explicitly political. While these two goals are almost always conjoined, they must initially appear to be somewhat separated.

Third, *agents, as citizens, mobilize grief over the deaths to call for political change.* That is, in addition to their role as mothers or brothers or members of the same union, they respond by taking their grief public and connecting the deaths to a political—not moral, not legal—solution. These political actors may be the bereaved, members of organizations affiliated with the dead or taking up their cause, or political elites. (However, not just anyone is positioned to be able to invoke deaths to call for change; the closer one is to a victim, the more vulnerable one is to being silenced by accusations of politicizing the death in ways that undercut the possibilities of success.) These called-for political responses can be diverse. Those who invoke the dead may demand changes in political structures and institutions: perhaps calling for new regulatory agencies, demanding enforcement of laws that already exist, or asking to be recognized as citizens whose losses deserve recognition and redress. In doing so, these agents position themselves as one of us, even though this invocation may be performative. When a young, black mother speaks directly to a news camera "as an American," she may be claiming an identity that others might deny her. This is rhetorically powerful. But the demands made by political agents may harden the identities of those assumed to be responsible for the suffering. The possibilities and limitations of political mourning hinge on how the events are framed by political actors, how large their audience is, what kind of demands they make, and the identities they project and embody.

Determining who the "we" of the polity is can be challenging. In *The Evidence of Things Not Seen*, Lawrie Balfour suggests that James Baldwin's destabilization and multivocality of "we" in his essays was productive.[79] In her masterful reading of Baldwin, Balfour writes, "By embracing his white readers in a racially ambiguous 'we,' he forces them to ask themselves how able they are to regard him, unself-consciously, as one of 'us.'"[80] Part of why Baldwin's prose lingers so powerfully is that it often exposes unseen worlds to readers who may be curious but ignorant. By using "we" to cover sometimes blacks, sometimes whites, sometimes all Americans, Baldwin forces perceptive readers to recognize their location with regard to the dominant (white) power structure and to begin to develop a more democratic orientation to fellow citizens. Are you, Baldwin asks us, one of those whose lives is deemed less worthy? Or are you ignorant that the polity is still marked by racial rather than democratic solidarity?

In a similar vein, Juliet Hooker suggests that the racial solidarity at the heart of American democracy has prevented the development of democratic solidarity. The question, then, is how to get whites to realize that they are "seeing whitely."[81] Whites, in a racial polity, seem to assume that losses are evenly distributed or are the result of poor (black) individual decisions, and are thus puzzled by intense responses by minorities to unequal losses. In "Black Protest/White Grievance," Hooker suggests that whites mourn symbolic losses (economic privilege, for example), while often ignoring the fatal harms suffered by people of color in the United States (black people killed by police).[82] Elsewhere, Hooker argues that the American polity must find a way to transform "the ethical-political perspectives of dominant groups," which involves "reshaping the public memory of the political community as a whole so its character as a racial polity is acknowledged."[83] I suggest that political mourning can contribute to this kind of transformation.

Fourth, the law tries but fails to hold any individual(s) responsible, thus exposing the impossibility of addressing *political responsibility* via legal means. The fourth component, then, helps us reconsider how we conceptualize responsibility, often by demonstrating the incomplete nature of legal responsibility. But at the same time, the polity may take up or reject their responsibility for conditions leading to the deaths. How collective political responsibility is assigned, rejected, or accepted, and to what ends it is used, is a central part of the analysis here. The losses I describe in the following chapters are integrally tied to the question of what law can and should do. The events that lead to the politics of mourning may form the basis of criminal or civil suits, but these legal processes prove unsatisfactory; they locate no one person to hold responsible, or they obviously scapegoat an individual when it is apparent (in a nonlegal sense) that the problem is far greater in scope. A blunt instrument for securing structural change, law is not particularly effective at locating responsibility in structures rather than holding individuals responsible.[84] Legislative responses to these failures of law demonstrate how the law is not a given, but changes as we change; our dissatisfaction with legal outcomes can prompt political change in the form of new laws that challenge the status quo. In this sense, then, the law can be understood as a means of attributing responsibility, even when it fails to do so satisfactorily. Law's failure can open us up to a sense of collective responsibility that law's success does not.

Responsibility, however, is tricky. It is relatively easy for those with power to manipulate or mislead the populace—the demos, who form the basis of democracy—about where responsibility lies, whether intentionally or not. For example, if the cause of African American poverty was a poor family structure, then a successful intervention would find ways to genuinely support and improve African American family units through enabling (rather than disciplinary) interventions. But if the root cause of African American poverty is white domination, an altogether different set of responsibilities emerges. The calls for political change based on these attributions are also very different. How political actors frame responsibility—who (or what entity) is responsible, and how we should ensure accountability to prevent such events in the future—is a crucial part of the process of the politics of mourning.

In general, I suggest that we can conceive of mourning as falling on a spectrum between more democratic and more sovereign. Democratic mourning seeks to foreground democratic relations of equality between citizens; it assumes that life chances should be roughly equal and that all citizens deserve roughly equal protection and support. Thus, if some group is bearing an unequal burden, the polity as a whole should respond by reforming institutions to address that unequal burden (even if those suffering are a minority). The challenge is that the American state has never been democratic across racial boundaries; we have long been a white democracy. Thus, with few exceptions, the response by the white majority to black loss has been a denial that that loss is a *collective* problem; instead, the response has been to blame particular individuals for what are collective problems.

This denial of responsibility for state actions that have generated unequally borne problems leads to undesirable sovereign mourning. As I argue in Chapter 4, the response to the events of September 11 led not to a foregrounding of the people and their needs but to a foregrounding of the state and its needs. This reverses the arrow in Dewey's terms, because for Dewey, the formation of a public precedes and enables the formation of a state. In Dewey's idealized version of democracy, the state's evolving functions are a result of the evolution of the problems faced by the demos. Thus, the state is not separate from the people; it should instead be the expression of the people. Sovereign mourning instead suggests that the state is the only means of preserving the people. As a result, its aims are to preserve itself (its institutions, borders, status quo, and—in a white democracy—white privilege) rather than taking stock of what is in the interests of the demos.

Finally, the combination of these previous factors helps ground calls for *political change*. Political actors must invoke the tragic event as the basis for political change. In the cases I consider, that change has been legislation. Once a death has served as the ground for calls for political change, political elites have taken up the charge and responded with some sort of legislative agenda. For the purposes of this inquiry, I leave aside the question of whether legislative efforts actually lead to political change. Obviously, they do not always do so; nonetheless, that political elites have taken on the question signals a shift that should not be disregarded. Thus, much like Verovšek's argument regarding the politics of memory—that political elites must take up the question—my suggestion is that the politics of mourning requires action in the domain of institutional politics, even if the effects are negligible or mostly symbolic.

It is possible and suggested by all of my cases that to be objects of a politics of mourning, victims are often successfully portrayed as apolitical and innocent, even when they may have been visible political agents previously. Miriam Ticktin suggests that this quest for innocent victims to ground structural change has considerable limitations, however. Innocence, Ticktin argues, relies on a quest for purity, displaces politics, and thus hides the structural and historical causes of inequality.[85] Ticktin rightly claims that those deemed innocent are politically powerful because once dead, their agency is evacuated; the memory of the dead becomes a palimpsest on which those still living project their own narratives.[86] Ticktin alerts us to the possibility that an invocation of innocence may insulate the situation from critiques of structural conditions of inequality, thus bypassing politics by relying on moral outrage and providing only comfort or assistance to victims rather than demanding change that addresses the conditions that led to their suffering. However, if we consider more fully the confluence between identity and responsibility, as I do here, we might argue that when successful, portrayals of innocence compel action by those left behind (made easier when those calling for change knew the victim well). That is, once a death has entered the politics of mourning that I describe, the deaths may enable the boundary of what counts as political to shift.

When that occurs, it provides cover for politicians to proclaim the urgent need to enter a new space or reopen a festering conflict. The space of mourning, cast as beyond politics-as-usual, might ironically enable us to address the perceived cause through politics. Yet as Ticktin points out, invocations of innocence can also insert a hierarchy of suffering, such that some suffering is visible and deplorable, while other suffering remains invisible and thus acceptable.[87] I share Ticktin's concern about bypassing politics through the production of innocent victims, as well as her desire to locate the possibilities and limitations of invoking innocence. Nonetheless, the figure of the victim portrayed as innocent is an important part of understanding why some instances generate a process of political mourning while others do not.

Calls for political change need not be successful to fulfill the criteria of a politics of mourning. Consider the example of the Scottsboro Boys. The National Association for the Advancement of Colored People (NAACP) and the Communist Party both engaged in sustained efforts to publicize the injustice suffered by the Scottsboro Boys in the 1930s.[88] Although this effort failed to generate the antilynching laws the activists had hoped to achieve, the movement generated cohesion and a Deweyan public that could identify a problem and articulate a political, democratic solution. As argued by Michael McCann, even a failed legal and political effort to challenge injustice can change identities in important and lasting ways; participating in the process can change people's perceptions of themselves as well as the legal system.[89] The three historical cases I consider resulted in institutional change, so the theory I lay out includes that as part of the process. But Black Lives Matter has not yet generated the same kind of significant political change that the other instances discussed here did (unless we account for the white backlash); it has, however, served to expose some of the most undemocratic impulses in contemporary America. I return to this question in Chapter 5 and the Conclusion.

A politics of mourning can challenge the political status quo when these components combine in the right way. Not all deaths lead to a politics of mourning, and not all deaths should. But there are moments when a loss and the law's inability to sufficiently respond to it so deeply disturb our collective identity that the polity is moved to take up its collective responsibility and call for political change. A privileged public learns of losses suffered by those of lower standing because these moments of loss expose the racial limits of our democratic solidarity, most often in the wake of some organized effort to gain visibility through more traditional means. After this connection across the borders of belonging is made, we seek to determine responsibility, often through the use of the law. When law fails, those affected or those in positions of power invoke the mourned to call for political changes directly related to a particular loss.

Tracing Political Mourning in Politics

The examples through which I trace the process model laid out above include the Triangle Fire, Emmett Till's murder, the events of September 11, and the unfolding of the Black Lives Matter movement. These examples highlight the possibilities and limitations of political mourning, which I discuss in the Conclusion. Some may object that these are not comparable, and in many respects that is true; in that sense, they are examples rather than case studies in the more specific definition used in the social sciences. The numbers of deaths vary: 146 in the Triangle Fire, Till's singular death, more than 2,000 on September 11, and the series of discrete deaths that have combined to fuel the rise of Black Lives Matter. Additionally, two of the events I consider occurred in New York City (Triangle Fire and September 11 attacks), the third was split between rural Mississippi and Chicago (Till), and Black Lives Matter has coalesced across the country. These all suggest that comparison in the sense required by a causal claim is futile. And yet all of the cases include the components I identify in the process model discussed above: contested identities, visibility, actors taking grief public, the inadequacy of legal responsibility, and political change. That they all share these components suggests that comparison may be constructive.

The examples were chosen in part for their different outcomes. Political mourning is fascinating precisely because it is unpredictable; if it always led to clearly democratic or clearly undemocratic outcomes, it would be far less interesting to study. Thus, I chose these examples because they have different democratically normative outcomes that significantly involve questions about race and belonging in the United States. If we think of a scale between democratically oriented outcomes and undemocratically oriented outcomes, the political mourning in response to Till's murder contributed to an expansion of the boundaries of identity and thus an expansion of white Americans' understanding of complex political responsibility—responsibility not merely to punish individuals but to change conditions such that similar deaths do not happen in the future. This is a democratically desirable outcome; it prompted reflection on the gap between ideals and practice and moved Americans to work toward lessening that gap. As a result, I would argue that it moved the polity in the direction of justice and democratic solidarity. The Triangle Fire is a mixed case. On one level, it expanded the boundaries of belonging and prompted the state to take action to regulate industrial worksites, which helped incorporate not-quite-whites into the polity. But on another level, that move toward democratic solidarity for some came at a cost for African Americans employed in domestic or agricultural settings. Their claims for workplace protection and regulation became even harder to see once not-quite-whites were transformed into whites. September 11 serves as the exemplar of political mourning that led to undemocratic white racial solidarity and injustice, what I call sovereign mourning. American conceptions of identity have been contracting ever since as we have come to eschew complex political responsibility, falling instead into a melodramatic sense of victimization that demanded heroic military adventures to rescue us. Black Lives Matter is an example of a racial minority public seeking to be included in the boundaries of belonging confronted with a state that has increasingly sought to shrink the scope of Americanness. Throughout all of these, race is a central category that shapes who counted as an American and defines those to whom we owe recognition and respect. In all these cases, I argue, the dominant understanding of identity shifted.

While I hope the examples here that use race as a central category of analysis are instructive, many other identity categories might productively be considered under the framework I lay out here on an axis other than race. For example, many have died because of their sexuality. The murder of Matthew Shepard in 1998 might be an example of political mourning that made visible the violence of everyday life in a heterosexist society, as might the devastation of the AIDS epidemic in the gay community in the 1980s. Similarly, using gender or gender identity as a category of analysis might demonstrate that the deaths of women who died from botched abortions, women killed by abusive partners, or trans women murdered for being trans motivated others to call for change. These examples might include the components of the process of political mourning I have laid out here, but they focus on gender rather than race as the most salient identity category. There might be some similarities in the response to abductions and murders of children or to deaths caused by drunk driving, though it is more difficult to see how a context of contested identities would matter for these cases. In these other instances, people took their grief public to demand political change, but race may not have been central; it is certainly possible that other identity categories are. This suggests that political mourning is a rich site for further inquiry, of which this project is a tentative first step.

Chapter 2 discusses the first example, focusing on the events preceding and following the Triangle Fire of 1911. During the winter of 1909–1910, workers at the Triangle Shirtwaist Factory had engaged in a widely covered strike for better working conditions, but they failed to achieve an industrywide settlement. In March of 1911, 146 workers died in a massive fire on the eighth, ninth, and tenth floors of the Triangle Factory. Thousands of New Yorkers witnessed dozens of girls leap to their deaths from the ninth floor to escape death by fire. About two weeks after the fire, a procession of mourning that included approximately 150,000 marchers and 250,000 observers silently wound through the streets of Manhattan demanding political action around factory safety. After a criminal trial in which the factory owners were charged and acquitted of manslaughter, the state legislature enacted sweeping progressive reform bills to regulate industrial employment. In that sense, the Triangle Fire led to positive change in the lives of everyday citizens. But less obvious was that it contributed to a shift in racial identification that helped make ethnic whites (such as Sicilians or Polish Jews) just plain white. On the one hand, this appears as a victory in terms of expansion of identity: more people are seen as belonging and thus protected by the state. By virtue of being seen as worthy of protection, these working-class not-quite-whites could begin integrating into the national identity, as their lives were deemed worthy of protection while at work. On the other hand, the inclusion of those groups on the margins made black suffering more invisible; domestic workers and agricultural laborers essentially fell off the map as the state sought to prevent harms to workers in industrial settings but remained absent at labor sites dominated by African Americans. While the boundaries of belonging expanded, the responsibility of the state stopped at those boundaries. Those who remained outside the newly formed boundary of whiteness did not benefit from the enlarged collective responsibility to protect labor from the excesses of industrial capitalism.

Chapter 3 analyzes the events before and after Emmett Till's lynching in 1955. His mother, Mamie Till-Bradley, refused to let the authorities bury her son in Mississippi, and when his mangled body arrived in Chicago, she displayed it for three days in a South Side church so that people could see what racism looked like. The result was massive interest by white media in newly discovered black suffering. The trial of Till's killers was well covered in the national press; television crews from all three networks flew footage to New York daily. It was a huge media event that set both blacks and whites talking and thinking about race relations in the United States. Till's death clarified for many black Americans that there was little left to lose; being young and black could be a death sentence even if you followed the rules. Till's death made clear to whites that what was happening in the American South threatened to rip the country apart and potentially threatened American hegemony internationally. The result was the substantively weak but symbolically powerful Civil Rights Act of 1957 that paved the way for black Americans to assert their identity not as blacks but as Americans. The American identity of blacks was asserted in *Brown v. Board of Education*, but it was made broader by executive and legislative actions after Till's death. With that new identity came additional responsibilities for the federal government to act.

Chapter 4 considers the events of September 11 as a manifestation of sovereign rather than democratic mourning. In the aftermath of the events, conceptions of belonging were re-restricted on racial, religious, ethnic, and gender lines, as Americans refused to acknowledge any responsibility for the conditions that led to the event itself. Patriotism meant unity; democratic dissent was betrayal. While grief could have led to a political effort to remedy the cause of the loss, as Judith Butler has argued, good-faith efforts seeking to explain why privileged young men joined al-Qaeda were met with irate criticism; American elites critiqued complicated explanations as nothing more than efforts to exonerate.[90] As a result, the American public, led by political elites, misread the complicated situation and misunderstood their own responsibility for the conditions that led to the attacks. Although events in the aftermath of September 11 follow a process similar to that in the other examples, the democratic potential of mourning was undercut by political elites who, rather than understanding the state as a manifestation of democratic will, instead imagined the state as a thin line standing against domination. Instead of seeing September 11 as a political event, Americans came to see it as an ontological threat, existing beyond politics in a world of good and evil. As a result, while law was used but found wanting in the other examples, law after September 11 was entirely bypassed; instead of criminal actions that demanded accountability, this was an existential threat that demanded war. Thus, for many Americans, "radical Islamic terrorism" has become an inexplicable manifestation of a violent culture, which served as a blanket justification for violent interventions against other nations and groups. This denial of responsibility and hardened distinction between us and them helped lay the groundwork for the rise of anti-immigrant discourse in the late 2010s, progressing from President Donald Trump's so-called Muslim ban to putting children in cages. The perception of existential threat after September 11 has made democratic solidarity internally and across borders increasingly difficult to maintain.

Chapter 5 takes up the contemporary example of Black Lives Matter (BLM). The assertion by activists in the wake of Trayvon Martin's and Mike Brown's deaths that Black Lives Matter, followed quickly by the largely white, social media response of All Lives Matter, served to expose the deeply undemocratic nature of an American state premised on white democracy and black subjugation. The rise of Black Lives Matter suggests that the American state is indeed a racial one, and that it remains an open question whether the United States will survive the transition from white democracy to multiracial democracy, given the partisan differences in the response to BLM.

The Conclusion offers an overview of the possibilities and limitations of political mourning, as well as identifying some questions unaddressed by this work. What do we learn about democratic values and the value of democracy by examining these events of political mourning? How might we respond to the deaths of everyday people to move toward democracy and away from sovereignty? Might the process hold true in other states, including ones that are not democratic?

2

The Triangle Fire

State Responsibility for White Workers

I n the fall of 1909 and winter of 1910, the Triangle Shirtwaist Factory was at the heart of a bitter struggle over labor rights. The industry-wide strike, dubbed the "Uprising of 20,000," came near the end of massive waves of immigration into the United States, and it prompted public sympathy for the mostly young, female, Jewish and Italian immigrants who worked in the booming garment industry in New York City. Such workers, although nominally white, were classified under bewildering racial-classification schemes premised on stark assertions of Anglo-Saxon superiority. The strike pitted recent immigrants against those who had been in America longer, and racialized lines were drawn between and among these new immigrants as well as between and among earlier arrivals. The strike also challenged some of these distinctions when, in the face of fears that the strike would cause a race war between Italians and Jews, the two groups worked together; instead of being separated by race, they found common cause in class. But widespread popular support was not enough to sustain the momentum, and eventually the strike failed. In early February 1910, the owners of the Triangle Factory offered higher wages and shorter hours, but not the right to bargain collectively; the offer separated liberal reformers (philanthropic women of the Women's Trade Union League) from the more radical labor activists and workers of the International Ladies' Garment Workers' Union. The strikers wanted to end egregious employment practices that controlled and divided workers (including property searches, arbitrary pay, and harsh working conditions), but the broad coalition of strike supporters could not survive the owners' offer.

Thirteen months later, on Saturday, March 25, 1911, the floors occupied by the Triangle Shirtwaist Factory—floors 8, 9, and 10 of a ten-story "fireproof" building—caught fire. Of the 500 or so workers present that day, 146 died within minutes. The building was located only a block away from popular Washington Square Park, and a large crowd quickly gathered at the sound of fire engines. Those in the crowd saw dozens of young girls plunge to their deaths from the ninth floor, many in flames; heard the screams of the workers as they caught fire; and smelled the burned flesh of the victims. The fire department could do little to help—its pumps were not powerful enough to reach the burning ninth floor, its ladders reached only the seventh floor, and its safety nets proved useless; some jumpers crashed through the nets and then through the vault lights in the sidewalk, coming to rest in heaps in the basement of the building.

The Triangle Fire was singularly riveting. Thousands witnessed the fire firsthand; tens of thousands viewed the bodies in a makeshift morgue over the next few days; the tragedy received nationwide media coverage; and hundreds of thousands participated in an immense display of public mourning on April 5, 1911 (originally planned to mourn the bodies of the unidentified, though the city did not release the bodies as hoped). About 150,000 people marched in the procession, while another 250,000 lined the streets. Even though the march of mourning was a general strike, involving members of more than sixty sympathetic unions, the mourners were intentionally silent and purposefully apolitical. Signs identified each participating union and said, simply, "We mourn our loss" or "We demand fire protection." The procession took more than four hours to pass under the arch in Washington Square Park. The tremendous display of silent mourning was an unusual, powerful call to attend to the pervasive, widely acknowledged, yet intransigent problem of perilously unsafe workplaces.

Observers, connecting the fire to the failed strike, commented on a new sense of racial unity that descended on the city in the wake of the fire. Spurred by the horrific memory of the fire, activists, union members, progressive reformers, and politicians all demanded strengthened laws to regulate industry and protect workers. The result, on June 30, 1911, was the establishment of the Factory Investigating Commission (FIC), tasked with a broad mandate to investigate the conditions of industrial manufacturing. Though terrible and tragic, the Triangle Fire accomplished what the Uprising of 20,000 did not.

By the time the FIC dissolved in 1915, it had fixed the plight of industrial workers in the public's conscience and established workplace regulation as being within the proper scope of government. By 1919, New York had institutionalized an industrial commission to administer industrial safety laws throughout the state. In less than a decade, industrial workers in New York, whose worksites before 1911 had been practically unregulated, could claim the most advanced sanitary and health protections in the world.

The mourning after the fire helped establish basic worker protections by enabling political intervention into industrial labor sites; part of that process included conversations about political identity and collective responsibility. Before the fire, the immigrant, not-quite-white striking workers were perceived by political elites as attacking American values and cherished ideals of self-sufficiency at the heart of American identity, particularly regarding the extent to which the state could intervene in business or commerce. This put those in positions of power and privilege on the defensive. The "good story"—that is, the widely accepted view—of laissez-faire economic policy was confirmed, and strikers, though found sympathetic by the public, were still seen as threats to the American way of life.[1] However, the fire and the outpouring of public sympathy after the fire recast the now-dead workers as victims of politically enabled negligence and racialized exclusion. Their victimhood—based in part on the workers' youth, femaleness, and ambiguous racial status—opened a space for political change that the strike had not. Their contested identities (identities assigned to them by a highly race-conscious, western European, Protestant majority rather than chosen by the workers) had made the public sympathetic to them during the strike, but public opinion changed when the owners offered more money. The difference between the two identities during the strike and after the fire—the difference between agents demanding political change and victims who confronted the public with the costs of failing to act—helped challenge the then-dominant understanding of the separation of public and private. It made what had been a good story about government absence in the workplace into a bad story. The fire and its aftermath helped labor reformers enact a broad slate of legislation that changed the landscape of American politics and that helped soften the bright line between white and not-quite-white, while still maintaining a hierarchical racial structure. These changes occurred in part because of the political mourning, which opened a way for the (more privileged) public and politicians to assume collective political responsibility for the conditions that led to these deaths. But while a politics of mourning helped achieve egalitarian goals via labor protection and industrial regulation, it also expanded the domain of whiteness in ways that benefited many recent immigrants. Certainly, this was an important move toward justice in terms of expanding the boundaries of identity and responsibility. However, this shift further marginalized those deemed unambiguously "not white" and thereby contributed to a slowly coalescing understanding of race as black or white that Matthew Guterl identifies as having occurred from 1900 to 1940.[2] In short, we see a shift in the conception of the borders of belonging so that those previously seen as "not-quite-white" could now be ushered into an expanded category of white ethnics rather than racialized others. At the same time, we also see an expansion in the larger understanding of political responsibility such that the workplace became a legitimate site of political regulation. These shifts occur in tandem; as those excluded from whiteness were ushered into whiteness, the state took up responsibility for their protection in workplaces.

The argument in this chapter proceeds as follows. The first section considers the plight of immigrant factory workers in New York to illustrate the challenges of visibility. The strike of 1909 generated tremendous visibility, but it failed to generate a sense of collective responsibility and thereby political change. The second section considers the public discussions about and attributions of responsibility after the fire and provides evidence suggesting that the fire inspired a sense of collective responsibility that demanded action. The final substantive section offers reasons why the Triangle Fire helped motivate political change even though another, comparable fire did not. It also suggests that while on one axis, the Triangle Fire moved the polity toward justice by expanding the boundaries of belonging and reenvisioning workplaces as sites of collective responsibility, on another, it made the losses suffered by people of color in less visible workplaces difficult to code as politically salient.

Making Loss Visible: The Strike, the Fire, and a March of Mourning

Though visibility alone is not enough to secure political change, it is a crucial step toward opening the necessary conversation about the collective responsibility and political will required to implement political change. Visibility helps transform a loss from a private problem (private in the sense that employment was a private endeavor) to public one. Visibility sometimes does not occur because the citizenry at large perceives certain types of death as inevitable and natural, given the existing social order—for example, it is widely known and accepted that some groups die younger or lose more children or suffer preventable poverty-related diseases. Such losses are difficult to invoke as the basis of political change because the privileged who rule in a given social order are predisposed to ignore the human costs of that order when losses are suffered by those outside their own group. Those who bear losses disproportionately face the hurdle of making these losses visible to the larger political community. But political mourning can pierce that veil; the bereaved (or those who speak on their behalf) may be able to make more privileged citizens and elites see the injustice of the deaths so that the ones with power will be moved to address the contributing conditions. Mourning might communicate unjust conditions in ways that explicitly political challenges and deliberation cannot.[3]

The 1909 ladies' garment workers' strike was an important moment for American labor history, feminist organizing, and Progressive politics.[4] Because of these different currents, the strike was a complex phenomenon, involving a complicated set of actors and demands. In general, scholars of the Triangle Fire have focused on the intersections between politics, class, gender, and labor. These analyses provide crucial insights and contribute to a story of progress and policy evolution. According to most scholars, the fire made evident the suffering of the working class. As a result, citizens in positions of privilege changed institutional structures, and American politics became more inclusive. But the standard story does not address how race shaped conceptions of belonging during the strike and how, after the fire, conceptions of identity shifted through reshaping racial categories. In excavating this untold story, I do not seek to downplay the considerable and important shifts that occurred after the fire in terms of industrial regulation. The addition of race helps reveal the limitations of political mourning. Racial conflict and hierarchy were visible during the strike itself, and limited the scope of political change that followed.

To remedy this, I supplement other works on Triangle history by explicitly examining the role of race in the strike, the fire, and the subsequent political changes.[5] With that in mind, I turn to the strike of 1909–1910 and its role in generating the visibility required by a politics of mourning.

The Uprising of 20,000

Strikes—like most overtly political actions—are efforts to garner support from the larger public by making visible some material injustice or harm. The strike of 1909 was no different. It erupted because of the grim conditions in the New York garment factories of the 1900s, where recent immigrants worked long hours in awful conditions for miserable wages because they could find no other work. About 60 percent of the workers in the Triangle Factory were Jewish immigrants from eastern Europe; about 30 percent were from southern Italy; and the remainder were native-born Americans, though mostly with immigrant parents.[6] Considered racially white but nonetheless inferior to Anglo-Saxons (not-quite-white and not yet considered American), these Jewish and Italian immigrants faced significant discrimination in their new home.

Most workers at the Triangle Factory were also women. While men held supervisory and lucrative positions in the ladies' garment industry, women did the bulk of the work.[7] Even though women made up 20 percent of the industrial labor force by 1910 and at least 20 percent of all women in the United States were working for wages, women lagged far behind men in terms of unionization rates, pay, and protection.[8] Women's organizations addressed this gap by advocating for women workers, who often had no other allies. Arguing less for political inclusion and more for the right to work in safer environments, women's organizations such as the Women's Trade Union League (WTUL) worked with and on behalf of the mostly young, immigrant, and Jewish and Italian workers.[9]

While one might think that labor unions would want to organize these workers to increase membership and influence, this was not the case. The dominant labor organization of the era, the American Federation of Labor (AFL), was nativist, masculinist, and craftwork oriented, and it showed little interest in organizing trades with large numbers of immigrants or women.[10] Furthermore, the AFL and other labor organizations reinforced racialized hierarchy in the workplace by perpetuating a racial-classification scheme that determined who received the best-paying and often safest jobs. David Roediger writes that the left and labor were "instructors in whiteness. . . . Unions that discriminated but opened to new immigrants more readily than to African Americans, Mexican American and Asian Americans reinforced the 'inbetween' position of southern and eastern Europeans."[11] Those in positions of power and privilege assumed that Anglo-Saxons were racially superior but disagreed about where other races—including those we today consider white—fit into a bewildering array of racial classificatory schemes. Meanwhile, "in-between" immigrants worked to ally themselves with people higher in the hierarchy.[12] This racializing process shaped how both privileged and marginalized groups viewed labor struggles.[13]

The workers at the Triangle Factory, like workers at hundreds of other factories in New York City, were hired under the contracting system, which set a male boss over a group of workers. The owner paid the boss for the output of the workers he supervised. In turn, he paid the workers according to a variety of factors: what he earned, how much he liked them, whether they had irritated him that day, and so on. As a result, pay scales were often unfair. Additionally, workers were searched each evening as they left, charged excessively for the needles they used, punished for speaking to one another, regularly insulted by their bosses, and occasionally even assaulted.[14] Finally, workplaces were unsafe. Fires erupted in factories of all types and were frequently fatal. One study showed that 99 percent of all suit-and-coat shops were defective in terms of safety. Another factory fire, the High Street Fire in Newark, New Jersey, in November 1910, provided a grim foreshadowing of the Triangle Fire. The details are eerily similar: a crowded workspace, a locked door, worthless fire escapes, the factory located high in the building, fire engines next door but useless, and a trial that determined no criminal responsibility.[15] Six girls burned to death, while nineteen leaped to their deaths, and yet the High Street Fire garnered little visibility and prompted no institutional change.[16] Workers, in short, were vulnerable on numerous levels. Their challenge "was to get New York to pay attention to the mistreatment of poor immigrants."[17]

In September 1909, workers from Triangle spoke with an organizer from the International Ladies' Garment Workers' Union (ILGWU), knowing the discussion might cost them their jobs.[18] Upon hearing of the meeting, the owners—Max Blanck and Isaac Harris, themselves recent immigrants—locked the workers out and hired prostitutes as strikebreakers.[19] Over the next two months, violent clashes between strikers and strikebreakers led to the arrests of hundreds of strikers. One chronicler noted that many "arrested women appeared in court with broken noses and bandaged arms and heads."[20] Law was clearly aligned with the owners, both on the books and in the streets. Police violence was justified as a reasonable response to the workers' lack of respect for the law. One judge condemned a striker for being "on strike against God and nature," while another swore to do "all in my power to stop this disorder."[21]

Middle-class women reformers of the Women's Trade Union League (WTUL), through assiduous cultivation of partnerships with working-class women, gained a respected though tense place in the struggle to protect workers. These reforming women were idealistic, well educated, and genuinely compassionate, and they made significant efforts to assist their less-fortunate sisters. Their influence enabled the strike's initial success (although it later proved to be its demise).[22] Their aid was crucial to the strike's visibility: matronly middle-class reformers, the majority from families of wealth and privilege, linking arms with young workers proved a public relations coup. Given the amount of labor unrest at the time, the public typically yawned at reports of violence against or the arrest of strikers. But when Mary Dreier, daughter of a wealthy businessman and president of the WTUL, was arrested after visiting the strikers, middle-class and wealthy citizens began paying attention.[23] When a judge later apologized to Mary Dreier for her arrest but sentenced the strikers arrested with her to hard labor, the story made front-page news on several New York papers (less for the disparate sentencing of the strikers than for the arrest of a society lady).[24] Deft managers of public opinion, the WTUL started seeding picket lines with college students practically indistinguishable from strikers.[25] The following report from the *New York Times* demonstrates how class differences were highlighted in news reports.

> Miss Inez Milholland, late of Vassar, appeared in the Night Court last night in behalf of three girl shirtwaist strikers, who were accused by Lewis Beerman . . . of calling him a "scab boss." One was fined $5 and two discharged. Miss Milholland, who was gowned for the opera, told Magistrate Harris that while she was with them the girls raised no disturbance, but she had been arrested at the door of the West Twentieth Street Station because she followed the three to the station, protesting against their arrest. At the station she was released. She was advised by the Magistrates to report this to the proper authorities.[26]

"Late of Vassar," "gowned for the opera," and the fact that Miss Milholland was identified by name while the strikers were not makes clear whose arrest mattered to readers. College students and society ladies were arrested and released while strikers were sent to the workhouse. The disparity of treatment drew sympathetic responses from many quarters of society.[27]

But the strike also exposed fault lines that bedeviled labor organizing then and continue to do so.[28] In particular, racial differences were used to divide workers who might otherwise work together. Factory owners adeptly used racial differences to keep workers estranged.[29] One organizer observed that "two girls will work side by side for weeks without knowing each other's names. Italians will be placed by the side of Jews, and race antagonism worked on to keep the girls at daggers' point, so that there will be created a distinct feeling against any sort of organization and fellow-feeling."[30] Because race structured the workplace, labor organizers feared that it would poison relationships between the strikers as well. Organizers were concerned that the strike would incite a "race war" because, as one WTUL leader bluntly said, "the strikebreakers are all Italians and the strikers Jewesses."[31] But these fears proved unwarranted as immigrant workers from diverse ethnic backgrounds collaborated. According to von Drehle, "Italians made up . . . between 6 percent and 10 percent of the shirtwaist strikers. . . . American-born workers constituted a similar portion. Eastern European Jews, who were two-thirds of the shirtwaist labor force, made up three-quarters or more of the strikers."[32] Observers expressed surprise that the strike brought workers together. One noted, "A good many girls . . . have come to know each other's names and to know a sisterly feeling for the first time in their lives."[33] By providing a common language of class, generating a sense of belonging, and downplaying discussions of racial differences, the strike helped overcome the cultural distance that made organizing new immigrants so challenging. But while racial tensions were partially overcome within the strikers' ranks, the differences between shades of white remained important to other workers as well as to the wider political community.

In late November, inspired by the Triangle strikers, more than twenty thousand ladies' garment workers in New York City walked off their jobs. Their demands included "an end to the subcontracting system, a 52 hour work week with unpaid overtime limited to 2 hours per day, and an end to wage deductions for supplies and electricity."[34] Jo Ann Argersinger writes:

> The shirtwaist strikers paralyzed the industry, demanded the recognition of the ILGWU, and called for improved wages and working conditions. Most of all they wanted respect. Many of them wore banners proclaiming, in Yiddish, "We Are Not Slaves." . . . They captured the imagination of the press and the hearts and pocketbooks of upper-class women, who joined forces with the strikers on the picket line, where they were dubbed the "mink brigade" by city newspapers.[35]

While the support from the mink brigade and the sympathetic coverage of the papers generated tremendous visibility for the strikers, the strike ultimately failed. To some degree, the failure was inevitable given the marked tensions between the aims of the ILGWU, the WTUL, and the strikers themselves. Each group had its own internal disagreements as well as disagreements with allies regarding primary goals: better pay, better conditions, industry-wide collective bargaining, fewer required hours, industrial democracy, or the empowerment of women. As a result, when owners in February 1910 made a calculated offer of higher wages and shorter hours without the right to bargain collectively, the proposal split the organizations and effectively ended the strike. Although workers had achieved impressive levels of visibility and had disseminated information about the deplorable conditions under which they worked, they had failed to obtain what they wanted most: respect paired with the right to bargain collectively.

As demonstrated by earlier legal contests about labor (for example, *Lochner v. New York* in 1905 and *Muller v. Oregon* in 1908), the strike was about where to draw the line between public and private and about whose interests the state would protect. As Elizabeth Mensch observes, the traditional understanding of business as private defined the era of "Classical Legal Consciousness" from 1885 to 1935, even as the first salvos of legal realism were fired in the 1920s.[36] Richard Greenwald contends that the Progressive Era in New York between 1900 and 1919 signaled the end of laissez-faire economics, in which all business relations were assigned to the private sphere and remained beyond government oversight.[37] The state's responses to the strike—overt harassment of and violence against workers, combined with judicial defense of owners' prerogatives—demonstrated that while buildings had public characteristics that required political oversight, what happened inside those buildings did not. Strikes therefore stirred debate over what counted as public and private, but for the most part, the status quo remained undisturbed. Relationships between workers and employers were generally viewed as private, and the state aligned itself with employers.

The failure of strikes, including the Triangle Factory strike, to provoke political change demonstrates that visibility itself is not always enough. A strike can expose poor conditions and overt violence suffered by workers. It also can help suture racial divisions that kept workers apart. Nonetheless, during this period, most strikes failed to generate a wider political sense of collective responsibility; the larger public did not act as if these industrial workers were citizens who deserved state protection in what was still understood as the private sphere and so the workplace remained beyond the reach of government regulation. As a result, any political change was limited in scope because the public and the law usually aligned with owners rather than workers. Owners deserved protection from government interference into their private affairs but workers did not deserve protection from concentrated private wealth.

The Triangle Factory strike also exposed the roles that race and gender played in constructing larger ideas about whose voices mattered. The young women, while often described as plucky, were considered rough and unladylike by both judges and their middle-class philanthropic sisters, who worried about the strikers' gaudy hats, heavy accents, and overt challenges to authority. Likewise, although many of the strikebreakers had been in America barely longer than the strikers, they were seen as defending the American way by protecting private enterprise from socialist incursions. The newer immigrants, meanwhile, were viewed as challenging these sacred tenets and disturbing the industrial peace. Thus, although the strike taught more sheltered citizens about the woeful conditions in the factories and the considerable violence suffered by members of the immigrant working class, this knowledge failed to generate any widespread call for political change. The responsibility for protecting workers lay on the shaky ground of the individual ethics of each business owner.

The Triangle Fire and a March of Mourning

But large-scale tragedies can move the political system to tackle thorny problems. The Triangle Fire performed this function. However, were it not for the visibility generated by the earlier strike, the Triangle Fire might have passed into history as little more than a footnote (like the Newark High Street fire in 1910).[38] This time, the public was predisposed to care about the workers in *this* factory, which had been at the heart of the 1909 strike and in the news for more than four months barely a year before.

The fire was ghastly to witness. Thousands observed it firsthand. It generated tremendous news coverage in New York and throughout the country.[39] The fire broke out near closing time on Saturday. At least ten thousand spectators crowded to the scene within a half hour of the first alarm.[40] The building that housed the Triangle Shirtwaist Company, the Asch Building, was designed to be "fireproof," meaning that the building itself could withstand fire without collapsing. But this had little to do with whether those inside could survive a fire.[41] It had unmarked exits, which were usually locked during business hours; one rickety fire escape; exit doors that opened inwards; and poor ventilation. At first, workers tried to extinguish the fire with buckets, but their efforts failed. Trapped by quickly spreading flames, workers faced two options: die by fire or jump. Dozens jumped. According to eyewitness William Shepherd, girls "fought each other to die by jumping instead of by fire."[42] Although firefighters had deployed safety nets, workers who fell into them broke through and hit the sidewalks with as much force as those who hit the sidewalks straightaway. Several fell through the vault lights in the sidewalk and crashed into the basement, while others lay where they fell on the sidewalk. In all, 146 employees of the Triangle Waist Company died within minutes: 123 were women, several of whom had walked picket lines the previous winter. The median age of the dead was twenty; the youngest was eleven. The witnessing crowd had swelled to twenty thousand by 7:00 P.M., when the dead were removed, placed in coffins, and hauled to a makeshift morgue. The mostly Irish policemen who had beaten and booked the strikers now respectfully handled their broken and burned bodies.

The next day, approximately one hundred thousand people visited the makeshift morgue, far more than the conceivable number of family members. One official estimated that six thousand people per hour passed through the morgue that day.[43] Families and friends had difficulty identifying the dead because many bodies were burned beyond recognition. Those closest to the victims identified the dead through their knowledge of intimate details: buttons on shoes, a signet ring, a capped tooth, a darned stocking.[44] Meanwhile, funeral processions flooded the Lower East Side; one funeral director performed eight funerals simultaneously.[45]

The ILGWU, journalists, and the wider public quickly connected the tragic fire to the failed strike. The ILGWU, in addition, saw an opportunity to make visible the human suffering that resulted from the owners' insistence on the right of privacy. The union wished to highlight the need for legal protection of workers in *all* factories. The ILGWU called for a general strike on April 5, 1911, organizing a vast procession to mourn and then bury seven still unidentified victims.[46] However, city leaders feared that the memories of the recent strike, unidentified bodies, public mourning, and the mass of "hysterical" immigrants would lead to violence. So the city refused to release the bodies to the ILGWU.[47] The union, nonetheless, forged ahead, supported by members of more than sixty sympathetic unions.[48] Approximately 150,000 mourners followed a single, empty, black hearse, and 250,000 onlookers lined the route from start to finish.[49] It took four hours for the marchers to pass under the Washington Square Arch. In all, close to half a million people participated in either this spectacular display of public mourning or in the other processions that day.[50]

While the ILGWU hoped the tragedy would reshape the political agenda, the political placards and banners that had characterized the Uprising of 20,000 were absent at this procession. The organizers of the march used more subtle techniques to express their demands. The union insisted that "no propagandist banners and no bands" be allowed.[51] The single exceptions were the banners held by ladies' garment workers, which said, "We demand fire protection."[52] Other banners, which identified the groups marching, said simply, "We mourn our loss."[53] Second, the procession was symbolic because the bodies themselves were not present. The willingness of mourners to march hours in the pouring rain (many, oddly, forsaking hats or overshoes) made a powerful impression on participants and observers, even more so since the procession with the actual bodies drew several thousand mourners to a Brooklyn cemetery.[54] Third, the silence of the procession was particularly powerful. No shouting or discussion occurred, perhaps because there was no single language in which the immigrant mourners could speak. Or perhaps it was because there was nothing that could be said that had not already been voiced. The silence was broken only as the procession neared the Asch building. There, the crowd let out "one long-drawn-out, heart-piercing cry, the mingling of thousands of voices, a sort of human thunder in the elemental storm—a cry that was perhaps the most impressive expression of human grief ever heard in this city."[55] Other than this, mourners did not shout, chant, or sing. They simply marched.

Like the earlier strike, this march was about making structural conditions that increased bodily vulnerability visible. The organizers of the march accomplished what Anne Norton suggests is rare but powerful: those on the margins, the liminars, calling for solidarity. Norton writes that "liminars become most active and powerful when they recognize not only their common experience of exploitation and subordination but also the formal resemblance of that experience to the experience of liminal groups in other structural relations."[56] Despite superficial similarities to a protest march, this expression of mourning attracted attention and achieved recognition through fundamentally different means. The difference between the rights asserted during the strike through the demand to "abolish our slavery" and the familiar rituals of mourning in the march expressed by "we mourn our loss" are significant. The first is a defiant assertion of equality while the second is a request for human recognition based on bodily vulnerability. The phrases convey different orientations toward viewers. Residents, workers, employees, firefighters, and politicians—basically everyone—knew that factories like Triangle were firetraps. But this common knowledge had failed to change public policy. The march self-consciously made what was generally considered a private matter—death and loss in the workplace—into a public spectacle, which demanded that New Yorkers *see* what the law allowed and what was being enabled in their names. The marchers asked viewers to do more than merely look, as, perhaps, many had during the fire. Marchers instead asked observers to feel the weight of these bodies and to consider that each person in the endless parade of workers could die the same death if nothing changed. Faced with a wall of bodies, all knowing and symbolically expressing their vulnerability to this kind of death, the public seems to have accepted the invitation to mourn and to turn that mourning into support for political change. As Judith Butler and Simon Stow have noted, a "mortalist humanism"—a recognition of shared bodily vulnerability—may be a necessary precursor to democratic politics, and this march of mourning seems to recognize and mobilize that insight.[57]

This expressive performance seems to have succeeded where logical demands had failed. Drawing on Sharon Krause's work, one might argue that the losses of the Triangle Fire aroused "a sense of what matters . . . [because] sentiments constitute the horizons of concerns within which practical judgment and deliberation transpire."[58] When this loss was so profoundly visible and so widely mourned, it seemed to help the public expand their sense of responsibility to include workers and worker safety, helping broaden conceptions of what constituted the public good. Certainly, the public nature of the tragedy contributed to its impact, as did the vulnerability signified by the bodies of young women. But the mourning that followed the fire helped spur action by the mourners and perhaps softened resistance by the public because knowledge was fortified by deep feelings that added emotional weight to specific calls for reform.

The 1909 strike familiarized observers with the plight of the workers at the Triangle Factory and in other factories throughout the city. When many of these same workers died in agony before the eyes of thousands of more privileged citizens, the public suddenly seemed open to considering whether the pressing political questions about the proper line between public and private were the right questions to be asking. To recall John Dewey's arguments in *The Public and Its Problems*, quoted in Chapter 1, the display of mourning, connected to the concrete demands of the strike, seems to have helped overcome the apathy and paralysis that make collective action impossible, by alerting the public to the indirect effects of failing to act.[59] The strikers' demands were no longer premised on abstract declarations of freedom from government intrusion but instead premised on a democratic response to collective, shared problems. And the public seemed to recognize that failing to intervene practically ensured that something similar would happen again. But to link the strikers and the fire's horror was only the second step in the process of political mourning. The contested identities of racial boundaries were overcome by the solidarity of the strike and the grief of the fire, while actors taking their grief public had certainly occurred. The next step in the process involved the effort to determine who was responsible for this horrific tragedy.

Agency, Collective Responsibility, and Political Change

The march of mourning helped participants and onlookers alike see workers' bodily vulnerability as politically meaningful. These losses were transformed; from private matters with private solutions, they came to be understood as requiring a larger structural solution because law itself had enabled this outcome. Prior to the march of mourning, many citizens acted as though they held a narrow view of political obligations, limited to minimizing the twin threats of anarchy and tyranny. This vision of a limited government, proposed by John Locke, partially taken up by the Founders, and later popularized by William Graham Sumner, understood the purpose of government as constraining these threats through citizen participation but preserving property and the space of business from state intrusion.[60] But as argued by Jane Addams and other Progressive Era reformers, the industrial era introduced a new threat to democratic government: concentrated wealth.[61] State institutions had failed to address this phenomenon. The Triangle Fire made the stakes of this failure apparent and enabled an expanded sense of responsibility toward fellow citizens: an obligation to protect fellow citizens from new forms of economic power. The strike and subsequent fire made it clear that these deaths resulted from a general, structural failure rather than merely one bad factory. Immigrants in New York asked little more than the chance to work. But the racialized composition of the workforce and the inability of organized labor to change the conditions of work meant that wage earners, and particularly these workers, had no real protection. The now palpable problem prompted many in New York to demand a new legal definition of what citizens owe one another as well as a new understanding of who counts as a citizen.

After the fire, journalists, politicians, the ILGWU, and the WTUL immediately asked about responsibility. Were the owners at fault for maintaining a substandard workplace? Did the fire department fail to inspect? Had the buildings department failed to enforce laws? Was this simply a sad and unfortunate confluence of events, perhaps a subspecies of natural disaster? Or was it a larger, systemic (and thus potentially political) problem?

Even though the owners of the Triangle Factory had a code-compliant workshop—in fact, one of the more sanitary and safe factories in contemporary New York—146 workers had died.[62] But the public came to see the owners as criminals: representatives of concentrated wealth who willingly sacrificed lives to maximize profits.[63] Many came to believe that the state itself must step in to address this threat. Though the owners might have been blameless according to the law, the fire made clear that the status quo was morally blameworthy. Repairing the situation required not only moral censure but political action. The new economic order demanded fair arbitration that balanced owners' right to accumulate wealth with workers' right to life.

But state institutions were not yet capable of performing this task. In a byzantine series of accusations, newspapers and politicians damned and then deemed innocent several entities. In the end, no single agency was responsible for inspection and enforcement of codes protecting workers. As a bitter fire chief remarked, "Those responsible for buildings . . . include the Tenement House Department, the Factory Inspection Department, the Building Department, the Health Department, the Department of Water Supply, Gas and Electricity and the Police Department to see that the orders of the other five departments are carried out."[64] But no agency was responsible for enforcing sanitary or safe working conditions for workers *within* these buildings. As a result, responsibility was pinned on the owners.[65] On April 10, 1911, barely two weeks after the fire, Blanck and Harris were indicted for manslaughter and criminal negligence. But after a trial in which the defense attorney relied on the witnesses' lack of facility with English, the owners were acquitted on all counts.[66] The *Literary Digest* reported "147 Dead, Nobody Guilty."[67]

This conclusion was unsatisfying to practically everyone. While there is no way to know for certain the extent to which the combination of strike, fire, and mourning took hold in the imaginations of everyday people, it seems plausible to infer from speeches made by labor activists, witnesses, and public leaders that these tragic events helped politicians and citizens reimagine the factory as public rather than private and to recast the condition of workers not as a private problem but as one of democratic politics. The series of events helped open citizens to consider revising institutional structures to counter a new threat. Leon Stein recounts several public speeches that make evident a sense of collective responsibility. He writes that a "sense of public guilt made itself felt at all the meetings."[68]

The following speech, delivered by well-known suffragist Dr. Anna Shaw, suggests that the mourning after the fire enabled an emotional shift toward identification with the dead and thereby contributed to a new understanding of political obligation:

> As I read the terrible story of the fire . . . I asked, "am I my sister's keeper?" For the Lord said to me, "where is thy sister?" And I bowed my head and said, "I am responsible." Yes, *every man and woman in this city is responsible.* Don't try to lay it on someone else. Don't try to lay it on some official. We are responsible! You men—forget not that you are responsible! As voters it was your business. . . . If you are incompetent, then . . . stand aside and let us try! There was a time when a woman worked in the home. . . . Now she can no longer regulate her own conditions, her own hours of labor. She has been driven into the market with no voice in the laws and powerless to defend herself. The most cowardly thing that men ever did was when they tied woman's hands and left her to be food for the flames. . . . Something's got to be done to the law. . . . And if it is not constitutional to protect the lives of workers then we've got to smash the constitution! It's our "instrument," and if it doesn't work, we've got to get a new one![69]

Shaw asks: What does it mean to be my sister's keeper? In the laissez-faire, Lockean and Sumnerian vision of limited government, it meant to protect her from anarchy and tyranny. But it came to mean something more. She, along with other workers, deserves to be protected from the ravages of corporate power aided and abetted by the law. Shaw argues that the only way to address this threat was to change the law: to make the Constitution do our democratic bidding rather than protect property at the expense of life.

Shaw also raises the question of who ought to be protected. She extends a democratic sense of responsibility to cover young, foreign-born, marginally white women. In her opinion, while everyone agrees that owners should be protected from unlawful seizures of property, we should also protect this subset of workers from deadly workplaces. Thus, Shaw not only identified a new threat (unconstrained profits) and proposed a solution (protective labor laws); she also boldly claimed that democratic government means more than protecting property: it also means protecting people. As a suffragist, she foregrounded the parlous position of women in the workplace. This enabled her to call for their political empowerment and for the right to vote as a means of self-protection. But the argument holds for a broader constituency, as well. People, her words suggest, deserve as much protection as property, and while some working-class persons may not have previously been recognized as worthy of protection, their tragic deaths have helped us see them as deserving.

Shaw, Clara Lemlich, and other mourners refused to keep their grief private, because the loss of their friends and compatriots was not a merely private loss; the loss of these individuals was a larger indictment of a too-distant state. These actors could have remained silent or could have continued to press their demands via traditional political channels. But the failure of the Uprising of the 20,000 had showed the limitations of that model. Their goal now was to use the reaction to this terrible loss of life to mobilize support for preventing similar losses in the future.

On April 2, a standing-room-only meeting at the Metropolitan Opera House led to the formation of the Committee on Safety, which advocated reformulation of factory safety laws. With the subsequent backing of Robert Wagner and Al Smith (eventually known as Progressive reformers but then Tammany Hall functionaries[70]), the Committee on Safety ultimately was incorporated into a legislative committee that then morphed into the Factory Investigating Commission (FIC). According to Richard Greenwald, "the fire's sheer horror propelled safety reform." As a result, the FIC enjoyed "unprecedented public support."[71] While the primary goal was to revise fire safety codes, Smith and Wagner expanded the FIC's mandate to enable investigation of other regulatory issues within factories and then expanded its jurisdiction to cover other workplaces. In its short life, the FIC enacted a remarkable slate of regulations dealing with fire safety, sanitation, dangerous trades, more stringent (and enforceable) labor laws, and the protection of women and children.[72] The FIC advanced the causes of organized labor and women's suffrage and laid groundwork for the subsequent rise of the Democratic Party, the New Deal (Francis Perkins, future labor secretary under Franklin Delano Roosevelt, witnessed the fire firsthand[73]), and the federal bureaucracy.

The fire helped shape future buildings—public venues where exit doors open out rather than in, illuminated exit signs, and adequate fire escapes are all legacies of the Triangle fire. The response of a newly invigorated regulatory state also seemed to signal the beginning of a change in the relationship between citizen and state as the state's intervention—for good or ill—into the space of formerly private business expanded. Richard Greenwald writes, "In the process of protecting women workers, the state remade itself . . . with the creation of new policies and laws."[74] It contributed to changing the boundary between public and private by including the workplace as a legitimate site of governmental intervention. The fire thus had considerable long-term political effects by virtue of happening in one of the major industrial sites in the United States, in the district of a politician who was rising to power (Al Smith), and during the Progressive Era.

I suggest that these changes happened in part because the public and politicians, as a result of the fire, were open to considering the factory as part of the democratic polity. In part because of the fire, in part because of actors who refused to accept the status quo, and in part because the demands for change found receptive listeners among political elites (such as Al Smith and Robert Wagner), previous beliefs about business as a purely private space changed. Places of business were now considered at least partly public, and citizens began to understand and accept political responsibility for what happened in those places. Moving forward, citizens began to view conditions within factories as reflections of the quality of American democracy.

Why Did This Fire Matter?

The deaths of twenty-six young working girls in the 1910 Newark High Street fire sparked little political response. Why did the Triangle Fire generate such a huge response while the Newark High Street fire did not? For one, the Newark factory was not involved in a highly publicized strike; because the 1909–1910 strike in New York garnered the attention of prominent women philanthropists and thus generated so much media coverage, a fire at Triangle was certain to be big news. Though the demographics of the workers were similar, concerns about racial differences were not as pressing because there was no priming event like the strike that made race salient. It also helped that the *New York Times* and other major news outlets in New York City provided considerable coverage of the Triangle Fire in comparison. The location mattered, too. While Newark was a major urban area, it has long been the city across the river from New York. In addition, that the Triangle Factory was a block away from popular Washington Square Park meant that people were already nearby when the fire broke out. In particular, the people nearby were those who had the leisure to visit a park rather than work on a Saturday. But perhaps most important was that the preceding strike meant that the ILGWU and other unions were willing and able to mobilize a massive march of mourning to call attention to dangerous factory conditions. Eliminating unsafe working conditions—including locked doors, crowded conditions, and a lack of respect or concern for worker safety—was part of the strikers' demands, so when working conditions led to a preventable accident, the utterly predictable nature of the fire was enough to motivate a response. The sheer numbers of marchers, any of whom might die in a similar factory accident, must have prompted serious reflection by the public about whether this is who we Americans are. That many of those who died in the Triangle Fire lived in the district of Al Smith—then well on his way to becoming speaker of the New York State Assembly and eventually governor of New York—surely also played a role. These objective differences help explain why one tragedy served as the basis of new kinds of government action to prevent similar occurrences in the future.

But on some level, the objective differences may not tell the whole story. The horror of facing the burned bodies of the dead must have moved even the staunchest capitalist to reconsider industry's ability to police itself, if for no other reason than accidents like this were terrible publicity and potentially ruined an industrialist's future. The larger question of the role of government in a capitalist democracy was pried open by the fire, partly because of a series of fortuitous circumstances, but partly because refusing to act exposed a gap between an assumed democratic norm of equal protection and the reality that workers had practically no protection. By remaining on the sidelines, the state was siding with business rather than workers. This was surely an important shift toward a normatively desirable outcome; it helped shift the boundaries of belonging to include not-quite-whites as well as industrial laborers, and it led to public support for government regulation of industry that had not existed before.

But while the Triangle Fire had democratically desirable outcomes for some, the outcomes for others were less positive. I have argued that the process of political mourning—contested identities, visibility, actors taking grief public, the inadequacy of legal responsibility, and political change—helped move the needle by expanding the boundaries of who counted as one of us and by taking up political responsibility rather than leaving the question of responsibility with the law. In the case of the Triangle Fire, the factory workers were between the poles of white and black. Mourning helped privileged citizens reconceptualize foreign women workers as citizens who deserved protection not only from anarchy or tyranny but also from the concentrated power of profit aided by law. These persons, who had previously been excluded from legal protection because the employer-employee relationship was not conceptualized as a *political* problem, were now incorporated into the bonds of citizen obligation. For the first time, the legal system recognized the public nature of the factory floor, and a judge allowed an indictment against the owners on a charge of public nuisance, which was diametrically opposed to the uniformly scathing denunciations of the strikers as disturbers of the peace by judges in 1909.[75] The strike, the fire, and the public mourning had made fire safety a public issue that demanded a political response, and helped labor relations more broadly to become a salient political issue.[76] These results have defined Triangle in our collective memory: a moment where business was opened to regulation and labor was empowered.

But missing from this story of democratic expansion is recognition of how perceptions of race affected the events. Triangle was a moment when intra-white racial differences were muted, and one of many moments in the long process of reconceptualizing the threat to Americanness as originating not from hordes of immigrants but from blackness.[77] By virtue of its location in a major northern industrial city bursting with confusing categories of whiteness, the Triangle Fire provided a moment when racially antagonistic working-class immigrants—made antagonistic by a political and social order that distributed jobs on the basis of race and immigrant status—came together to demand workplace reform. The strike, followed so quickly by a terrible tragedy, helped the public view these not-quite-white immigrant workers as potentially belonging within the network of citizen obligation. Italians and Jews continued to work together after the fire as the domain of whiteness expanded to include European immigrants, who became white ethnics rather than racial others; this was a long process that seems to have begun in earnest only after immigration was restricted in 1924, but events like the Triangle Fire may have helped.[78] According to Clara Lemlich, a primary instigator of the strike, the strike helped encourage workers to move beyond racial prejudices that separated them.[79] A contemporary religious leader likewise stated in reference to the Triangle Fire, "This calamity causes . . . racial lines to be forgotten, for a little while at least, [as] the whole community rises to one common brotherhood."[80] The scholar William Greider writes more recently that in 1911 New York City was

> bitterly divided by its multiplicity of hostile ethnic groups—immigrants against immigrants. The Triangle catastrophe pulled these different people closer together and helped them recognize their common humanity. A friend from New York once explained to me how that happened. "The Irish cops were picking up the bodies of the Jewish girls," he said, "and that changed New York politics forever."[81]

Such comments convey a sense of relief, as if the authors welcomed the resolution of a racialized hierarchy of whiteness.[82] The citizens of New York embraced a reduction of racialized tension in a city already bursting at the seams with new immigrants. While there is no evidence that anyone had a conscious goal of expanding the domain of whiteness to dampen conflict between immigrant groups, a rejuvenated notion of a unified white race meant that immigrants could now be folded into the dominant racial order without disturbing American commitments to whiteness.

Matthew Guterl argues that Manhattan, with its innumerable ethnic enclaves, was at the center of race-making in the United States. Thus, how race was constructed in New York had significant implications for how race was constructed throughout the United States. Perhaps unsurprisingly, this shift toward a broader conception of whiteness occurred when the African American population of New York was skyrocketing.[83] Thus, while there is no way to know for certain, there could have been strong if unspoken incentives for (white) New Yorkers to coalesce around a re/constructed white identity, in much the same way that Clarissa Rile Hayward shows that residential segregation in Columbus, Ohio, intensified as the result of the Great Migration of blacks from South to North paired with decreased immigration as the United States invoked country and racial quotas in the early 1920s.[84] The momentary immigrant unity after the fire may have contributed to this trend by briefly minimizing the significance of intra-white racial distinctions, possibly easing the transition from "racial" differences to "ethnic" ones.[85] When working-class immigrants were seen by themselves and by policy makers as legitimate claims-makers—as democratic citizens who bore economic responsibility for themselves and thus deserved protection from the harshness of workplaces that prioritized profit over workers' lives—it perhaps laid the groundwork for a shift from hostile race relations toward friendly ethnic rivalries that helped pave the way to full citizenship for white workers within a racialized democracy.

Because the women in the factories had done what was expected of them, their status as innocent victims meant their deaths could be used to promote a broader sense of whiteness. They had come to America, supported their families, and labored in factories for pay. They followed the rules of decorum for new immigrants, with the possible exception of the strike's unrest. However, by the strike's conclusion, the local press had begun to interpret the strikers' challenge to authority as a proper exercise of freedom, even if officers of the peace disagreed. Although newspaper coverage of the strike often focused on markers of the workers' difference— gaudy hats, funny accents, peculiar words, and strange food—these differences disappeared in descriptions of the dead bodies. What marked these girls as different from their WTUL benefactresses—their distinctive hats, speech patterns, and diets—had literally melted away. Newspapers portrayed the victims as Gibson Girls, simultaneously romanticizing and de-emphasizing the less Anglo-Saxon features of the victims.[86] The naive Jewish and Italian girls of the strike became simply the poor innocent girls of the fire.

Because of social circumstances that constructed identity on the basis of racial categories, this mournable moment was one of many that led to an expanded conception of whiteness. While the identities of participants were determined by dynamics beyond their control, participants in the struggles for labor and women's rights drew on extant identity categories and remade them. The strike made the workers sympathetic, but it also maintained their racial and social differences. The fiery deaths and subsequent mourning, however, may have helped onlookers begin to view the dead workers as whiter, thus contributing to the incorporation of Jews and Italians, as well as women, into the body politic. But this incorporation of not-quite-whites into whiteness, which Guterl argues was completed by 1940, did *not* challenge the notion of a racial hierarchy or the discourse of white supremacy. Instead, the boundaries of the concept of whiteness were expanded as the dead at Triangle were enfolded into the discourse of white supremacy. The Triangle Fire thus reveals the importance of race in the construction of politically grievable lives as well as how mournable moments may contribute to the transformation of racialized categories.

The transformation of racial categories like Jewish or Italian into white constitutes an important part of the political-identity formation process in early twentieth-century America.[87] The racial status of the Triangle employees was unclear before the fire. After the fire, the concerned citizens of New York viewed the victims differently—as invocation-worthy objects of mourning who, regardless of intra-white ethnic differences, deserved the rights of citizens. This moment was one within a much larger shift in identity categories. But I suggest that it is not an insignificant one, in part because of how the focus on not-quite-whites and responsibility for protecting industrial workers obscured the plight of others farther down the racial hierarchy.

The process of political mourning contributed to an expansion of labor rights for white people in the places white people worked. It failed, however, to make visible the violence and discrimination perpetrated daily against nonwhites.[88] Indeed, the mourning that followed Triangle may have actually *increased* political resistance to recognizing the challenges and losses experienced by those at the bottom of the racial hierarchy—people of color more generally and African Americans in particular. This was increasingly important as African Americans fled the Jim Crow South to find jobs in industrial northern cities during the Great Migration.

In some ways, the process is analogous to the struggle over same-sex marriage described by Judith Butler.[89] Butler argues that the movement to claim the right to same-sex marriage reinforces the marginalization of some nonheterosexuals by limiting the meaning of livable lives to coupled gays and lesbians. The demand for same-sex marriage challenges narrow boundaries of inclusion, but it fails to disrupt and might even bolster larger structures of exclusion. Thus, the extension of marriage rights to "good" (as in coupled and monogamous) homosexuals further legitimizes the violent oppression suffered by those even further on the margins (uncoupled, nonmonogamous, gender-queer, and so on). Once that horizon is established, the extension of rights—and recognition of losses—beyond that horizon becomes increasingly difficult.

We can see parallels between the marriage movement by gays and lesbians and the movement to make *white* workplaces safe. Efforts to protect newly white workers in factories likely lessened support for efforts to expose the injustices against workers of color in less obviously *public* workplaces, such as farms or in domestic service in households, where the overwhelming majority of blacks worked.[90] The oppression and losses experienced in these more private workspaces receded from public or political view and continued to be understood as social rather than political in origin. It was not until the rise of the civil rights movement, as discussed in Chapter 3, that the social exclusion of blacks from government benefits and protections came to be seen as a political matter and thus a site of political responsibility.

In the aftermath of the Triangle Fire, the question of what constituted an appropriate political intervention into private space was resolved through the development of regulatory agencies in Progressive-Era New York. This notable achievement—arguably encouraged by a racializing dynamic that tied visibility and protection to a white identity performed by a particular type of laborer in a particular location—foreshadowed and potentially enabled the later collective failures to protect nonwhite workers at sites of employment that remained coded private. Recall Dewey's notion that as a public coalesces, state institutions express that public's proposed solution to a collective problem. The public that coalesced after the fire was one made up of not-quite-white industrial workers—recent immigrants who worked in factories rather than blacks who worked in homes. The progressive state that resulted was one that addressed that specific need rather than others outside the boundaries of that public's identity. The institutional response to Triangle foreshadowed, for example, the race-based exclusions of the New Deal. By focusing on particular kinds of employment that were now firmly on the public side of the public-private split and by embracing an expanded definition of whiteness, the events in New York heralded the disappearance of the private side of the public-private split from political discussions altogether. Rather than directly confronting the separations and exclusions that characterize an American state built on racial exclusion, the events involving the Triangle Factory smoothed the path to a more inclusive whiteness for those then deemed not-quite-white while making the losses suffered by black Americans even more difficult to see.

3

Mourning Emmett Till

Federal Responsibility for Racial Violence

Born in Chicago, fourteen-year-old Emmett Till persuaded his mother to let him visit her uncle in Mississippi in August 1955. Before he left, his mother stressed that he was to do anything, including getting on his knees and begging forgiveness, to avoid white wrath. Emmett, outgoing and exuberant, waved her warnings off with a smile. A few days into his visit, Till went to the local, white-owned corner store with a group of cousins and friends. Till allegedly made verbal advances toward or whistled at Carolyn Bryant, the white woman working at the store. She walked to her car to get a gun, and Till and his cousins departed in a rush. Several days later, two men—Carolyn Bryant's husband, Roy Bryant, and brother-in-law, J. W. Milam—barged into Till's host's house in the middle of the night and dragged Emmett to their car at gunpoint. Shortly after, they tortured and killed him, tied a fan from a cotton gin around his neck, and threw his body into the Tallahatchie River. Till's body surfaced on August 31.

Challenging the local sheriff's order that the body to be buried in Mississippi immediately, Till's mother demanded that her son's body be shipped to Chicago, where she displayed his body in an open casket covered by glass so people could see what race hatred could do. For four days in September, tens of thousands viewed his mangled and waterlogged body. Many fainted at the sight. Every major African American paper of note published pictures of his body, and his funeral—at once a condemnation of white racism and a homegoing for young Emmett—was covered in most national news outlets.

Till's killers were tried later that month. The courtroom was racially segregated, the sheriff testified for the defense, and several members of the jury donated to the defense fund. Journalists from most major American papers (as well as several international ones) and all three television networks reported daily on the trial. The all-white jury took slightly more than an hour to exonerate the accused. Less than two months later, a grand jury refused to indict Bryant and Milam for kidnapping, despite their earlier confession to the crime.

Shortly after the Mississippi jury failed to convict, a handful of northern Republican congressmen pushed the Justice Department to investigate. While the FBI and the Justice Department asserted that there was no federal jurisdiction, the attorney general began working on proposed civil rights legislation in direct response to Till's murder and the failure of Mississippi law to hold his killers accountable. The proposed legislation eventually led to the 1957 Civil Rights Act, the first successful civil rights bill in two generations.

The civil rights movement is one of the most exhaustively researched social movements in the history of the United States. While each discipline and subdiscipline uses different lenses to interpret the events and contexts in which actors moved, I offer here a different way to read the subtle shift that occurred in America regarding civil rights in the middle of the 1950s: as an example of political mourning, with a focus on the murder of Emmett Till in 1955. I offer this rereading of well-traveled ground not as a challenge to compelling theories that focus on movement building, legal tactics, or the impact of international relations on the American government's interest in civil rights, but as a supplement to these analyses.[1] That is, I want to consider how the mobilization of political mourning in the wake of Emmett Till's murder contributed to subtle but important changes that helped draw African Americans into the movement while also helping the white majority see African American activism in a more sympathetic light.[2]

Till's death helped expand the audience to the contest over the role of white supremacy in the South after other events—notably *Brown v. Board of Education* but also lynchings of African American political activists in Mississippi that very summer—had not.[3] Till's death accomplished this in part because it mobilized white sympathy and encouraged reflection about racial justice in America in 1955 by white citizens far removed from the conflict over African American civil rights in the South. This is not to discount the effects of organizing within the African American community, but rather to add to that literature by considering how Till's murder enabled the larger white public to see such activism differently. After Till's death, a politics of mourning was mobilized by African American political agents to challenge the political status quo of a white supremacist state and nation. The politics of mourning succeeded in two ways.

First, it exposed the difference between formal law and law on the ground (*Brown v. Board* as compared to a segregated Mississippi courtroom). It was an unusually visible death of someone defined by his youth, and Till's apolitical youthful identity could more easily be used by agents to generate visibility and support for political ends. Till's murder and the publicity that followed during the display of mourning changed the interpretive context and provided whites with a new way to understand the growing political demands by African Americans for full citizenship.[4] In essence, Till's broken body breathed life into the law by pulling the abstract claims about equality of *Brown v. Board* into the realm of flesh and blood. Claims about the successful achievement of formal equality could not withstand the reality of a segregated courtroom in Mississippi, and the jury's failure to hold Till's murderers accountable highlighted the vast differences between the formal, abstract language of legal cases and law on the ground. Till's death generated political mourning that linked the vulnerability of actual bodies to the vulnerability of the political body of the United States; if the United States could not protect or procure justice for its citizens of all colors, its standing in the world was vulnerable to pointed challenges from the Soviet Union.[5] The juxtaposition of these bodies—actual and political—contributed to an important change of tone and shift of center in the national debate about civil rights.

Second, Till's murder challenged northern whites' ability to maintain what James Baldwin called "innocence" about their identity in a democracy that privileges whiteness.[6] The widespread media coverage—the first time a "race story" was extensively covered by a white northern press in more than twenty years[7]—made it impossible for northern whites to pretend that things in the South were not that bad. They *were* that bad, and Till's death made the circumstances abundantly clear. Certainly, this moment was overlaid by other structural and cultural trends that helped the civil rights movement coalesce, as argued by McAdam.[8] My goal here is not to minimize the importance of big, overtly political moments like *Brown v. Board* or the Montgomery Bus Boycott, moments often considered the beginning of the civil rights movement. Instead, I argue that focusing only on these movement-building events does not adequately recognize how a tragic death helped generate the visibility necessary to mobilize popular support to challenge a formerly stable political status quo.[9] A politics of mourning over Till's death gave white American liberals—who had apparently come to accept the Jim Crow status quo—a clear instance to reflect on the calls of the nascent civil rights movement for racial justice and to see how the reality of Jim Crow violated aspirations to actual American democracy. As Jane Addams argues in *Democracy and Social Ethics*, this experience of perplexity when confronted with two competing value systems can help citizens reevaluate values and potentially change their actions moving forward.[10] Thus, failing to recognize the role of mourning as a means to cultivate a sympathetic white audience leaves explanations and conceptualizations of political change during the civil rights movement incomplete.

I now turn to the events surrounding Till's racially motivated murder to analyze how and why the politics of mourning helped expand the boundaries of belonging in the months and years after his death. The remainder of the chapter traces the components of a politics of mourning by considering contested identities, visibility, actors taking their grief public, legal failure that contributed to a taking up of collective responsibility, and political change.

Contested Identities: Race and Law

The long history of extralegal lynching provides crucial context to the mourning following Till's murder, and the use of lynching as a means of controlling African Americans has resurfaced as an area of scholarly inquiry.[11] As Robert Cover reminds us, law is about violence, though that violence is given meaning through social cooperation and processes or norms of legal interpretation.[12] However, for African Americans in the 1950s, there was no veneer; southern law was little more than violence.[13] Between the end of Reconstruction and the Civil Rights Act of 1957, the federal government made little effort to stop the violence perpetrated against blacks in the South, a position reflecting white apathy in the North.[14] Black civil rights activist Ida B. Wells and the National Association for the Advancement of Colored People (NAACP) advocated for federal antilynching laws beginning in the early years of the twentieth century, but to no avail.[15] Proposed legislation would have enabled federal prosecution of lynching perpetrators when local justice failed.

Practically every scholarly work that discusses Emmett Till links his death to this history of "lynch law"; the NAACP did so immediately after his death in 1955, and the killers' later confession to *Look* explicitly connects the threat of interracial sex to their decision to kill Till.[16] Hugh Steven Whitaker, in his 1963 groundbreaking master's thesis on Till's murder, foregrounds the significant role that sex played in the justification for lynchings, and he links that history to Till's murder.[17] Stephen Whitfield's *A Death in the Delta* similarly begins with the tortured relationship between white fear of black male sexuality and the violence that often accompanied that fear.[18]

But while the purported reasons for lynching were often accusations of rape or attempted rape by African American males, Ida B. Wells demonstrated that these claims were often pretextual; lynching was, in fact, an all-purpose means of dominating and controlling southern blacks that could be triggered by a wide variety of transgressions, including black economic success, failure to be appropriately subservient, efforts to gain political power, and so on.[19] However, in the minds of white southerners, lynching remained tied to the specter of uncontrollable black male sexuality set loose upon helpless white women. White southerners interpreted the threat of integrated schools, a threat embodied in law by *Brown v. Board*, as the first step toward breaking down the racial barriers that miscegenation laws maintained.

Although the nature of lynching as communal carnival decreased around the start of World War II, by the 1950s, it remained an important cultural, economic, and political referent meant to remind African Americans of "their place" in the southern world.[20] As Christine Harold and Kevin Michael DeLuca write, "By the time of Emmett Till's murder, lynching was no longer an acceptable public spectacle, though it was still an acceptable community practice. . . . By 1955, lynching had become an invisible public event."[21] Invisible, perhaps, but dangerously omnipresent. Because the federal government refused to seek redress for the civil rights violations that produced all-white voter rolls, any violation of an African American citizen's rights, whether criminal or civil, was investigated by white law enforcement officers, prosecuted by white attorneys, heard by white juries, and sentenced by white judges. The status quo in Mississippi in 1955 utterly disenfranchised and silenced African Americans, a situation enforced by the constant threat of extralegal violence and a good deal of legally sanctioned violence. To observers seeking change, the very existence of lynching as practice indicted not only individuals who lynched but entire communities who condoned or tolerated it. While lynching as a public event had gone underground, its silencing effects had not diminished.

Earlier in the summer of 1955, two other black men had been murdered in Mississippi. Both George Lee and Lamar Smith had been working to register and organize black voters and were murdered as a result.[22] Although his head was filled with lead slugs, George Lee's death was ruled a traffic accident. Lee's wife left his casket open at the funeral, and while the African American community in Mississippi and Chicago widely mourned him, his death failed to capture the attention of whites.[23] Lamar Smith was shot in the middle of a town square in the Mississippi Delta shortly after noon on a weekday; although the square was filled with bystanders, including several law enforcement officers, no one could identify the shooter.[24] Neither murder led to an indictment.[25] These examples serve to illustrate just how unlikely it was that a young black man's murder in Mississippi would cause more than a ripple in the national news.

In addition to the context of a long history of lynching, the nation was uncertain of the impact of *Brown v. Board I* and *II*. Throughout the United States, blacks were visibly segregated, ranging from ghettoization and redlining in the North to the pervasive culture of violence against African Americans in the South. Born, raised, and educated in the North (although in predominantly African American schools) but killed in the South, Till's mutilated body signified the South's intention to reject the vision of racial integration and equality offered by the Supreme Court in *Brown v. Board*, a refusal accomplished through a spectacular act of violence against the image of a new generation's promise: a smart, confident, African American youth.

After years of pursuing a federal denunciation of de jure segregation with a particular focus on education,[26] the NAACP finally succeeded. On May 17, 1954, the Supreme Court issued its landmark decision *Brown v. Board of Education of Topeka*. Southern states responded with a weak series of saber-rattling statements (bolstered by outrageously racist tracts and strong grassroots activism against integration[27]). While *Brown* overturned *Plessy v. Ferguson*, it provided little clarity regarding compliance or implementation. This was instead to be provided in *Brown II*, the implementation decision, released a year later on May 31, 1955. *Brown II* ordered desegregation with "all deliberate speed," but left timing and responsibility for compliance up to local school boards under the supervision of the federal judiciary.[28] Given the centuries-long subjugation of African Americans at the hands of whites in the South, any effort to meaningfully desegregate schools through the courts seemed doomed from the start, in part because the NAACP's strategy of seeking legal victories failed to generate a mass movement. According to Aldon Morris, "White repression, the NAACP's bureaucratic structure, and the complexity of the legal procedures that absorbed its attention all discouraged mass participation." Thus, although the NAACP had widespread support, at no point did its membership rolls exceed 2 percent of the nation's African Americans.[29] Furthermore, a federal court ruling meant little to local white school boards, who could effectively stall for years via legal and extralegal means. Nonetheless, *Brown* was a considerable symbolic victory that provided a real boost to the morale of the African American community. It provided some hope that the federal government had at last recognized their exclusion from the political community and might offer substantive help contesting it.[30]

These two legal worlds—the abstract legal equality pronounced by the Supreme Court paired with the always-present threat of physical violence ignored or enabled by southern law—coexisted in Mississippi in 1955 (as they do still). Northern whites were perhaps pleased with the Supreme Court's decision, but they could avoid knowledge of the violence borne by African Americans in the South. Southern whites tried to avoid implementation of the court's decree, while holding fast to their racial privilege through undisguised threats and acts of violence. African Americans, then, were caught between two realities of the law—an abstract, federal court decision that gave them hope and some standing paired with the reality of a state legal system that rarely, if ever, delivered justice for African Americans. But while African Americans in the South were caught in a twilight zone between two legal realities, the legal contests up to and including *Brown* had finally succeeded in making their status as second-class citizens a question rather than a given. Their position as second-class citizens had been visibly challenged, even if the outcome of that challenge was not yet clear. The explicit contest over the place of African Americans in the American political community set the stage on which the events surrounding Till's death played out.

Making Loss and Mourning Visible

Young Emmett Till was outgoing, self-reliant, whip-smart, thoughtful, and protective.[31] His peers confirm his leadership, geniality, and general good humor.[32] Although his mother, Mamie Till-Bradley, had been born in Mississippi, her parents left for Chicago shortly after her birth. She stayed in Chicago and raised her son within the protective confines of Argo, Illinois, a mostly black enclave with plentiful industrial employment, where African Americans could exhibit "runaway ambition" within the confines of familiarity.[33] Till-Bradley was a model citizen in many ways; graduating first in her high school class, she was one of the first African Americans to gain civil service employment in Chicago.[34] Despite deep reservations about Emmett's request to visit relatives in Mississippi, she relented, but only after delivering a sharp lecture to her son. Assured by Moses Wright, her uncle, that he would watch out for young Emmett, she finally agreed.

A few days after arriving in Mississippi, Emmett and a group of friends and cousins went to the local white-owned store to buy some candy on August 24, 1955. What transpired between Till and Carolyn Bryant, the white woman behind the counter, remains disputed. Carolyn Bryant on September 2 told her attorney, "I waited on him and when I went to take his money, he grabbed my hand and said how about a date, and I walked away from him, and he said, 'What's the matter, baby, can't you take it?' He went out the door and said 'Goodbye,' and I went to the car and got [the] pistol—didn't do anything further after he saw [the] pistol."[35] Till's cousin, however, "insisted that the only mistake he made was to place his candy money directly in Carolyn's hand rather than put it on the counter, as was common practice between whites and blacks."[36] Regardless of what happened, Till's cousin Simeon was worried enough that the dozen African Americans there quickly dispersed.[37] Till's cousin, an eyewitness, claims that as Emmett left the store, he turned to look at Bryant and said either "goodbye" or "bye baby." Till also might have "wolf-whistled" at Bryant as she walked outside,[38] at which point an older African American man forcefully suggested that the young folks leave.[39] Emmett and his cousins did so, but at Till's insistence none of them spoke to Till's uncle and host, Moses Wright, about the incident. Whatever occurred, Bryant did not call out to her sister-in-law in the next room; she walked to her car rather than simply lock the shop; and she did not inform her husband about the incident when he returned home later that day. These, taken together, suggest that either she did not find the breach significant enough to mention or knew that mentioning it to her husband would produce a violent response. It seems that "whatever happened in that store made her more mad than fearful."[40]

But Roy Bryant eventually heard about the incident (possibly from one of the young black men present that afternoon).[41] On August 28, Bryant and his half-brother, J. W. Milam, knocked on Wright's door at 2:00 A.M. and demanded to see "the boy from Chicago" who did the talking.[42] Disregarding Wright's entreaties to give the boy a whipping and be done with it or his wife's offer to take what cash they had and leave, Milam and Bryant kidnapped Emmett and headed toward the town of Money.[43] Fearing for his family's safety, Moses Wright put his wife on a train to Chicago before reporting Till's disappearance to local authorities the next day.[44]

Once alerted to her son's kidnapping, Till's mother immediately sought local, state, and federal assistance to locate her son, including sending a telegram to President Dwight Eisenhower directly.[45] She called Chicago-area newspapers, the NAACP, and labor leaders, imploring them to do whatever they could to raise awareness of Emmett's disappearance.[46] Within days, Mayor Richard Daley of Chicago, Governor William Stratton of Illinois, and U.S. Representative William Dawson were all involved.[47] These efforts helped ensure widespread knowledge of Till's disappearance. But they also signal a shift in Till-Bradley's understanding of what she could ask from the larger community. She experienced a fundamental shift in her conception of herself and the world she lived in; she had become someone who could speak, even as the intention of those who abducted her son was to silence.[48]

On August 31, Emmett's battered body was discovered floating in the nearby Tallahatchie River. His body was so unrecognizable that Wright could only identify him because he was wearing his father's signet ring. As an indicator of the significance of this event in Chicago, local television stations interrupted *I Love Lucy*—the top-ranking television show in the nation at the time—to report that Emmett's body had been found.[49]

In accordance with the local sheriff's order to "get the body in the ground" immediately, Wright and his family gathered at their Mississippi church to bury Till. As they were about to lower his body, they received word that the body was to be shipped to Chicago at Till-Bradley's insistence and expense.[50] As a result of widespread newspaper, radio, and television coverage of Till's disappearance and death in Chicago, a crowd of about one thousand gathered to meet Till's body on September 2.[51]

As a result of Mamie Till-Bradley's quick and decisive effort to make her son's disappearance a public issue, as well as her upstanding position within the black professional class of a mostly white northern city, Emmett's demise—unlike the deaths of so many blacks in the South—immediately reached headlines across the nation. A few weeks later, *Life* magazine, with a circulation of 5.3 million,[52] published an image of Till-Bradley greeting her son's casket at the train station in Chicago, with this extraordinary caption:

> Homecoming of a Lynch Victim: A grief-torn mother, Mrs. Mamie Bradley, received in Chicago the body of her son, Emmett Till, 14. Visiting on a farm near Greenwood, Miss., he had been dragged from his bed, beaten and slain. Mississippi's governor deplored the deed and local authorities arrested two white men on kidnap charges. Emmett's alleged offense: he whistled at a white woman.[53]

The accompanying image shows a distraught young woman overcome with grief, supported on all sides by professionally dressed men. All are African American and appear middle-class. They are the very image of respectable people, and yet they are bowed by grief.

Till-Bradley recalls that officials in Mississippi would release her son's body only if the casket would remain sealed. Her response to the undertaker's word of caution that she could not open the casket because it would violate signed documents was, she later said, "'I didn't sign any papers . . . and I *dare* them to sue *me*. Let them come to Chicago and sue me.' I just couldn't imagine a judge anywhere finding me guilty of viewing the body of my boy."[54] Although she knew of the potential backlash, Till-Bradley needed to confirm that this was her beloved son. To that end, she asked the undertaker to open the casket.

Her description of this experience is profoundly disturbing. Recollecting her arrival at the funeral home, she writes, "It was the most terrible odor. We began to smell it about two blocks from the funeral home. . . . I will never forget that smell. It was Emmett. At Rayner's funeral parlor, they were shooting off bombs so people wouldn't become ill from the smell."[55] When she entered the funeral home and approached the body, Mr. Rayner, the undertaker, explained that the body had been packed in lime, presumably "to make the body deteriorate faster, to make it even harder to identify."[56] Till-Bradley, overwhelmed by grief, but determined to discover if this was her son, started her intimate examination at his feet. She writes:

> At a glance, the body didn't even appear human . . . [but] none of Emmett's body was scarred. It was bloated, the skin was loose, but there were no scars, no signs of violence anywhere. Until I got to his chin. . . . I saw his tongue resting there. It was huge. . . . I forced my-self to keep going on one small section at a time. . . . I was putting him back together again, but only to identify the body. . . . From the chin, I moved up to his right cheek. There was an eyeball hanging down, resting on that cheek. It looked like it was still attached by the optic nerve. . . . [R]ight away, I looked to the other eye. But it wasn't there. It seemed like someone had taken a nut picker and plucked that one out. . . . I looked at his teeth. . . . [T]here were only two now. . . . I looked at the bridge of his nose. . . . [I]t had been chopped, maybe with a meat cleaver. It looked like someone had tenderized his nose.[57]

Till-Bradley, unsure or perhaps unwilling to believe that this was her son, looked to his ears only to discover that his left ear was missing. She then realized that her son had been not only brutally beaten but also shot; she could see daylight through his head. She writes that at that moment, "my momentum was broken. With all the grisly things I had just witnessed in silence, it was that one bullet hole that finally caused me to speak. 'Did they have to shoot him?' I mean, he had to be dead by then."[58]

Riven by grief, Till-Bradley asked that her only son's body be available and in public view for four days, so that "the world could see what I've seen."[59] Her decision to share the experience of viewing her son's disfigured body sparked a tremendous outpouring of grief and mourning by Chicago-ans and others appalled at Till's murder. The mangled body, enclosed in a casket covered by glass, was accompanied by three images of a smiling Em-mett from the Christmas of 1954 taped on the lid of the casket, a juxtaposi-tion that made his degradation all the more shocking. At least one hundred thousand (and possibly up to six hundred thousand) people witnessed Em-mett Till's mutilated body in person as it lay in the church or funeral par-lor.[60] Medical personnel stayed near because people kept fainting at the sight.[61]

While the sanitized vision of a mother's grief in *Life* reached millions of Americans, with Till-Bradley's permission, only the African American press published images of Till's mutilated body. (Although his mother asked that the body be displayed untouched, the funeral home director apparently removed Till's hanging eye and bulging tongue, and sutured the torn-in-half scalp back together. Thus, the images of Till's body that circulated were already sanitized.) Images of his body reached far more than those who viewed the body in person.[62] *Jet*, with a 1955 circulation of 425,000,[63] published the two images of Till's body and reproduced them at least two additional times within weeks. The first issue with images of Till's body sold out immediately, and for the first time ever, *Jet* went to press a second time for a single issue. Although *Jet* held exclusive rights to the images of Till's body,[64] the *Chicago Defender*, the *Pittsburgh Courier*, the *New York Amsterdam News*, and the *Crisis*—basically every paper of record in the African American press—published reproductions of these images.[65] Nonetheless, it was not until the broadcast of Henry Hampton's *Eyes on the Prize* in 1987 that most white Americans saw Till's mutilated body.[66]

In making her son's body visible and taking her grief public, Till's mother put young Emmett into circulation in what Sara Ahmed has termed "affective economies." Ahmed argues that emotions are not possessions of individuals, but that they "play a crucial role in the 'surfacing' of individual and collective bodies through the way in which emotions circulate between bodies and signs . . . [suggesting] that emotions create the very effect of the surfaces or boundaries of bodies and worlds."[67] By putting her son's body into circulation in the affective economy of 1955 America, Till's mother made an implicit statement about the wider exclusion of African American bodies from state protection.

In footage from the days after Emmett's death, Mamie Till-Bradley stated, "I know the whole United States is mourning with me,"[68] a surprising assertion of belonging by a woman who had just suffered an immense blow. And yet her claim was reasonable on many levels. The huge turnout at the funeral, the unprecedented white media coverage of his death, and blanket coverage in every African American media outlet of note could all be interpreted as an experience of national mourning: mourning that called attention to the terrible scourge of white violence while at the same time comforting mourners with hope of a better future.[69]

While the mourning was certainly concentrated within the African American community, it resonated outside this group, in part because the images of maternal grief that were published in the white press were visible and legible across racial lines.[70] While the white press did not publish images of Till's body itself, it did publish images of the mourning that followed his death. As Gene Roberts and Hank Klibanoff write:

The press responded sympathetically to Mrs. Bradley's sorrow, in effect linking arms with her in portraying the evils of race discrimination in the South. The coverage in turn linked her with an empathetic nation. With all the reporters and photographers around her, Mamie Bradley, a heretofore anonymous face in America, had the overwhelming feeling that much of the nation was standing beside her, crying with her. Much of the nation felt the same way.[71]

Till-Bradley's implicit claim was that of a full citizen, one whose loss deserved recognition and recompense. It was a remarkable response to an event meant to silence and dehumanize her and every other African American.

The very words "I know the whole United States is mourning with me" are a powerful rhetorical construction. First, it implied that her loss was, and should be, recognized as a loss not only within her racialized community but by the entire nation. This was an extraordinary assertion of shared identity that defied the intent of the men who had murdered her son. Her loss, rather than leading to isolation or silence, enabled a moment of visceral connection between white and black communities. To use Ahmed's language, Till's body and his mother's provocative display evoked emotions that aligned "individuals with communities,"[72] drawing whites for the first time in years across the boundaries of race and into the community of those who mourned racially motivated violence. Few but the most ardent racists could look upon the body of a young boy and not be repulsed by the excessive violence visited on him because of his race. Upon the discovery of the body, many white southerners expressed outrage at the crime, but when Till's mother displayed the body to make visible the effects of racism, these same whites condemned her actions as politicizing the death.[73]

Consider, for instance, the lack of a similar affective draw across the lines of racial difference in the days after *Brown v. Board*. Jesse Jackson notes, "In 1954, *Brown* v. *Board* broke the legal back of segregation. But the murder of Emmett Till broke the emotional back of segregation. Emmett's death—and Mamie's life—gave us the backbone to resist racism. . . . When Emmett Till was killed, unlike with *Brown* there was no need for definition."[74] Unlike the law's layers of knowledge and remove, Till's body offered an immediate emotional connection to the realities of southern racism.

Second, Till-Mobley's statements—in both words and deeds—were a call to action for the African American community, because her son's death was caused by racism.[75] Her action effectively circumvented any effort by southerners to say that Emmett Till got what he deserved. That lynching occurred in the South was not news to African Americans. But something about this particular incident stirred individuals to recall instances of humiliation or fear that refused to be put to rest. Several people who became prominent civil rights activists recall that Till's death prompted widespread discussion for months.[76]

Third, while she suffered more directly than the rest of the nation, this tragedy was not only about her loss but also about a larger problem that affected every citizen in the nation. Till's mother writes that as a nation, we had "averted our eyes far too long, turning away from the ugly reality facing us. . . . I was guilty of the same thing. . . . People had to face my son . . . [but] people also had to face themselves. They would have to see their own responsibility in pushing for an end to this evil."[77] While she was shaken by losing her son, her hope was that the rest of the nation would be similarly shaken and moved to act. By asserting that the whole nation was mourning with her, she claimed that her loss—and, by extension, all similar losses suffered by African Americans on account of their race—deserved recognition, could have been prevented, and should not recur. This assertion of equality unnerved white Mississippians and planted the seeds of a bitter resistance.

The Failure of Law and Recognition of Collective Responsibility

Immediately after Till's body was located, white Mississippians condemned his murder as a heinous crime. But when the terms of the debate shifted from murder to lynching, they closed ranks. Against "outside agitators" (code for the NAACP and African Americans from the North), white Mississippians asserted that the state legal system would do its duty without interference from others.[78] Whites in Mississippi impugned Till-Bradley's decision to display the body as "uncivilized" and tied NAACP advocacy on her behalf to the threat of Communism as a way to minimize her loss;[79] rather than accept any communal responsibility for the death, Mississippi whites invoked undisguised assertions of racial inferiority and threats to the nation's wellbeing. Milam and Bryant, identified by Moses Wright as the men who abducted Emmett, were originally charged with kidnapping. Both confessed that they had in fact taken Till from Wright's home but had released him later that night after determining that he was not the young man from Chicago they sought. When his body was found three days later, the charge changed to murder, although it moved from Leflore County (where the kidnapping occurred) to Tallahatchie County (where the body was found).

Within weeks, the case was brought to trial in Sumner, Mississippi. At the start of the trial, reporters invaded the town of Sumner (population 550). About seventy reporters covered the five-day trial, including reporters from across the nation.[80] Every paper in Chicago, plus *Life*, the Associated Press, the United Press, the *Washington Post*, the *New York Times*, the *New York Post*, and the *New York Daily News*, sent reporters. Also represented were papers from St. Louis, Atlanta, Memphis, Detroit, London, and Toronto. All three major television networks—NBC, CBS, and ABC—flew film back to New York daily for use in national news coverage.[81] For the first time in more than twenty years, the trial of Till's killers broke the seal of silence that had surrounded the South.

This trial was also the first time in memory that an African American stood in a southern court to accuse white men of any crime, much less murder. When asked to identify who had taken his nephew, Moses Wright stood up, identified Milam and then Bryant, and said, "There he is."[82] Wright also pointedly stopped using the requisite "sir" after every response to the defense attorney.[83] Wright himself said, "It was the first time in my life I had the courage to accuse a white man of a crime, let alone something [as] terrible as killing a boy. I wasn't exactly brave and I wasn't scared. I just wanted to see justice done."[84] Wright's decision to stay in Mississippi in the days between Till's death and the trial took enormous courage. Having sent his family to Chicago, he stayed in Mississippi, sleeping some nights in his car and some nights in the woods for fear of suffering the same fate as his nephew.[85] Wright departed for Chicago immediately after the trial, leaving a full crop of cotton unharvested.[86] Stephen Whitfield quotes Dan Wakefield, a reporter for the *Nation* who covered the trial, as noting that Jim Crow was a

> "system in which a Negro citizen doesn't call the police if a boy is dragged from his bed in the night by white men[,] because the police are white too, and therefore the enemy. It is not really strange or remarkable that the people who are victims of such a system have begun to fight it with so little fear. They have, after all, nothing to lose." . . . Wright had raised not only his own stature but elevated that of other subjugated Negroes as well.[87]

Thus, while Till's death was shocking, it was almost more surprising that Wright stood up in court and condemned the men who took his nephew. In a world where a whistle could get you killed, one can only imagine the response to sworn testimony in a murder trial.

A handful of other African American witnesses followed Wright's courageous testimony after extraordinary efforts to locate them by activists and journalists. The prosecution had done little investigation—hampered by time constraints and the fact that the chief law enforcement officer and investigator (Sheriff Clarence Strider) was a witness for the defense—so local NAACP leaders (including Medgar Evers, Amzie Moore, Ruby Hurley, and Aaron Henry) and a cross-racial coalition of reporters went to work.[88] They located a handful of witnesses who saw at least two, perhaps as many as eight, additional people involved with Till's death and identified a cotton gin missing a fan in a storage shed owned by a member of Milam's family.[89] The prosecutors used this information to the best of their ability, but it was coolly received by whites in the courtroom, including all twelve white men on the jury.

The defense's case centered on an assertion that it was not Till's body they found in the Tallahatchie River, an assertion made by Sheriff Strider—rotund, arrogant, and stridently racist—and supported by testimony of two medical experts.[90] These two experts also claimed that the body from the river had been there so long that they could not tell whether it was white or black (even though Strider had called a black undertaker rather than white) and that it was so waterlogged that it must have been there for at least two weeks. All three testified that the body was unidentifiable. Mamie Till-Bradley courageously testified against this claim.

The national press agreed that the prosecution and judge were as fair as could be expected given the circumstances.[91] In the end, though, no one in the courtroom was surprised when Bryant and Milam were acquitted. The African Americans who had been attending the court proceedings vacated the courtroom before the verdict was read for fear of suffering violence.[92] When the verdict of not guilty was delivered, the whites left in the courtroom and the surrounding white countryside turned celebratory; the courtroom itself erupted into cheers as the verdict was read.[93] Till-Bradley, staying about an hour away in Mound Bayou, recalled hearing several shots as whites fired guns in the air in celebration. The acquitted are pictured in the next day's papers smoking cigars, kissing their wives, and accepting congratulatory handshakes from their neighbors and friends.

The racial order was upheld, even though, as most jurors admitted later, they believed that Bryant and Milam had killed Till. This was because, as Till-Bradley later wrote, the defense focused not on the murder of a young man but on "showing who was in charge."[94] The courtroom became the site of a virtual lynching. Removed in time from the actual death, it nonetheless affirmed a white supremacy that was not to be stymied by the rule of law; the communal and carnivalesque aspects of lynchings past resurfaced in that Sumner courtroom, almost inverted. While only a handful of men had perpetrated the crime, the entire community celebrated their acquittal. Lynching moved from the backwoods to the courtroom, and no one in Washington or anywhere else intervened to demand a trial that approximated justice. This is a lesson the South learned well, demonstrated by a legal system in which African American men continue to receive racially disproportionate sentences for the murder of whites.[95]

While Mississippi was not surprised, the rest of America and the world were stunned. Condemnations from national news outlets were harsh, and those of international news outlets were even harsher. As reported by a later survey of European opinion and press coverage, American prestige abroad was severely damaged as a result of this incident.[96] But perhaps more importantly, America's perception of itself was gravely affected by the murder and following trial. It was a stark moment that required the nation to do something to maintain the ideology of liberal inclusion. White northerners responded by identifying the South as exceptional. Lassiter argues that "Southern exceptionalism" contributed to the North's unwillingness to address the de facto racism that ran rampant and unchallenged in northern cities.[97] It was easier for white northerners appalled at Till's death to assert white southern responsibility than it was for white northerners to see that they, too, might bear some responsibility for enabling the southern way of life to continue unchecked by federal intervention.

The trial itself, then, generated a second moment of mourning; beyond the loss of life, there was a loss of idealism. No longer could the rest of America pretend that paternalistic stories told by southern whites about happy Negroes were true. The miscarriage of justice was too obvious, too great; the willful innocence of white northerners had been disturbed, even as they sought to limit their responsibility to fixing the South. This feeling of unease was confirmed when a grand jury blatantly disregarded Bryant and Milam's confession to kidnapping and refused to indict them on kidnapping charges in Leflore County only a few weeks later.[98]

Mobilizing Mourning for Political Change

In her discussion of how images of lynching have been used and contested, Dora Apel argues in reference to Till's death:

> It was crucial that his body was not quickly and quietly buried but turned into a public occasion of mass mourning that was widely publicized, and that the circulation of the image of his mutilated body took place not among the white supremacists of the South but in the arena of the national black press and on television. Whereas such images formerly served to unite the white community across class lines, they now united the black national public with the left and liberal white public. "Grief was collective," remarked black writer John Edgar Wideman, who noted that "the stolen face of Emmett Till" began to haunt the nation.[99]

Instead of a broken black body being used to entrench white supremacy, it was now being used to contest it; rather than a cautionary tale to be whispered, Till's body became a provocative image to be displayed.

Till's murder helped push two groups to challenge the unjust exclusion of African Americans from the rights of full citizenship: African Americans and liberal whites in the North. While there was a long tradition of political and social activism in the African American community before Till's murder, something changed in the wake of Till's death. In the weeks after Till's killers were acquitted, Till-Bradley spent weeks traveling the country and speaking on behalf of the NAACP. Several thousand citizens, mostly African Americans, attended events in New York, Chicago, Detroit, Cleveland, Youngstown, Baltimore, and Los Angeles.[100] There is also considerable evidence that Till's death inspired many African Americans to stand fast in their support of the civil rights movement or to do more. If Amzie Moore, Charles Diggs, Myrlie Evers, Anne Moody, Eldridge Cleaver, Cleveland Sellers, Ruby Hurley, Shelby Steele, Michael Eric Dyson, Kareem Abdul-Jabbar, and Muhammad Ali all reference Till's death in their memoirs as a turning point, it is a plausible inference that many more, less widely known black people had a similar experience.[101] Michal Belknap notes that African Americans across the country were particularly outraged at federal inaction regarding the Till murder and felt that they had been completely abandoned by the federal government, which was particularly painful coming so soon after the tentative promise of recognition in *Brown v. Board*.[102]

In her memoir, Mamie Till-Mobley recollects that she and Rosa Parks became friends later in life. Parks informed Till-Mobley that she was thinking of Emmett as she stayed in her seat less than two months after the conclusion of the Till trial.[103] We cannot know, of course, what motivates people to participate in mass actions like the Montgomery Bus Boycott, but it is worth asking if some events are more effective than others. While the literature of political science rightly looks to big moments of collective political action, it is surely worthwhile to ask what motivates people to put their lives on the line. Till's death contributed to a deepened sense of solidarity among African Americans, a solidarity crucial to survive the decades of struggle that loomed ahead.[104] Whitfield notes, "Within the span of a decade, the impetus had passed from white supremacists to Black activists, and it had been lifted out of the courts and into the streets."[105] This shift from abstract legal decrees to politics on the ground held great democratic potential.

Fredrick Harris argues that Till's death is an example of how collective identity drives collective action, and his argument aligns with my larger point (though I am focusing primarily on loss as the central claim rather than visibility more broadly).[106] Using the results of a 1966 national survey of African American respondents, Harris's work shows that knowledge of

Till's death was more motivational to political activism than knowledge of *Brown v. Board* or of the Montgomery Bus Boycott.[107] Harris observes that "when entrepreneurs appropriate events after determining whether environmental conditions are ripe for collective action they then construct frames for cooperative action."[108] To apply Harris's insight to mourning, I suggest that when put to work by political agents, mourning can help people see the status quo differently, which can plant the seeds for a changed subjective response to the objective conditions that surround us. The theory of political mourning laid out in this account considers how loss and mourning are a resource for politics but can also explain the roles of identity and the uptake or rejection of a larger sense of political responsibility. Thus the theory helps make sense of how a highly visible event like Till's death provided a space to reflect and a dissatisfaction with the status quo that could lead to greater collective action when Smith's and Lee's murders in the summer of 1955 did not. General knowledge of unjust conditions is important, but knowledge of a specific unjust incident—one that comes with a handsome young face brutally disfigured after torture—forces a particular kind of knowledge; if we do not push it away, it can help us recognize our failures and speak plainly for a future that must be different. Furthermore, mourning helps make clear that this newly envisioned future can only come to pass if we engage politically. After Till's death, there was little question that, left to the local power structure, little would change in Mississippi or anywhere else in the South.

But Till's death and the mourning that followed it also sparked a changed response by white northerners to claims to full citizenship by African Americans in the South, even as they continued to be cold to such claims in the North.[109] Like people in New York in 1911, who knew that factory fires were a persistent reality, everyone knew that events like Till's death happened. But when these events were publicized in a context preceded by celebrated assertions of equality (such as those in *Brown v. Board*) and of freedom (as compared to the totalitarian nature of Soviet Communism), northerners could no longer pretend ignorance or innocence. While the murder itself was disturbing, the failure of the legal system was even more so and indicated the need for wholesale political change. To restate Apel's insight above, Till's body provided a means to reconstruct a coalition across racial lines. While African Americans had long advocated specific political measures to achieve racial justice, their demands, made only by a minority population, could not be realized without white support. Till's death helped mobilize white support for recognition of African American claims about justice.

To be clear, I am not arguing that this concern about Till's death occurred in a vacuum. At the same time Till's death was front-page news, there were at least three other political contests under way. First, the Cold War context was crucial.[110] In October 1955, the American Jewish Committee (AJC) reported that the impact of Till's death on public opinion in Europe was unusual in both scope and vehemence:

> Europe's condemnation came from all sections of public opinion, all political directions, and was expressed immediately and spontaneously. Surprisingly, on this occasion the Communists were less vociferous than many of the liberal and conservative elements. These protestations were expressed in hundreds of newspaper editorials, statements by public leaders in every country of Western Europe, and by men in the street. . . . Seldom has a trial at such distance been reported so extensively.[111]

The AJC report made specific policy recommendations meant to repair America's image abroad. These recommendations included institutional empowerment of civil rights investigatory and enforcement mechanisms, as well as suggestions that attacks on the basis of race should be interpreted as a violation of federal civil rights statutes.[112]

Second, electoral concerns continued to matter. African Americans were increasingly important to northern electoral strategies.[113] As reported by Representative Emanuel Celler, head of the House Judiciary Committee, in July 1955, there were seven antilynching bills before his committee, but none were likely to succeed.[114] As reported by the *New York Times*, the October AJC report about the impact of Till's death on public opinion abroad "appeared to foreshadow another and more intensive drive when Congress reconvenes in January for enactment of the long-pending civil rights program. It got nowhere in the first session."[115] Celler and Senator Paul Douglass publicly approved of the AJC report, and Celler suggested an "additional legislative 'remedy' to [ensure] strict enforcement of civil right law. He would deny Federal aid to states that in his opinion were lax."[116]

Third, there was interbranch conflict over the proper location of civil rights advocacy within the federal government. In *A Death in the Delta*, Whitfield describes the Eisenhower administration's refusal to intervene in part because they believed no federal law had been broken. He recounts a December 1955 cabinet meeting, chaired by Vice President Richard Nixon, where the idea was floated to punt the problem of civil rights to Congress since there was no chance the Dixiecrats would let it through.[117] Southern Democrats had refused to support any civil rights bill for the previous eighty years and there was little reason to believe they would change course now. But Till's murder pushed the administration to act. Throughout the summer of 1955, Attorney General Herbert Brownell Jr. had declined Representative Celler's request to appear before the Judiciary Committee's subcommittee on civil rights, while Eisenhower's Justice Department had refused to support any civil rights bills. Till's death helped change that reluctance into support. Historian David Nichols reports that by the end of 1955, the White House had received "three thousand communications as well as petitions with eleven thousand names protesting [Till's] murder."[118] Historian Michal Belknap writes, "The Till case had convinced Brownell that the attorney general needed more power to protect the constitutional rights of United States citizens," and it was becoming increasingly obvious that power could only be obtained via federal civil rights legislation.[119] After a December 1955 meeting organized by White House aide Maxwell Rabb to discuss with civil rights leaders the "mob violence in Mississippi,"[120] Rabb urged Eisenhower to directly address civil rights in his 1956 State of the Union address, which Eisenhower did.[121] In response to this new commitment to civil rights, the Justice Department began work in December 1955 on a civil rights bill to send to Congress.[122]

After a year and a half of political maneuvering, these proposals became the Civil Rights Act of 1957. Unfortunately, this act was a sadly watered-down version of a civil rights bill. After much debate and compromise, aided by Dixiecrat intransigence and executive ambiguity grounded in Eisenhower's desire to maintain a distant federalism, the result was an act that "protected from physical abuse and other forms of coercion only persons attempting to exercise the right to vote for candidates in federal elections."[123] While no more than a "mild victory for the forces of civil rights,"[124] it did create the U.S. Commission on Civil Rights charged with upholding the civil rights of all Americans. Although the act was not exactly a robust statement of support for African American claims to political equality, it *was* the first federal civil rights law since 1875. The 1957 Civil Rights Act demonstrated that African Americans' civil rights were now an issue with national significance, a significance not limited to the judiciary. Till's death had helped pull a reluctant executive into the battle over civil rights. The failure of the 1957 Civil Rights Act to justify a robust federal response to the crisis in Little Rock, Arkansas, demonstrated that more effective federal statutes and responses were necessary to protect civil rights.[125]

James Patterson points out that the murder of Emmett Till garnered international attention, exposed the depth of violence used by southern whites against southern blacks, and "bared a range of white sexual concerns." The latter was surely foremost in the minds of southern whites in the fight against desegregation.[126] It matters, then, that young Emmett Till was school-aged and that Bryant and Milam tied their decision to kill him to his purported confession that he had a white girlfriend. His killers looked at him and saw a confident, smart, African American boy who might befriend their white children or marry their white daughters if given half a chance. Threatened by the abstract specter of equality proposed by *Brown v. Board* and tales of civilization's demise circulated by the Mississippi Citizens' Councils, they lashed out at a body in real life. But their actions might have spurred the very thing they meant to challenge.

The rhetorical power of Till's body consisted of showing white Americans in the North what racial oppression looked like. The horror of that image, combined with the farcical trial, provoked mourning that demonstrated the necessity for society-wide change in ways that no protest, speech, or rally could—a mourning not for Emmett's family and friends alone but for our own skewed image of reality. Could white Americans, particularly those in the North, see Till's face and not be shamed into action? It made Americans ask if this was who we were and whether this was the future we wanted. It also gestured toward the possibility that we were all complicit in enabling the conditions that led to Till's death. This is the moment of solidarity that mourning can generate: not just passing sympathy, but a deeper appreciation of shared complicity and an abiding commitment to work toward a new future generated by a visceral sense of loss that reason alone cannot produce.

In her memoir, Mamie Till-Mobley writes that "somewhere between the fact we know and the anxiety we feel is the reality we live."[127] The facts known by white and black Americans in 1955 were that African Americans in the South led lives of exceptional difficulty where breaching the unwritten rules of a racial caste system was a potentially fatal mistake. The anxiety felt was that this situation was unjust and correctable in a nation that claimed to be democratic and equal. The unwillingness to bear the costs and consequences of relieving that anxiety coexisted with that certain knowledge. Till's death and his mother's efforts to mobilize his mourning to call for political change compelled Americans to address the distance between facts and unspoken anxieties through making racial injustice an explicit conversation rather than something unmentionable in polite society. Mourning helped generate a new interpretive framework that objective facts about racial violence in the South had not.

Without understanding the politics of mourning, it is difficult to make sense of why some deaths lead to political change while others do not. Of the hundreds of black men lynched in Mississippi, Till's death stands out in our minds. Why? Till's murder was different because it occurred shortly after a widely visible battle over contested identities, achieved stunning visibility, prompted his mother to unprecedented public action, demonstrated the failure of the Mississippi legal system to attain anything like justice, and catalyzed social mobilization to call for political change. The contest over the standing of African Americans in the United States had truly gone public with *Brown v. Board*, and the political uncertainty generated by that decision provided an opening for advocates to raise questions regarding the federal lack of protection for black victims of extralegal violence in ways unthinkable prior to May 1954. Second, through Till-Bradley's willingness to share her private grief and the NAACP's ability to generate media coverage, Till's death achieved a visibility that no other lynching victim had before. Third, the failure to convict Till's confessed killers made it obvious that the law was not the same as justice and that leaving such cases in the hands of state courts in the South was a farce. Fourth, political agents—including Till-Bradley, the NAACP, and northern congressional representatives— used Till's death to, finally, argue for a wider sense of responsibility that required political change. Till's death generated a nationally significant moment of mourning that drew both reluctant political agents and citizens into the fray as well as empowering those already fighting to continue. Although Till's killers and the jury that acquitted them meant to quell their own anxieties about the place of African Americans in a changing world, their actions sharpened the rest of the nation's resolve to address them.

A widely visible loss—when it occurs at the right time, when the law fails to approximate justice, and when it coincides with a movement able to keep the loss in view—can focus citizens on issues we would prefer to ignore. While we desire to remain blissfully ignorant, the affective power of loss and grief rivet our attention by exposing our collective political failures and demanding that we act collectively to change our shared future. This is the power of political mourning; it can expand our conceptions of belonging in powerful ways that approximate our stated ideals of justice and democratic inclusion.

But while the story told here is a mostly positive one, where mourning provoked a just and correct opposition to an oppressive political status quo, it is a story that also illustrates the limitations of political mourning. While liberal whites and the vast majority of African Americans supported civil rights activism, Till's death and the trial that followed solidified southern white opposition in dangerous ways. Although southern whites initially called Till's murder inhuman and unjustified, the display of Till's body provoked their widespread denigration of both Till-Bradley and the NAACP. Southern whites, cast as villains by northerners and the southern black population they meant to control, responded to national interest in the case by becoming even more set against what they considered outside agitators. Their steadfast resistance has continued for decades. For many white southerners, then, a politics of mourning hardened their opposition to desegregation, federal intervention, and "race-mixing" of any kind. The story was cast by the media and liberal northerners as having only one side, but white Mississippians tried to change the story from Till's death to the death of their way of life. It might be argued that white southerners also invoked a politics of mourning for the South's second defeat. But this mourning failed, at least in the short term, to produce a movement that matched the civil rights movement.

September 11

*Sovereign Mourning—Rejecting
International Responsibility*

On a crisp, sunny September morning in 2001, members of al-Qaeda flew a hijacked commercial passenger jet into the North Tower of the World Trade Center complex in Lower Manhattan at 8:46 A.M. Seventeen minutes later, as efforts to evacuate the North Tower and extinguish the raging fire in the upper stories had just begun, a second plane struck the South Tower. About thirty minutes later, at 9:37 A.M., a third commercial airliner crashed into the Pentagon across the river from Washington, D.C. Less than an hour after the South Tower had been struck, at 9:59 A.M., the building collapsed. Only minutes later, a fourth plane slammed into Pennsylvania farmland after United 93's passengers, alerted to the other hijackings, rushed the cockpit, where hijackers had taken control. Less than two hours after first impact, at 10:28 A.M., the North Tower collapsed. By 11:00 A.M., five stories of the Pentagon had also collapsed. In just over two hours on September 11, 2001, three iconic American buildings—two symbolizing American economic power, the other its military might—had been destroyed or grievously damaged. The death toll, initially feared to be in the tens of thousands, was eventually determined to be 2,977.[1]

The American public—indeed, the world—stopped. Stunned, Americans rushed to the nearest television, riveted by the endless, impossible repetition of images. We gathered in living rooms, called people we had not heard from, and huddled together to find comfort in chaos. At least that is what people outside New York and the D.C. area did. Those where the planes crashed struggled to reach their homes and determine whether loved ones were safe as both cities went into lockdown. Thousands never heard their loved ones' voices again; they put up fliers, seeking information about the missing, many of whom never returned home. Thousands more, traveling, were stranded at airports they never intended to visit after American airspace was shut down.

Those who lived through that day—Americans old enough to remember as well as millions around the world—can never forget its horror. After an outpouring of sympathy from other nations, allies as well as those long perceived as hostile to the United States, the United States responded to the terrorist attacks by demanding that Taliban-controlled Afghanistan turn over the architect of September 11: Osama bin Laden. After the Taliban refused, the United States bombed sites in Afghanistan and then invaded in October 2001, launching the so-called War on Terror. The War on Terror metastasized into a weakly justified invasion of Iraq in 2003, which prompted millions of people to protest in the United States and around the world—possibly the largest protests ever.[2] Though the name—War on Terror and its eventual sibling, the "axis of evil"—was eventually dropped, its effects persist, as several thousand American troops remain on the ground in Afghanistan and Iraq as of 2020.

The endless war that the September 11 attacks began has spawned much greater death and destruction than the event itself. By November 2017, 6,771 Americans had died in these two war zones, more than twice the number of deaths on September 11.[3] But civilian deaths in the affected areas dwarf American losses. By 2015, Physicians for Social Responsibility estimated that "the war has, directly or indirectly, killed around 1 million people in Iraq, 220,000 in Afghanistan and 80,000 in Pakistan, i.e. a total of around 1.3 million."[4] In addition, the Middle East as a whole has been destabilized, contributing to the rise of the Islamic State and the horrors of the conflict in Syria, which has caused an estimated 500,000 deaths.[5]

I argue here that rather than leading Americans into a democratic or tragic orientation in response to deaths, September 11 generated sovereign rather than democratic mourning. Recalling the centrality of tragedy to Greek democracy, Simon Stow reminds us that thinking through the effects of our actions on others can help us see from different perspectives. For example, although performed before an Athenian audience, Aeschylus's *The Persians* depicts the aftermath of the Persians' defeat at the naval battle of Salamis from the Persian perspective. Stow argues that this opportunity of Athenians to view victory from the perspective of the defeated helped the victors see the humanity of their opponents, which he suggests is a crucial precursor to politics of any kind. Considering the effects of the September 11 attacks from this perspective, Stow argues that the events of September 11 led to mourning without end (drawing on the *álaston pénthos* in Aeschylus's *The Persians*) that brings on "a grief-wrath the Ancients called *mênis*." This *mênis*

> manifests . . . in a particular form of blindness that prevents its suf-
> ferers from comprehending either their interests or their actions.
> Identifying the complex ways in which this blindness undermines
> the political and strategic capacities of the afflicted, [Stow] points to
> the ways in which America's postplanes response was undone by the
> grief it embraced and assiduously cultivated in the years following
> the attacks.[6]

In sum, while I argue in previous chapters that political mourning may move the polity in democratic directions—toward an expansion of the boundaries of belonging and a sense of responsibility for those who share our fate—in different circumstances and with different actors, it may serve instead to harden or contract the boundaries of belonging and undermine democratic responsibility. When the latter occurs, it is not the people but the legitimacy of the state itself that is threatened. The state's response, then, is less a manifestation of the people's will and more aimed toward preserving its own power. This sovereign mourning bypasses the will of the people—the very foundation of a democratic state—and focuses instead on preserving sovereign power.[7] The events of September 11 serve as a recent and catastrophic example of this sovereign sleight of hand. Like war memorials that edify the state while obscuring its own responsibility and the human costs of war, the American response to the September 11 attacks has served to strengthen sovereignty at a considerable cost to democracy.[8] Given that previous chapters suggest that political mourning may be mobilized for normatively desirable and just democratic ends, how did the events of September 11 lead to the opposite response?

Contested Identities and American Responses to Terrorism before September 11

In this section, I remind the reader of how questions of identity and the problem of terrorism were framed prior to the September 11 attacks. First, I discuss the problems of American identity after the Cold War. With the United States having emerged from the Cold War on top, what did it mean to be an American? How could we define ourselves in the absence of an external threat? Second, terrorism was not a new phenomenon that emerged only on September 11; there had been numerous instances of terrorism both domestically and abroad. Yet none of these events prompted the proclamation of a global War on Terror.

First, the end of the Cold War posed a problem for American identity. Without a clear enemy to focus our energies, it was unclear who we were to ourselves and in the world. As noted by scholars across the political spectrum, America had no singular enemy in the period between the fall of the Soviet Union and September 11. Francis Fukuyama, Samuel Huntington, Madeleine Albright, Charles Krauthammer, Michael Mandelbaum, and dozens of others puzzled over the role of America in the world without a clear adversary.[9] The lack of consensus about what America should do with its massive military power led to a series of military exploits during the 1990s that failed in terms of moral clarity and achievement. From Desert Storm forward, the U.S. military had either not gone far enough (stopping short of Baghdad in 1991; air strikes in Kosovo in 1999), been too late to prevent the worst genocides in fifty years (Rwanda in 1994 and Bosnia in 1995), been ineffective (Somalia, 1993), or relied on missiles to send a half-hearted and misguided message about terrorist attacks (Sudan and Afghanistan, 1998). Conservatives and liberals alike worried that, by failing to use its power, America was in danger of losing its way in the world. American hegemony and identity were in danger without an enemy to focus its energies. The fear of a return to a Vietnam-era malaise and sense of inefficacy loomed.

The American sense of place in the world has long been associated with imperial military interventions abroad. But American interventions in the Middle East and elsewhere have not been universally welcome, because American foreign policy has often prioritized stability over democracy. Ussama Makdisi, for example, argues that anti-American sentiment in the Middle East is grounded in modern politics, not in some eternal hatred of the "American way of life" or, still more elusive, "freedom." Makdisi writes that in the Middle East today, "The United States is at once admired for its affluence and technology (and by some for its secularism, law, and order) and resented for its contribution to a repressive Middle Eastern status quo."[10] Makdisi chronicles a promising start to American interventions in the Middle East in the years after World War I, but then demonstrates a negative shift in popular opinion in the last few decades. American support for dictators and widespread feelings of betrayal at America's unshakable support of Israel have eroded previous goodwill. Given this history, Makdisi asserts that while bin Laden is no more a representation of Arabs or Muslims than David Koresh is of Americans, "bin Laden *is* a manifestation of a deeply troubled Arab world beset by Arab government authoritarianism, a rise of Islamic fundamentalism, Israeli occupation and settlement of Arab lands, continuing Palestinian exile, and, finally, by American policies toward the region during and after the Cold War that have done little to encourage justice or democracy." Both Arabs and Americans, then, need to "move away from narratives of innocence and purity—whether of religions or of nations," Makdisi writes.[11] No one side is innocent of responsibility for the rise of groups like al-Qaeda.

But this Manichean division of good and evil—a path that often runs alongside racialization—is essential to American conceptions of identity.[12] Consider, for example, Roy Harvey Pearce's examination of the development of white, colonial identity in the early encounters between Europeans and native peoples in what is now New England.[13] Examining British colonial and early American literature for traces of this identificatory process, Pearce writes in *Savagism and Civilization* that "what Indians signified was not what they were, but what Americans should not be. Americans were only talking to themselves about themselves. But they had succeeded in convincing themselves that they were right, divinely right. Only with such conviction—cruel, illogical, and self-indulgent as it was—could they move on."[14] In essence, from the very start, American identity has been built on racial exclusion and white domination.[15] One main branch of critical race theory has considered how immigrants and immigration law shape our conceptions of citizenship.[16] This offshoot of critical race studies draws on the concept of racial formation first articulated by Michael Omi and Howard Winant.[17] Scholars of the evolution of the identity category of whiteness argue that various immigrant groups have sought to be recognized as white and that we can locate these moments of inclusion and exclusion in political contexts and legal decisions, as well as in cultural artifacts such as literature or film.[18] These scholars argue that race is a fundamental concept that has shaped and continues to shape American life, but they also contend that the meaning and construction of race is fluid, contextual, ambiguous, never seamless. While they all agree that race is a social construction, they all also argue that race has significant material consequences that shape our actions, cognition, and chances in life.

Yet religion was a considerable part of the equation of exclusion as well. While we may think of race and religion as separate categories, the two categories often intertwine in popular conceptions of race in the United States. Nadine Naber, following Junaid Rana, argues that the Spanish, as they conquered the New World in the wake of expelling Muslims from the Iberian Peninsula, transferred their racial classification of "religious infidel" from Muslims to Native Americans.[19] This early transfer put racialization and colonization on paths that often converged. A more recent conflation of race and religion was the inclusion of Hindu as a racial classification in the 1890 U.S. Census.[20] Similarly, David Roediger points out that for U.S.

immigration officials in the early 1900s, "Russian birth plus Yiddish mother tongue plus Jewish religion equaled 'Hebrew race.'"[21] Racial categorization efforts in the United States have not infrequently conflated several categories (including nation, culture, geography, religion, and phenotype) and have relied on religion as a marker of racial difference for a variety of immigrant groups.

In the last two decades in the United States, religion has been conflated with geography and race to become part of a larger category that includes persons from the Middle East or North Africa, persons who appear to be Arabs, and those who are or are perceived as Muslims. The result is that Middle Eastern, Arab, and Muslim have merged in the white American mind. Naber writes, "Religion coupled with civilization discourses support the construction of 'the Arab' as different from and inferior to white Americans," a difference constructed on the basis of religion *and* race.[22] This process intensified after the discovery of vast oil reserves in the Middle East in the 1950s and 1960s and after the 1967 Arab-Israeli war. Naber notes that it was only after these events that "hegemonic discourses on the 'Arab Other' in the United States increasingly deployed the assumption that all Arabs are Muslims and that Islam is an inherently backward and uncivilized religion." As a result, U.S. "government policies that were directed at individuals who were associated with a constructed 'Arab enemy' came to be directed at a constructed 'Arab Muslim' enemy."[23] The Middle East came to figure into this hypercategory as well, because of the United States' strong alliance with Israel and subsequently contentious U.S. relationships with Islamic Middle Eastern and North African nations.

There is considerable evidence that even before September 11, Middle Eastern, Arab, and Muslim immigrants fell into the ambivalent middle ground described by theorists of whiteness: they were not quite white but not black either. While the question of whether this differentiation is racial, cultural, or religious in origin is an open one, I am persuaded by claims that these groups have been the subject of racialization, defined by Howard Winant as "the extension of racial meaning to a previously racially unclassified relationship, social practice, or group."[24] Sarah Gualtieri, for example, demonstrates that Syrian immigrants to the United States in the late 1920s were vulnerable to the same extralegal violence as their African American neighbors even though they had won legal recognition as white and were eligible for naturalization.[25]

As argued by Louise Cainkar, instead of seeing differences in terms of ideologies—the dominant Cold War trope—Americans have come to believe that "the Arab enemy was about innate cultural dispositions to violence." As a result, the social exclusion of Arabs in the United States has been a racial project because Arab inferiority has been constructed and sold to the American public using essentialist constructions of human difference. In the 1990s, when Islamist challenges to American global hegemony became more powerful than Arab nationalism, these constructions were extended to Muslims and became grander; they became civilizational.[26]

Any challenges to American hegemony or differences regarding American foreign policy were then imputed not to political differences but to innate, unchangeable essences.

While the specifics of racialization may differ for each group in the United States,[27] in the case of Arabs, Muslims, and Middle Easterners, a new category has arisen that combines race, religion, and geographic ancestry. In doing so, it erases differences between Arabs (many of whom are Christian), Middle Easterners (many of whom are not Arabs), and Muslims (not all of whom are Middle Eastern or Arab). These categories have grown together in the American mind. Amaney Jamal explains why: "In a society that is already constructed along racial lines, any perceived difference between the dominant mainstream and a minority 'Other' tends to conform to racism's framework. . . . This form of racism is not contingent on differences in appearance but on differences in cultural attributes."[28] As pointed out by Sara Ahmed, the negative emotions that adhered to these "Other" bodies help build the illusion of coherence among those who believed themselves superior.[29] Thus, white, Christian, European Americans can build a collective identity on the negation of this other racialized category, much as Pearce demonstrated that early British settler colonists constructed the identity of "savage" for Indians that essentially defined "civilized" as "not savage."

Second, in addition to the complex identity questions the United States faced after the Cold War ended, to more fully recall the context in which the events of September 11 occurred, it is helpful to think about how the United States and the rest of the world responded to terrorism before September 11. I offer this brief review of terrorism and American responses to it to compare them to the vast political and institutional mobilizations after September 11. Beginning in 1970 and continuing to the year 2000, there had been an average of one terrorist attack per year using airplanes, none of which prompted the level of airport security the United States has enacted in the years since 2001.[30]

In the years leading up to 2001, there had been several terrorist attacks on American military hard targets. These include the bombings of a joint

Saudi-U.S. training facility outside Riyadh, Saudi Arabia, in 1995 (5 Americans and 2 Indians killed); the bombing of Khobar Towers in Dhahran, Saudi Arabia, in 1996 (19 Americans killed, 372 injured);[31] the simultaneous bombing of U.S. embassies in Nairobi, Kenya, and Dar es Salaam, Tanzania (killing 224, including 12 Americans, and wounding approximately 5,000), in 1998;[32] and the USS *Cole* in Yemen (17 Americans killed, at least 40 wounded) in 2000.[33] Although the vast majority of these were perpetrated by attackers who were themselves from the Middle East, were Arabic, and/ or were Muslim, none of these attacks led directly to a war on terror abroad or a significant spike in the incidence of violence at home against persons perceived to be Middle Eastern, Arabic, or Muslim. However, these attacks certainly contributed to the growing identification of "terrorist" with persons who were Middle Eastern, Arabic, or Muslim.

The first effort to bring down the World Trade Center (WTC) occurred in 1993. Although six were killed and over one thousand injured, the American response was painstaking police work, followed by prosecutions in courts of law rather than a global war on terror. The perpetrators were loosely tied to bin Laden, but there is little evidence that bin Laden had anything to do with the WTC bombing in 1993 (al-Qaeda did not yet exist). The *9/11 Commission Report* notes that this incident was significant post–September 11 in four ways. First, this was a new kind of terrorism, "whose rage and malice had no limit," in which a high body count and visibility were twinned goals; second, "the FBI and Justice Department did excellent work investigating"; third, the civilian legal system successfully prosecuted and convicted those responsible; and fourth, "although the bombing heightened awareness of a new terrorist danger, successful prosecutions contributed to widespread underestimation of the threat."[34]

Thus, although it was a terrorist attack on American soil, aimed at the same symbol of American economic power that would later fall to an attack with similar goals, this incident was deemed a crime rather than an existential threat. The response was contained by the law (meaning no invocation of sovereign power was necessary), led to far less extralegal violence against those deemed Muslims, and did not provoke a global war on terror. These efforts institutionally empowered both the law and law enforcement in ways (mostly) consonant with the rule of law. The response, then, deemed a legal framework and legal institutions capable of responding to the threat of vulnerability. The law was enough. Here we can use the distinction discussed in Chapter 1 between ordinary politics and moments of rupture. After the 1993 WTC bombing, we remained on the terrain of ordinary politics, which required no invocation of sovereign power. In Carl Schmitt's terms, "sovereign is he who decides the exception" to ordinary law; the sovereign deemed the 1993 WTC bombing not exceptional enough to warrant the suspension of normal law.[35] And as Jade Schiff argues, during "ordinary politics," narratives of limited legal responsibility work well enough that they are unquestioned by the majority. Ordinary politics, however, are exploded by extraordinary moments of crisis or rupture "that can engender profound disorientation" because they "disturb our sense of ourselves and the world, and draw attention to both through that very disturbance."[36] The American response to the September 11 attacks, though, seems not to have drawn our attention to the world; rather, our attention turned inward. Rather than seek to understand what happened to us and why, we sought to blame others. This might offer a clue about why our response was sovereign mourning rather than democratic.

The Oklahoma City bombing in 1995 comes closest to the scale and loss of life suffered in 2001. With 168 dead and almost 700 injured, it was the deadliest incident of domestic terrorism prior to September 11. Observers were shocked that such things could happen in the heartland of America. A *New York Times* reporter who interviewed witnesses on the scene writes, "One by one they said the same thing: this does not happen here. It happens in countries so far away, so different, they might as well be on the dark side of the moon. It happens in New York. It happens in Europe."[37] In quotations like this, Americans reinforced a misguided belief in their right to a privileged invulnerability while also heightening fears of its breach. Americans projected such violence as normal and acceptable in places like New York, Europe, or "countries far away." Recognizing this kind of violence as it happens elsewhere might serve as a step toward democratic mourning, leading us to recognize that we have a responsibility to prevent harm to others (even if they live far away). But in this instance, it seems that citizens of the heartland displaced this violence as foreign, distant, and none of their concern. Instead of a shared experience of profound vulnerability that might be mobilized to build solidarity across borders, these responses disavowed connection to the everyday violence suffered elsewhere.

After Oklahoma City, the federal government enacted a series of counterterrorism measures, including the Comprehensive Terrorism Prevention Act of 1995.[38] Significantly, the day after the bombing—perpetrated by Timothy McVeigh, a white, American-born male, trained by the U.S. Army, and with ties to the militia movement—there were reports that investigators were interviewing men of "Middle Eastern appearance."[39] In the immediate aftermath, there were 220 incidents of hate crimes against Arabs and Muslims reported nationwide, which "reflect the existence of a reflexive association of terrorism with Arabs and Muslims that has developed over a course of decades."[40] Although McVeigh had already been arrested and admitted that he was responsible for the bombing of the Murrah Building, this bill nonetheless included several sections on international terrorism prevention.

This suggests a deep but unstated connection between terrorism and racialized foreigners in the American mind; although the perpetrator was neither foreign nor nonwhite, the threat from that direction should nonetheless be neutralized. On April 21, the *New York Times* editorialized that the initial draft of this bill was "misguided" because it allowed "the Government to deport aliens who have committed no crime but have made charitable contributions to organizations branded 'terrorist' by the Government. It would permit the use of evidence from secret sources in deportation proceedings without fully disclosing the nature of the information or where it came from." A later *New York Times* article describes how the bill allowed the president to determine which international organizations were terrorist; made donations to such organizations criminal acts; expedited deportations of aliens suspected of terrorism; and instituted a "terrorism court." All of these foreshadowed and enabled the eschewal of traditional legal machinery in favor of a war footing that followed September 11.[41]

It is difficult to square this response with the reality of the Oklahoma City bombing without understanding how race influences American perceptions of belonging and vulnerability. Within days, it was obvious that McVeigh was the main perpetrator. Nonetheless, the antiterrorism bill after Oklahoma City focused on terrorism as an *external* threat. There was no similar concerted effort to curb domestic terrorism by white men, such as public mass shootings or bombing abortion clinics.[42] Leti Volpp argues that "Timothy McVeigh failed to produce a discourse about good whites and bad whites, because the public conceptualized McVeigh as an individual deviant, a bad actor. His actions were not considered representative of an entire racial group."[43] McVeigh was simply seen as a bad apple, an individual who was in no way a stand-in for all the other good (white) men who would never do such a thing. Curiously, then, even as a white man admitted guilt for the largest act of terrorism on American soil at that time, the law responded by targeting and racializing Middle Easterners, Arabs, or Muslims in a stated effort to prevent similar instances in the future. This suggests that terrorism had become linked to Arabs/Muslims/Middle Easterners in the American mind. The 1993 WTC bombing seems to have secured in the American mind that Muslims were terrorists; this story was not dislodged even when a much more deadly terrorist attack was perpetrated by a white man only two years later. And rather than fight to quell violence within our own house, we sought enemies abroad.

To conclude, given the long history of racialization of different groups in the United States and the lack of a clear international adversary, the United States was primed and ready to find or construct an enemy on which to project an existential threat. The events of September 11 provided a ready outlet: Arabs/Muslims/Middle Easterners could replace the Russians as the existential threat we needed to know who we were. At the same time, while acts of terrorism had been none too infrequent, the visibility and horror of September 11—paired with journalists and elites who depoliticized the context, denied American responsibility for creating the popular unrest that fueled terrorism, and turned terrorism instead into an existential or civilizational threat—spurred action that went far beyond previous responses to terrorist violence.

Depoliticizing Visibility: Intimate Loss and Public Spectacle

There is no question that the events of September 11 were spectacularly visible. They were witnessed in real time by a substantial number of Americans on the ground in the New York and Washington, D.C., metro areas. But far more people watched on live TV, followed by newscasts that repeatedly replayed the crashes, falling buildings, and explosions. As with many important historical moments, most Americans can recall precisely where they were when they heard the news, which—even in the absence of widespread high-speed internet connections—spread very quickly. A communication survey done on September 13, 2001, in New Mexico—far from New York, Washington, D.C., or Pennsylvania—showed that within three hours of American Flight 11 crashing into the North Tower, over 90 percent of those surveyed knew what was happening (within six hours, it reached 99 percent), and 69 percent of those surveyed informed someone else.[44] Of the 127 individuals surveyed in New Mexico, 75 of them "said they were personally affected by the terrorist attacks of September 11, 2001." They offered statements about the effects ranging from "I am depressed, sad, upset and angry" to "[The attacks] reaffirmed my patriotism" to "I no longer want to move to New York" to "I am in the military and ready to fly."[45]

Though a minority of Americans witnessed the events firsthand, life in the United States ground to a halt for days as Americans turned on their TVs and did not turn them off. Pew Research found that between September 14 and 17, 81 percent of Americans said they were "constantly tuned in to news reports."[46] At that time, 63 percent of respondents agreed that they "can't stop watching news about the terrorist attacks," even though 92 percent agreed that watching the coverage made them feel sad, 77 percent said it made them feel frightened, and 45 percent said it tired them out.[47]

And yet unlike the other mournable moments this book considers, the bodies of the September 11 dead were not displayed as bodies; I suggest in this section that the bodies themselves were obscured, leading families to mourn their losses in ways that became privatizing and individualizing, while the political nature of the event was obscured by public spectacle rather than properly political mourning (a view enabled by elite political actors, as I argue in the following section). Recall that thousands viewed the Triangle Fire as it happened, tens of thousands more viewed the bodies in the morgue, and images of the dead from the fire were published in news reports. The march of mourning that followed—essentially a general strike—was conceived as a way to honor the bodies that remained unclaimed. Similarly, Emmett Till's body was displayed for tens of thousands to see firsthand, and images of his body and his grieving mother were published in the popular press. In both these prior instances of political mourning, then, the body itself was central; the humanity, mortality, and fragility of the human body was an important component of the collective responses. Even the iconic images of prior terrorist attacks centered on bodies; recall the smoke-blackened faces of those leaving the World Trade Center after the 1993 bombing or the firefighter carrying the lifeless body of a toddler out of the Murrah Building in Oklahoma City.

But the events of September 11 eclipsed the bodies of the victims so completely that human deaths became practically invisible. Instead, the focus was on the event as a whole. Jenny Edkins suggests that, as with most trauma, the event itself was unspeakable, so that all the media could show was endless images of buildings exploding or collapsing; the destruction of the buildings, endlessly repeated, stood in for images of destroyed bodies.[48] What bodies we did see in pictures were—at least in most published images—not yet dead. They are instead in extremis, waving shirts or tumbling down. The most memorable of these images was "The Falling Man," photographed by Richard Drew and released on the Associated Press wire; the image was published in hundreds of newspapers around the world on September 12.[49] In this iconic though controversial image, the man is still alive. We know his fate, but we never see his end. We know, too, that scores more died the same way. The discomfort of sitting with the questions faced by those who jumped—Would you jump? How bad would things have to be for your best option to be a leap from the hundredth floor?—was a step too far for many Americans. In response to sustained and heated criticism from the American public, the image was quickly scrubbed from coverage. Tom Junod writes, "In most American newspapers, the photograph that Richard Drew took of the Falling Man ran once and never again."[50] According to Junod, the rest of the world saw these images, while the American public did not.

There are few exceptions to this pattern. Images of body parts either never appeared or appeared then quickly disappeared. One such image, by Todd Maisel, was titled "The Hand, 9/11, New York, 2001." It appeared in the *New York Daily News* on September 12 but caused an outcry and was removed from later editions of the paper. In fact, I have been unable to lo-cate the original image. A search of the *Daily News*'s archive online yielded nothing, as did an online search of the *Daily News*'s photo archives. While several websites show the image and mention that it appeared in the *Daily News*, Jeffrey Green's "Eyewitnesses to History" directly addresses the con-troversy in a ten-year retrospective. Green writes:

> The Sept. 12 edition of the *Daily News* contained several of Maisel's photographs, but two, in particular, generated a lot of discussion in and out of the newsroom. Many already shell-shocked New Yorkers who read the *Daily News* on Wednesday may not have been prepared for the black-and-white photo on page 12. "There are a lot of mixed feelings about that photo, whether that photo should have been used," Maisel acknowledged. In fact, later editions of the paper did not carry it. "I felt it was very appropriate because I don't think we should understate the true horror of the day."
>
> The photo's tabloid caption said it all: GRISLY REMAINS: Severed hand of World Trade Center victim lies in street after terrorist at-tack. "I saw lots of body parts, but the hand was intact," Maisel said. "The hand was kind of spooky to me. It was pointing at me and right next to the hand was this piece of Hershey's chocolate."[51]

Maisel, though disturbed by the image he captured, believed its publication was an important part of the record, a record remarkably free of depictions of bodily harm but filled with images of structural damage to buildings.

Tom Junod suggests that this refusal to look at the bodies, to witness these deaths, is a departure from previous coverage of important tragic events. There are numerous iconic photographs of moments of death or ter-rible pain. And yet we Americans refused to look at pictures of the jumpers of September 11. Junod argues:

> What distinguishes the pictures of the jumpers from the pictures that have come before is that we—we Americans—are being asked to discriminate on their behalf. What distinguishes them, historically, is that we, as patriotic Americans, have agreed not to look at them. Dozens, scores, maybe hundreds of people died by leaping from a burning building, and we have somehow taken it upon ourselves to deem their deaths unworthy of witness—because we have somehow deemed the act of witness, in this one regard, unworthy of us. . . .
>
> The picture went all around the world, and then disappeared, as if we willed it away. One of the most famous photographs in human history became an unmarked grave, and the man buried inside its

frame—the Falling Man—became the Unknown Soldier in a war whose end we have not yet seen. Richard Drew's photograph is all we know of him, and yet all we know of him becomes a measure of what we know of ourselves. The picture is his cenotaph, and like the monuments dedicated to the memory of unknown soldiers everywhere, it asks that we look at it, and make one simple acknowledgment.

That we have known who the Falling Man is all along.[52]

Clément Chéroux's statistical analysis of September 11 photographs in U.S. newspapers confirms what seems like a tacit agreement to focus coverage on buildings rather than bodies. According to Gérôme Truc's review of Cheroux's work *Diplopie*, it demonstrates that the news coverage focused not on the suffering of the victims but on the disintegration of the buildings. Truc offers the following summary of Chéroux's findings:

Based on a sample drawn from the covers of 400 US newspapers for September 11 and 12 (out of a total of 1,500), he concluded that the photographs fall into six image types. He found that beyond slight formal variations such as differences in framing, 41% of the images portray the explosion of the South Tower at the moment of impact of Flight 175, 17% the smoke cloud above Manhattan, 14% the ruins at Ground Zero, 13.5% one of the planes approaching the towers, 6% scenes of panic in the streets of New York, and 3.5% the American flag. Only 5% of the cover photographs fall outside of these six categories, and the World Trade Center is omnipresent; as Chéroux observes, "it is the suffering of the building that dominates," taking precedent over the suffering of the victims.[53]

The focus on the buildings—abstract architectural icons, themselves abstractions for a host of concepts, including capitalism, American economic hegemony, masculinity, New York itself, and sovereignty—contributed to the surreal quality of the day. Surely, we knew that the buildings were not what we mourned. And yet it was easier to focus on and see those losses over and over than it was to see the effects on human bodies. In this sense, the losses became more public spectacle than a properly political invitation to reflect on the responsibility of the audience to consider the effects of their actions on others, as in Aeschylus's *The Persians*. It is as though our greatest fear was the loss of power rather than the loss of people.

Perhaps, though, this confusion is understandable. While there were shrines to the dead and missing in and around Lower Manhattan for weeks, few bodies were recovered and even fewer were recognizable. Of the 2,753 dead in New York, where the majority of the casualties and devastation occurred, "seventeen were recognized by 'remains viewed'; 305 by fingerprints; 25 by photo; 78 by personal effects; 534 by dental or body X-rays; six by tattoos," while 21,744 remains had been recovered by 2009.[54] As of 2009, the New York City Office of the Chief Medical Examiner was still finding bone fragments near the World Trade Center; they continue to work toward positively identifying more than 1,100 victims via DNA analysis.[55] As the result of improvements in DNA technology, one victim was positively identified through DNA testing as recently as 2018.[56]

In response to the baffling immateriality of 2,700 deaths in New York, the *New York Times* ran a special section called "Portraits of Grief," in which it offered snapshots and brief bios of those who died. Simon Stow argues that the individualization of these images made grief personal in dangerous ways. By focusing on individuals—whose stories sound the same because so many of the individuals who died were remarkably alike—the mourning after September 11 limited critical political faculties that might have helped dampen the calls for revenge. Likening these portraits to pornography, Stow writes, "It was not enough simply to catalogue the dead, as in previous individual memorializations; the dead had to be made attractive to the living in a kind of emotional necrophilia."[57] The result was a too-personal hold on grief that focused solely on individuals rather than the larger political conditions and ramifications of this event. That is, rather than viewing these dead as citizens, we mistakenly viewed the victims as pure and apolitical individuals whose lives bore no relationship to American political and economic hegemony. The mourning for the individuals killed on September 11 was privatized—few if any funerals were open to the public—and thus removed from the political domain while simultaneously thrust into the realm of the public spectacle. These factors worked together to evacuate the space where mourning could become political.

On the one hand, then, the media attention dedicated to the events of the day directed the public's focus toward spectacular explosions and collapses, broadcasting and printing images that essentially made the event colossal: almost inhuman in scope and impact. The scope of the event ushered the public into a sense of awe and potential paralysis as the complications of American interventions in the Middle East made easy attributions of responsibility difficult. It was less demanding to focus on terrorists hating freedom than to engage with the tortured history of colonialism and neocolonialism. As a result, the event was inexplicable to most Americans; following the lead of political leaders, Americans resorted to the readily available racialized tropes of a backward culture and a violent religion. The events induced a kind of helplessness that enabled those with hawkish agendas to more easily shape a military response while the magnitude of events made critique of sovereign power's protection difficult. Who could critique

108 / Chapter 4

capitalism after watching two of its iconic symbols fall? Who could critique American militarism after its very center had been struck so devastatingly?

On the other hand, the focus in the days after was on the individuals who died. This directed us not toward the dead as citizens but toward the dead as purely private persons, whose work in the World Trade Center or the Pentagon was without political significance. This, too, obscured how power and political ideologies around gender and race led to a particular subset of the population to be in those particular spaces. The death certificates issued by September 2009 for the World Trade Center indicate the ratio of men to women is about 3 to 1 (2,100 males to 623 females) and most of the dead were "non-Hispanic, white" (2,064, or 76 percent).[58] While those who died came from many nations around the world (115, according to *New York* magazine), four out of five were born in the United States (2,155, or 79 percent). The dead in New York were mostly white, mostly male, mostly native-born American citizens in one of the most diverse cities in the world.[59]

While the other instances considered in this book force us to look at the bodies and realize that we, collectively and democratically, bore political responsibility for the conditions that led to those deaths, that connection was severed in the depictions of the events of September 11 and our mourning of the individuals who died. The buildings collapsed, and we mourned the individuals who perished. But we failed to connect what the buildings stood for and how those ideals may have played a role in enabling the deaths that happened within the buildings.

Our response was, instead, to create heroes. To be clear, many humans did, in fact, act in accordance with the highest ideals of self-sacrifice and genuine heroism; there were a thousand instances of strangers going to great lengths to help one another, often by taking great personal risk. Seeking to inspire courage rather than dwell in grief, the media focused on the heroism of first responders. There are numerous iconic photographs of that day: of the towers, horrified onlookers, bodies tumbling through space, rescuers. The images of the living tend to be of two groups—horrified onlookers (often women) and rescuers (primarily men). While the rescuers were slightly more than 10 percent of the total dead on September 11, their images were by far the most reproduced. Most of us can recall the image of Father Mychal Judge's lifeless (though seemingly whole and unbloodied) body being carried out by rescuers; a firefighter working his way up the steps of the World Trade Center as civilians work their way down; and the flag raised over ground zero by three New York Fire Department firefighters. This impulse to see patriots rather than citizens may be related to the identities of those who died. They fit well into a masculine patriotic identity in which, according to George Kateb, what counts most is "a readiness to die and to kill for what is largely a figment of the imagination."[60] That is, rather than seeing images of torn, wounded, everyday people whose lives tragically ended without warning, we recall images of patriotic heroism and agency that reaffirm collective identities that became more salient that day and that contribute to a suppression of critical citizenship. This focus helped prefigure and bring into being a protective sovereign state; it was easier to imagine ourselves (and thus our state) as heroic rescuers than to imagine ourselves as the anxious audience or the annihilated victims. We craved the protective power of Thomas Hobbes's sovereign.

And yet at the heart of sovereignty, too, lies violence. Like David Hume and Edmund Burke, Jenny Edkins argues that how we remember events—in particular how states memorialize moments of disruption and violence—suggests an effort to obscure the forces of violence that are foundational to the creation of sovereign states. In the mythic social contract, the decision to create a state is driven by our rationality. And yet Hobbes himself notes that while some sovereigns may be created by "institution," most are created through "acquisition" and conquest.[61] Most sovereign states now in existence came to be through violence and trauma. Yet to retain its legitimacy under the mythic social contract, sovereign power must reframe this violence as heroic and redemptive. To explain, Edkins writes:

> Memory is central to relations of power. Dominant powers can use commemoration as a means of *forgetting* past struggles. For example, they can use accounts of heroism and sacrifice that tell a story of the founding of the state, a narrative of glorious origin. This obscures trauma. In this context practices that insist on remembering [the costs to individual and societies during conflict] can be insurrectionary and counter-hegemonic. They remind us that power is provisional and contingent, and that it entails violence.[62]

In short, "remembering is intensely political: part of the fight for political change is a struggle for memory."[63] Remembering the heroism of the first responders rather than the civilian deaths—of Americans or of countless persons killed or displaced by American foreign policy in the Middle East—makes it easier *not* to ask about the role of American sovereignty and imperial militarism.[64]

This spectral, invisible death was, perhaps, more difficult to absorb and easier to abstract than a bier bearing three thousand bodies. The collective disappearance of the dead removed the focus from the sheer physicality of the deaths—from the achievement of mortalist humanism that Stow suggests *The Persians* and other instances of tragic mourning help create—and toward the replayed spectacle of speeding planes slamming into monumental buildings. Surely this was an obstacle to locating shared experience of bodily vulnerability in the wake of the attacks. The absence of bodies focused American fear not on the mundane reality of bodily vulnerability but on fears of a more abstract character.

Although September 11 was highly visible across the globe, the focus was not on bodies but on symbols. Furthermore, the scale of the event boggled the mind, which set the stage for a national anger that invoked bodies of the dead while simultaneously occluding their location in complex configurations of political power and denying any American responsibility for the conditions that gave rise to al-Qaeda. The effect was to obscure the space of politics altogether. This depoliticized space enabled a response that disregarded costs of military interventions for others: particularly those living in lands Americans invaded or destabilized. By focusing on individuals rather than citizens, we missed a chance to foster a larger, critical view of the political situation. We felt sympathy for abstracted patriotic selves, for the wound to our idealized country whose seemingly impermeable borders had been so spectacularly breached. (Though this presumed impermeability is itself hardly gender-neutral.[65])

Political Actors Taking Their Grief-Wrath Public to Make War Instead of Law

In the days immediately after September 11, Columbia University's Oral History Research Office and Institute for Social and Economic Policy collected oral histories from people in New York "who experienced the most direct and traumatic aspects of the disaster, through either proximity or loss,"[66] in an effort to determine how collective memories are formed around an event of such magnitude. Carefully distinguishing the purported national consensus from the local responses to the attack, they found that

> an official public interpretation of the meaning of September 11 was generated soon after the events occurred. This dominant account portrayed a nation unified in grief; it allowed government officials to claim that there is a public consensus that September 11 was a turning point in the nation's history that has clear implications for national and foreign policy. It is important to remember that this consensus was constructed not by those who lived through the terrorist attacks and their aftermath, but by those who observed it and had political reasons to interpret it as they did.[67]

In contrast to the presumed and constructed national consensus, this study found that many directly affected by the events of September 11 in New

York "feared that the violence they lived through would spark greater violence. Many . . . wanted publicly to record their reluctance to pinpoint the enemy in a way that would rationalize an invasion. . . . [Their] statements rejected revenge as the only official response and revealed how the vulnerability of eyewitnesses and survivors translated into sympathy for other potential victims."[68] Put together, this seems to indicate that support for the immediate bombing of Afghanistan was markedly lower in New York City than it seemed to be in the rest of the nation. Many hoped—aloud and in public—that the United States would choose a different response: that Americans would stop to reflect and consider our role in the histories that led to these events. Many New Yorkers, in particular, did not want to purposefully rain this destruction on others. For example, a friend related her experience of being in New York at that time. She wrote:

> In the days that immediately followed, there was such a strong sense of shared mourning in the city, such a powerful solidarity and longing for peace, that it seemed things might finally change, for the better, and for good. But the subsequent decade has been a long unraveling of that fragile sense of kinship, and I know many New Yorkers feel personally betrayed and disgusted by the politicization of our shared grief.[69]

She expresses here the response of many. In New York, there really was a sense that things could change—a hope that dimmed when the first bomb fell in Afghanistan and was soundly extinguished as America expanded the War on Terror at home and into Iraq. But my friend's use of the language of "politicization" is perhaps too broad. I would argue instead that she meant "instrumentalization" or even "manipulation." That is, the promisingly democratic aspects of witnessing such devastation on our shores—devastation that Americans have generally been a comfortable distance from—could have generated for Americans a sense of solidarity across borders as we came to understand just how brutal such events are. But these glimmers of democratic mourning were quickly overtaken by the assertion of sovereign power, accomplished in part by political elites who shifted the question from the terrain of politics to ontology.

The abstracted, mediated images the rest of the country and world saw did not provide them with the experience of what war might feel like to those on the other side, an experience for which many New Yorkers gained a new and profound respect. Many in New York realized that what they experienced on September 11 was unusual only in place, not in scale or type, and it provoked a profound hesitation to inflict that kind of terror on others, while many removed from the experience itself seemed to have no such hesitation.

While New Yorkers may have been reluctant for the country to go to war in their names, it was quickly evident that the Bush administration would seek precisely that. As related by Bob Woodward in *Bush at War*, twice on September 11, President George W. Bush called the events of that day "an opportunity."[70] George Kateb asks: An opportunity for what? Kateb posits that Bush was pursuing an "overarching aim that is barely avowed and that, when avowed, is expressed in an anodyne and patriotic rhetoric. That aim is to guarantee the existence of a long-term project that will serve to justify the national security state (an ensemble of bureaucratic structures) and the economy that serves it and is served by it. Only an ideologically defined enemy can justify this system."[71] The aim is to preserve American sovereignty and hegemony.

The events of September 11 were employed to assert a national unity that did not exist and shut down any effort to challenge the overly simplistic narrative of "saving freedom" offered by the Bush administration. In addition, there was an immediate determination that these events, unlike previous terrorist attacks on U.S. soil, could not addressed by legal mechanisms. Instead, they required military ones. To support this, unity was constructed by reiterating a simplistic view of American innocence that located all fault in places and people coded foreign. Given that narrative, overwhelming military force was the only option.

John Hutcheson, David Domke, Andre Billeaudeaux, and Philip Garland demonstrate how, in the days after September 11, a "patriotic press" gave more weight and coverage to "government and military officials [who] consistently emphasized American core values and themes of U.S. strength and power while simultaneously demonizing the 'enemy.'"[72] As a result of the press prioritizing these voices, the conflicting emotions of the wider populace after the event were given focus and articulation by those with access to the media: primarily government and military officials. Hutcheson and colleagues demonstrate that, when interviewed by the press, "first, U.S. government and military officials were more likely than other U.S. elites and U.S. citizens to include national identity-related themes in their comments; second, President Bush engaged in the highest usage of such discourse."[73] Similarly, U.S. government and military officials were far more likely to immediately attribute blame to terrorists (94 percent), while U.S. citizens were slightly less sure (80 percent blamed "the terrorists"), and other U.S. elites were far more skeptical (about 58 percent declaring terrorists the cause of the attacks).[74]

There was still more variation between government officials, the public, and nongovernmental elites regarding American values. About four-fifths (81 percent) of U.S. government and military officials who referenced "American values" did so in a positive manner.[75] For example, recall President Bush's first statement on the day itself: "Freedom itself was attacked this morning by a faceless coward. And freedom will not be defeated."[76] U.S. citizens tended to be in agreement; 80 percent "mentioned U.S. values in a positive manner."[77]

In contrast, barely half (51 percent) of other U.S. elites referred to U.S. values in a positive manner, while 20 percent were critical of U.S. values, and 29 percent offered a mixed appraisal.[78] To make sense of this disparity, the authors claim:

> The overwhelmingly positive valence of government and military officials' statements about U.S. national identity suggests the presence of *conscious, strategic* communications on their part to mobilize public sentiment. In contrast, statements by other U.S. elites were relatively much less affirmative of U.S. identity, particularly in the categories of blame attribution for September 11, American values, and U.S. strength. This finding may be a combination of the likelihood that opinion leaders not affiliated with government are more likely to offer analysis of the U.S. position, rather than outright advocacy for the U.S. position.[79]

One way to read this apparent difference is that government and military leaders *asserted* unity (the unity required for sovereign power to seem legitimate) to avoid having to build democratic consensus; their language was truly constitutive in this sense. The administration's constant invocation that other countries and peoples were with us or against us helped create the effect it named, by compelling citizens and countries to support or reject its position regardless of whether the premise itself was correct. Journalists uncritically followed their lead, offering coverage that was too simplistic in its support of American values and too confident in its assertion of American innocence.

Many scholars have considered the media coverage of September 11, including the mobilization of emotion, the dualism of victim and perpetrator, and thinly veiled invocations of a contemporary crusade. Elisabeth Anker offers a provocative reading of news coverage as melodrama, which "employed emotionality to provide an unambiguous distinction between good and evil through clear designations of victimization, heroism, and villainy."[80] Denise Bostdorff reads George Bush's rhetoric in the days after September 11 as a form of "covenant renewal," which "depicted evil as a cause rather than an effect . . . depicted a benevolent God and placed primary blame for the nation's problems on external sources, rather than his 'parishioners.'"[81] These academic analyses generally agree that the American state worked hard to create a unity that did not necessarily exist.

Furthermore, the space of critique by nongovernmental elites was quickly shut down by government elites. In fact, government officials actively called out anyone who dissented from the call to unity. Administration officials used their bully pulpits to publicly dress down anyone who made comments critical of the United States. Two examples should serve to support this claim. First, Bill Maher made a provocative statement on his show, *Politically Incorrect*, that those calling the hijackers cowards were wrong; what was cowardly, according to Maher, was launching missiles against targets thousands of miles away. In response, White House Press Secretary Ari Fleischer denounced Maher, saying of news organizations and all Americans that, in times like these, "people have to watch what they say and watch what they do."[82] Second, in response to citizens raising legitimate concerns about the Patriot Act, Attorney General John Ashcroft responded as follows: "To those who scare peace-loving people with phantoms of lost liberty, my message is this: your tactics only aid terrorists for they erode our national unity and diminish our resolve. They give ammunition to America's enemies, and pause to America's friends."[83] Statements such as these by leading administration officials contributed to a "linkage of national identity to national security [which] helped create a climate in which dissent and opposition became equated with anti-Americanism."[84] The message of these administration officials was that critiquing or questioning state power was not a patriotic duty of a democratic citizen; dissent was, instead, a graver threat to the security of the state than terrorism.

As a result, by September 16 most Americans were "willing to accept dramatic changes in law enforcement policies," according to a Pew Research survey.[85] Even so, the public did not give blanket approval to all proposed antiterrorism measures. The report notes that a two-to-one majority rejected the idea of establishing internment camps in response to the question "Would you favor or oppose . . . allowing the U.S. government to take legal immigrants from unfriendly countries to internment camps during times of tension or crisis?" but three in ten Americans said they *would* favor that option. About 70 percent of the public wanted to prevent the government from accessing private communications such as telephone and email, but 70 percent also supported establishing a national identification card to be carried at all times and 67 percent approved of allowing the Central Intelligence Agency (CIA) to conduct assassinations overseas.[86]

Overall, Pew Research found that Americans were nearly split on the question of who should be feared more: the government or terrorists. When asked, "What concerns you most? . . . That the government will fail to enact strong, new anti-terrorism laws, or that the government will enact new anti-terrorism laws which excessively restrict the average person's civil liberties?" 39 percent worried that the government would fail to enact strong enough laws, while 34 percent worried that new laws would excessively restrict civil liberties.[87] From this we can infer that Americans were far less united than officials pronounced or than news outlets portrayed, in particular about the conflicted desire for a strong, protective state. There were deep divides regarding what should be done, and who should be more feared.

Eschewing Law and Responsibility

The American response to the prior instances of terrorism had been to treat them as crimes, with a focus on investigation and prosecution through existing legal institutions. Unlike the response to the World Trade Center bombing in 1993, in the days after September 11, domestic law and international legal regimes were deemed incapable of responding to the threat posed by future terrorist activity. Recall that in 1993, several perpetrators were apprehended, tried, and convicted in domestic courts by the end of the year. As stated previously, the 9/11 Commission reported that legal success in locating and convicting the men who orchestrated the 1993 bombing brought with it a failure to comprehend and respond to the real and growing threat of terrorism.[88] This reading of what happened in the months after the 1993 World Trade Center bombing conflates two aspects of law: deterrence and prosecution. It also obscures the connection between law and politics. Finding international terrorists and bringing them to trial in federal court was a stunning legal accomplishment and is what a state should do in response to such a terrible event. But finding someone guilty for a heinous act in a court of law can make it difficult to ask questions about why they undertook these actions; legal guilt can obscure political responsibility. As a result, the successful prosecutions of the 1993 perpetrators potentially made coming to terms with how American foreign policy was contributing to the spread of terrorism more difficult to see because of our confidence in the power of law as a deterrent. Prosecution is meant to be an after-the-fact response that signals to potential criminals that the costs of violating the law are significant enough to dissuade them from such activity. In the face of a movement promising a blessed afterlife, however, deterrence through punishment will generally be ineffective. Thus, while the 9/11 Commission analysis may be correct that the success of the 1993 investigation and trial prevented the nation from understanding the necessity to prevent such acts in the future, my suspicion is that this failure was because of a misunderstanding of political responsibility. Rather than focusing solely on disrupting international terrorist networks through traditional law enforcement, why did we not pause to consider how our foreign policy interventions were driving those networks?

Comparing these two events, however, provides an opportunity to consider how and why a similar if less spectacular crime in 1993 was pursued via traditional prosecutorial means aided by international cooperation and yet the events of 2001 were so easily turned into a call for war. Much turns on how responsibility was conceptualized, and American neoconservatives conceptualized responsibility as a minimally regulative security state. The result is that unlike the other cases I analyze, law did not fail on its own terms (as a result of the limitations of a legal understanding of responsibility); rather, political actors deemed the law incapable of responding to the threat. That is, the more reactive prosecutorial model of law and law enforcement was edged out by calls for a military response, which secured the *state itself* rather than the demos.

This was not a foregone conclusion. Public opinion surveys and oral histories done in New York tend to show a much more reflective period of trying to sort through why this happened, whereas administration officials presented a unified front and the media dutifully followed their lead. James Berger writes:

> Linguistic control of the event was a sign of social and political stability. At first, for the most part, the names were rather general: "catastrophe," "tragedy," and, most broadly, "event," or simply the date, 9/11. The word "attack" was used in these early days and weeks but markedly less often than the other, more general terms. By October 11, however, the "event" had become "the attack." What is the difference? An attack requires a particular kind of response: a counterattack. . . . Once the destruction of the World Trade Center had been definitely named a terrorist attack, the paralyzed, nameless agony of that event, that thing that happened for which every attempt at meaning was inadequate, was converted into the beginning of a war.[89]

Joan Didion notes a similar change in the weeks immediately after "the event," drawing on an interview with Stephen Weber, a political science professor at the University of California at Berkeley who was in New York on September 11. Weber observed that, in New York bookstores,

> on September 12, the shelves were emptied of books on Islam, on American foreign policy, on Iraq, on Afghanistan. There was a substantive discussion about what it is about the nature of the American presence in the world that created a situation in which movements like al-Qaeda can thrive . . . but that discussion got short-circuited. Sometime in late October, early November 2001, the tone of the discussion . . . became: what's wrong with the Islamic world that it failed to produce democracy, science, education, its own enlightenment, and created societies that breed terror?[90]

Acknowledging that these sources are thin, it still seems plausible that there was a moment after September 11 when many engaged in the kind of collective questioning that *could* have led to a more democratic response. But that is not what happened. I suggest that *how* political actors—in particular, administration officials and hawkish elected representatives—framed the event short-circuited the public's initial response of tragic mourning (as Stow describes it): mourning that moves us to imagine the world from another perspective and work to minimize the vulnerability of all.[91]

Law's perceived inadequacy was largely the result of the immediate response of American hawks, including Senator John McCain and President George W. Bush, who framed the event not as a crime defined by the laws of the United States or as a crime against humanity (for which a persuasive argument can be made) but as an act of war, which it manifestly was not.[92] On the one hand, then, the slow and painstaking mechanisms of investigation and prosecution attendant upon treating it as a crime was, according to the president, an improper response to such an colossal act. On the other hand, the Bush administration's antipathy toward the United Nations was well known, and an American invocation of international law to locate and prosecute the criminals who perpetrated the crime would have countered the administration's stated goals. Law was characterized as incapable of addressing the events of that day. Rather than "ordinary" politics, then, this event was construed as extraordinary, requiring sovereign power rather than leaving events to run their course through ordinary law and democratic politics.

As Schmitt writes in *Political Theology*, "Sovereign is he who decides on the exception."[93] In the language of Bonnie Honig, September 11 was clearly a moment of "emergency politics." The United States simply had to act. The question, Honig says (following Bernard Williams), is whether we can live with the aftermath of our actions, given that there may be no good option. As Honig writes, "Political emergencies rarely occur as a result of mere innocent wanderings. Instead, emergencies are usually the contingent crystallization of prior events and relationships in which many are deeply implicated."[94] Given the long history of American intervention in the Middle East that consistently supported authoritarian states and prioritized stability over democracy, surely the United States bore some responsibility for creating the conditions in which the nineteen hijackers came to see terrorism as a legitimate choice.

Lawrence Wright's Pulitzer Prize–winning book *The Looming Tower* carefully details the road to the events of September 11. Wright identifies a double bind experienced by those who became hijackers or members of al-Qaeda: being recipients of globalization's promise in the form of education and international mobility while feeling displaced both in one's home and abroad. He writes:

> What the recruits tended to have in common—besides their urbanity, their cosmopolitan backgrounds, their education, their facility with languages, and their computer skills—was displacement. Most who joined the jihad did so in a country other than the one in which they were reared. They were Algerians living in expatriate enclaves in France, Moroccans in Spain, or Yemenis in Saudi Arabia. Despite their accomplishments, they had little standing in the host societies where they lived. Like Sayyid Qutb,[95] they defined themselves as radical Muslims while living in the West. The Pakistani in London found that he was neither authentically British nor authentically Pakistani; and this feeling of marginality was just as true for Lebanese in Kuwait as it was for Egyptians in Brooklyn. Alone, alienated, and often far from his family, the exile turned to the mosque, where he found companionship and the consolation of religion.[96]

I want to be clear that to explain is not to exonerate. As Judith Butler argues in *Precarious Life*, attempts to explain why any person might do what the hijackers did in no way seek to exonerate their actions.[97] I do not include Wright's characterization of al-Qaeda members in an effort to exonerate their actions, which were categorically wrong and unjust. But it is important to explain why they might have come to believe the things they did and what events or actions prompted them to take such radical, nihilistic steps.[98] What drove bin Laden and al-Qaeda was American support for dictators throughout the Middle East, the extreme fundamentalism of Wahhabism in Saudi Arabia, and the tortured series of American interventions in Afghanistan.

Al-Qaeda only appeared on the international scene when bin Laden announced his "Declaration of War against the Americans Occupying the Land of the Two Holy Places" in 1996.[99] Wright describes a motley crew of followers in the years immediately before and after the declaration of the group's founding. Shortly after bin Laden's declaration of war, CNN's Peter Arnett traveled to Afghanistan to interview bin Laden. When asked what kind of society he wished to see on the Arabian Peninsula, bin Laden replied:

> We are confident, with the permission of God, praise and glory be to Him, that Muslims will be victorious in the Arabian Peninsula and that God's religion, praise and glory be to him, will prevail in this peninsula. It is a great pride and a big hope that the revelation

unto Mohammed, peace be upon him, will be resorted to for ruling. When we used to follow Mohammed's revelation, peace be upon him, we were in great happiness and in great dignity, to God belongs the credit and the praise.[100]

Wright observes that "what is notable about this response, filled as usual with ritualistic locution, is the complete absence of any real political plan, beyond imposing Sharia, which was already in effect in Saudi Arabia. The happiness and dignity that bin Laden invoked lay on the other side of history from the concepts of nationhood and state."[101] Wright correctly diagnoses the lack of a *political* vision offered by bin Laden. What bin Laden envisions—and what all other religious fundamentalists envision, including many Christian fundamentalists in the United States—is fundamentally *anti*political, not *a*political (as in apathy) but *anti*political (as in antipathy). The vision of the good life bin Laden presented is one in which democratic politics is not only unnecessary but dangerous and evil. Rather than a democratic state having access to sovereign power, such visions prioritize an embodied sovereign acting at the behest of an immortal one. As a result, dialogue must be tamped down to preserve the revealed purity of God's law, and as Wright says, "Whenever purity is paramount, terror is close at hand."[102] In these fundamentalist visions, there is no need for contested yet collective discovery of shared goals; instead, revelation is privileged. There is one right way and there is every other way. (To be clear, this is not a battle between secularism and religion, because both Islam and Christianity include traditions that value debate and contestation.[103]) Later in the Arnett interview, bin Laden stated, "The U.S. today has set a double standard, calling whoever goes against its injustice a terrorist. . . . It wants to occupy our countries, steal our resources, impose on us agents to rule us . . . and wants us to agree to all these. If we refuse to do so, it will say, 'You are terrorists.'"[104]

In May 2001, months before September 11, the Middle Eastern editor for the *Guardian*, Brian Whitaker, came to a similar conclusion about how the United States applied the label "terrorist" by analyzing the definition of terrorism offered by the U.S. State Department in 2000.[105] Whitaker points out that the State Department's definition of terrorism—"premeditated, politically motivated violence perpetrated against noncombatant . . . targets by subnational groups or clandestine agents, usually intended to influence an audience"—makes it clear that states themselves cannot be terrorists.[106] As a result, Palestinian mortar attacks on Israeli settlements are, by definition, acts of terrorism, while Israeli rocket attacks on Palestinian communities are not (but are treated by the State Department as a "human rights issue" in a different report). In fact, Whitaker writes that "the American definition of terrorism is a reversal of the word's original meaning, given in the Oxford

English Dictionary as 'government by intimidation.' Today it usually refers to intimidation of governments."[107] Whitaker concludes that the American definition of terrorism can be essentially summed up as "violence committed by those we disapprove of."[108] What is striking is how much agreement there is between a news analyst from the *Guardian* and Osama bin Laden regarding American judgment of others' acts. Bin Laden successfully identified America's foreign policy hypocrisy; although American foreign policy included lofty rhetoric about freedom and democracy, U.S. actions provoke distrust in its assertions about the priority of either freedom or democracy. It is this contradiction that al-Qaeda correctly recognizes, even if its response was reprehensible and unjust.

Betraying the early promise of understanding our *political* responsibility—a responsibility that rests on the achievement of seeing others as our equals—America denied our responsibility for creating the conditions in which terrorism festered and found succor (most obviously in Afghanistan) as our ability to see honestly was wiped away by the magnitude of September 11. The language of an "axis of evil"—used by President Bush in the 2002 State of the Union address—included no sense of the enemy's humanity or a shared global fate. As Simon Stow argues in *American Mourning*, this refusal of the enemy's humanity comes at a considerable cost. He writes:

> The grief-wrath of *mênis* embodied in and cultivated by the nation's responses to loss dehumanized the enemy, making them something to be destroyed rather than someone with whom to engage. As such, the polity denied itself the possibility of a measured response to the attacks, one based on careful deliberation, good judgment, and reasoned debate, values central to the democratic ideal. It led to blindness and the eliding of important distinctions that, among other things, paved the way for the Bush administration to shift—in a tragically self-defeating way—the focus of the War of Terror to Iraq. American mourning practices thus helped undermine domestic politics, denied the possibility of a politics beyond the polity, and adversely affected the execution and formulation of the military strategy it adopted as an alternative to political engagement.[109]

In other words, the American response replaced politics with force. Denying any responsibility for the conditions that led to the attacks enabled a portrayal of terrorists as pure evil, and evil must be eradicated, not negotiated with. Stow's arguments about our inability to contain or direct our grief-wrath seems particularly apt in the Trump presidency, as the president's response to an anonymous editorial from a senior administration official was to tweet, "TREASON?"[110] Stow's most sobering insight is that mourning practices after September 11 have undermined domestic politics in the United States by making those who disagree about policy enemies rather friends. By denying the humanity and equality of those who attacked us, it has become easier to deny the humanity and equality of those we must call friends if democracy is to continue.

Political Change: The Patriot Act and the War on Terror

Actors invoked the events of September 11 to call for specific political changes. The most obvious example is the Uniting and Strengthening America by Providing Appropriate Tools Required to Intercept and Obstruct Terrorism (USA PATRIOT) Act of 2001.[111] While there has been sustained debate over the constitutionality of certain provisions in the Patriot Act, it was embraced by the American public and sailed through Congress to be signed by President Bush on October 26, 2001. While little research has been done to determine the Patriot Act's effectiveness at preventing further acts of terrorism in the United States, the Patriot Act has certainly led to an increase in popular hostility toward Arabs, Middle Easterners, and Muslims in America, as well as increased surveillance and more aggressive policing of this same population.[112]

In "Forget September 11," Maja Zehfuss argues that September 11 has helped produce an "us" that is drawn into an "exhortation to remember" that becomes "justification for both a military response abroad and for curtailing civil liberties at home."[113] Like Judith Butler in *Precarious Life*, Zehfuss points out that the experience of vulnerability has not "led us . . . to find the best way of living with it . . . but to a strong desire to overturn its inevitability and thus to search even more aggressively for an elusive security."[114] The result is that regimes have shifted from "rule of law" to a "rule of prevention"[115]—rather than being bound by collectively agreed-on norms and rules, the state becomes an intrusive, militarized apparatus that exists primarily to ensure security from terrorist attacks. And this inertia is hard to interrogate, because the "innocence" of the dead provokes a kind of (false) piety, such that pointing out the ways in which a security state overrides freedom is read as a failure of proper respect for the dead. The result is that a limited and exclusive "we" of the West has been constructed, and that September 11 is seen as an exceptional moment.[116] This second component— the creation of a moment that is on the one hand exceptional, but on the other hand expected as just another instance of terrorism—leads to a dangerous flexibility of state power. The state can call on the threat of war (a regular problem of the state) *or* of terrorism (an exceptional moment) to expand its reach.[117] In short, the will of the demos was overcome by the will to power of the sovereign security state.

Conclusion: Sovereign Mourning

I argue here that the events of September 11 might have generated a democratic rather than a sovereign mourning. In New York City, many citizens—including those most affected by the events of that day—engaged in exactly the kind of questioning and critical interrogation that Stow praises as tragic mourning and David McIvor calls the "democratic work of mourning."[118] There was a brief opening when we, as a country, caught a glimpse of our complicity in creating a world where reasonable people could fall prey to unreasonable ideologies. For a moment, having experienced or watched on TV utter devastation on the streets of America's greatest city, we could imagine similar experiences in other countries funded by American support for dictators. But this brief moment of a vision of "politics beyond the polity" was eclipsed.[119] Surely it was not fear that al-Qaeda would successfully invade the United States. The differences in resources and sheer size, not to mention being on another continent an ocean away, made any such claim perverse.

The reanimation of American sovereignty was not a foregone conclusion. That outcome came to be through a shutting down of democratic dialogue and debate, as well as a dehumanization of our enemies (and our friends—remember "Freedom Fries"?). Rather than accept the invitation to view death as a tragic, unavoidable part of life, we chose to engage in a fantasy world of good and evil, where any introduction of gray into the world of black and white signified cowardice. Jenny Edkins argues:

> The events of 9/11 exposed the contingency of everyday life and the fragility of the taken-for-granted safety of the city. The intrusion of the real of death and devastation into New York on a sunny September morning was a brutal reminder that all security is a fantasy. . . . [But] the attacks were not a protest against state violence. . . . Nor were they an attack on the state as such. The events of 9/11 were rather an instance of state-like violence, a reflection of the state. Like the state they produced life as nothing more than bare life—life that could be taken with impunity. . . . To the state, this action was a direct challenge to its monopoly. It was a throwing down of the gauntlet to sovereign authority. The terrorists had shown that they too could exercise what they would claim as justifiable violence. They could treat people the way the state does: as bare life.[120]

What might have happened had America taken responsibility for our actions? What might have happened had we chosen to mourn rather than flee into a fantasy of sovereign security?

Steven Johnston writes, "Perhaps a political order that must make a point of fostering patriotism does not deserve the love it represents; conversely, perhaps one that does deserve it has no need to concern itself with its cultivation."[121] The calls to patriotism in the wake of September 11 helped Americans interpret what happened as an irrational, civilizational challenge to freedom rather than a call to consider American responsibility for the conditions that made those acts possible, even likely. In the aftermath of that day, George Kateb writes, the "American public remains incurious about the possible background causes of September 11, as if that tragedy could have no sources in grievance or the sense of being wronged or despised."[122] With the invocations of patriotism in the days after September 11 came a yearning for righteous certainty and invulnerability, which mapped onto a return to mythic ideals about belonging in America.

David McIvor argues, following Melanie Klein's object relations theory, that loss is a fundamental part of human experience, and that this foundational aspect of human subjectivity has significant political implications. When confronted with political events in which loss plays a significant role, we may choose a certainty that drives us to see the world as a battle of good and evil, or we may choose to see the complicated good and evil that makes up any entity.[123] Similarly, Simon Stow urges Americans to develop a tragic orientation to mourning: to take up "tragic public mourning—understood as a response not as a condition—predicated on a worldview that is pluralistic in outlook, critical, and self-consciously political," in which "tragedy as response seeks to generate ambivalence in its audience as a productive response to tragedy as condition."[124] Taken together, these two authors suggest that the American state's response to September 11 heightened the fragility of our democracy by invoking not an ambivalent, democratic response but a certain, sovereign one.

Having dwelled on aspects of responsibility for some time, let me return to questions of identity. Recall from earlier in the chapter that America has a seemingly clear preference for racialized responses. The Bush administration quickly—perhaps too quickly—determined that the United States was blameless. This strategy might have failed without the deep strain of American racism that draws lines of belonging on the basis of race. Sabine Sielke points out a distinct shift toward deracialization in the language of collective trauma: from aboriginal displacement to the horrors of slavery to the industrial genocide of the Holocaust, race was a foundational justification of the perpetrators' acts.[125] In contrast, the victims of September 11 are now "raceless."[126] Sielke asks the extent to which a story of trauma depoliticizes, even as it psychoanalyzes a city, in the process "making a blatantly political matter . . . appear all too personal."[127] Because this strain of racialization already existed in the United States, the trope of irrational Middle Eastern/

Arab/Muslims could be quickly and easily mobilized. In essence, what might have been political mourning in the way I define it earlier became a depoliticized mourning that denied any American responsibility and hardened the boundaries of identity.

Like "the communists" in earlier eras, "the terrorists" were not bound by geography; instead, the enemy was now "an amoebic 'ism' that could take up residence in any number of surprising places."[128] But the attributions of responsibility located those deemed responsible in a now-racialized conflation of geography, culture, and religion that did not value freedom or life. As Chad Lavin argues, liberal conceptions of responsibility only see individual accountability, but this vision conflicts with racialized American citizenship that attributes negative traits to *all members* of a minority while reserving positive traits for *individuals* in the privileged racial majority.[129] This move from individual accountability of those who hijacked planes and killed thousands to civilizational accountability of those who support or even fail to adequately condemn terrorism indicates that even a sacred American concept like individual autonomy crumbles before a deep-seated need to racialize the Other.

In this case, it seems that rather than engaging in *political* mourning, Americans turned instead to a sovereign anxiety for security and certainty that could only be assuaged by forcefully reasserting racial and gendered orders. Unlike other instances of a politics of mourning that led to institutional change by expanding incorporation into the body politic, September 11 involved primarily the deaths of adult white men. Although those who died on September 11 came from well over half the countries in the world, and were of all religions and races, white men quickly became the dominant face of the tragedy. And not just any white men: these white men were mostly well-off (many were in the financial sector) or were cast as heroes and warriors (police and firefighters)—in short, they sat atop the pinnacle of the "inegalitarian ascriptive Americanism" that helps determine whose losses rise to the level of recognition necessary to achieve political change.[130]

Leti Volpp argues that three dimensions converged in the racialization of Arabs/Muslims/Middle Easterners after September 11: "the fact and legitimacy of racial profiling; the redeployment of old Orientalist tropes; and our conception of the relationship between citizenship, nation, and identity."[131] Volpp argues that, like its European cousin, American Orientalism is deeply gendered. As a result, although the oppression of women was rhetorically used to generate popular support of an American invasion of Afghanistan, "there has been a complete elision of the U.S. role in creating conditions in Afghanistan in the closed circular link made between women's oppression, Taliban evil, and Islamic fundamentalism."[132] Women's oppression happens only over there (despite a number of attacks by private

American citizens on women wearing clothing that identified them as Muslim) and by Islamic zealots rather than American ones.[133] Lila Abu-Lughod makes a similar argument regarding Laura Bush's speech celebrating the newfound freedom of Afghani women in the wake of the American invasion. Abu-Lughod notes that Bush's speech confirms the dynamic Gayatri Spivak identified of "white men saving brown women from brown men."[134]

The American desire to keep chaos at bay abroad ended up reestablishing the racial and gender order at home, as well. Although emasculated by a long decade without an identifiable enemy and a wounding attack on our tallest towers, American masculinity and the consequent gender order could be recovered by winning a war. This deployment of a foreign policy grounded in conquest had significant gendered dimensions. Volpp argues that "post-September 11 nationalist discourses reinscribe both compulsory heterosexuality and the dichotomized gender roles on which it is based: the masculine citizen-soldier, the patriotic wife and mother, and the properly reproductive family."[135] More recently, Bonnie Mann's *Sovereign Masculinity* suggests that there is a connection between the national shame of failing to remain impervious and over-the-top displays of sovereign masculinity.[136]

In one of the more intriguing ruminations on the interplay of gender, race, economics, and power in the international system after September 11, Anna Agathangelou and L.H.M. Ling argue that hypermasculinity is a reactionary stance that "arises when agents of hegemonic masculinity feel threatened or undermined," and that we can extend this meaning beyond individual agents and into "security and economic domains, especially as one hypermasculine source (e.g., U.S. foreign policy) provokes another (e.g., al-Qaeda) to escalate with iterative bouts of hypermasculinity (e.g., 'jihad'/'war on terror')."[137] As a result, jihad and the war on terror form "mirror strategies of imperial power politics."[138] The coalescing of the Islamic State in the last decade suggests that Agathangelou and Ling diagnosed an important dialectic that seems unlikely to end soon.

In many ways, the American response to September 11 has been a manifestation of dialectical fundamentalism. Roxanne Euben defines fundamentalism as a lack of contestation, which "places fundamentalists in an epistemologically privileged position from which to determine, once and for all the one and only authentic way to live in a collectivity as a Muslim, a Christian, a Jew, an American."[139] Similarly, in *Orgies of Feeling*, Elisabeth Anker argues that September 11 was cast as a melodrama, which requires heroes, villains, and victims. She writes, "*Melodramatic political discourse* casts politics, policies, and practices of citizenship within a moral economy that identifies the nation-state as a virtuous and innocent victim of villainous action. It locates goodness in the suffering of the nation, evil in its antagonists, and heroism in sovereign acts of war and global control coded as expressions of virtue."[140] As a result of this melodramatic framing, our access to imagining our own responsibility in creating the conditions that prompted bin Laden and al-Qaeda's response was obscured. In short, though clothed in the language of secular state sovereignty, we have taken up the path of fundamentalism.

Fundamentalists refuse to compromise, and rely instead on purity, historical obfuscation, an idealized past that never actually existed. What if the war on terror and jihad both lead to an end of politics itself? To a consistent demand for unity and purity not only in bin Laden's reading of the Qur'an but in an American reading of our own history and Constitution? The rapidly growing calls for political purity demonstrated through a refusal to compromise (exemplified by the rise of the Tea Party—the political version of the congressional Freedom Caucus—and the resounding attraction of many to Donald Trump's calls to "make [white] America great again") might be read as a dialectical manifestation of al-Qaeda's success in destroying a democratic order. Fundamentalism of all types seeks to create a world of absolutes in which the give and take of contested ideas is a mark of weakness rather than a sign of strength. As Richard Devetak argues, what we risk when we see those who challenge us as monsters (Saddam Hussein) or ghosts (bin Laden) is becoming exactly the monster we fight—terror, tyranny, "dictatress of the world."[141] Devetak concludes that, like for Dr. Frankenstein, the American obsession with chasing monsters might well destroy the chaser as well as the chased.

American military interventions in the Middle East and the war on terror generate new resistance wherever they go, as assertions of sovereignty spawn counter-assertions. Errant bombs in Pakistan, mistaken firefights in Afghanistan, tortured prisoners in Abu Ghraib, perpetual detainment in Guantanamo, denial of asylum to refugees at our southern borders—all of these contribute to real physical pain that results in substantial and located grievances, many of which have been turned into recruiting tools for still more violent opposition. It is as though our military exploits have freed us to return to a Hobbesian state of nature. Deeply wounded and anxious, we focus on being the first to strike in order to stay alive even when our survival is not necessarily threatened. As Roxanne Euben observes, "Wherever it occurs—in Oklahoma, New York City, Bosnia or the medical clinic next door—the toll of violence on the life of the body politic is immeasurable. In addition to the victims who suffer directly from such violence, in the words of Hannah Arendt, the 'practice of violence, like all action, changes the world, but the most probable change is to a more violent world.'"[142] In short, our sovereign, de-democratized mourning may have ushered in an era where loss is constantly inflicted but never adequately or democratically mourned.

The Democratic Deficit of All Lives Matter

I f September 11 turned America inward, leading us to desire order and security over justice, abdicate responsibility for our actions abroad, and narrow and harden our conceptions of identity, Black Lives Matter has exposed this order and security as reserved for white citizens, demanded that white Americans take responsibility for harm done, and sought to expand identity through democratic equality. While sovereign mourning for the wounded state led Americans to ignore the loss of life abroad, it also served to obscure how white/American security has long depended on black/international insecurity. The rise of Black Lives Matter, then, is an antidote to the narrow conceptions of identity and responsibility that sovereign mourning established. The work of Black Lives Matter (BLM) movements are steps toward remaking American identity and responsibility to be more truly democratic. This is in part because BLM is not so narrowly focused on legal reform or institutional politics (though it advocates for these, too); it also attends to dialogue and demands that we recognize dignity, giving us a vision of democracy more akin to what John Dewey imagined.

BLM accomplishes this in part by exposing the limits of white empathy for black suffering. As Juliet Hooker argues, whites readily equate symbolic losses (increased competition with people of color for jobs, status, wealth, and power) with material, bodily losses suffered by people of color (earlier deaths, violence, poverty, police killings, etc.).[1] White Americans' response to deaths like those of Trayvon Martin and Mike Brown (among many others), which other scholars and activists directly tie to the rise of BLM, demonstrates just how willing white people are to accept violent black death. The immediate birth of the slogan "All Lives Matter" in response to Black Lives Matter signals a false equivalence and an embrace of the willful racial innocence James Baldwin identifies in *The Fire Next Time*.[2] It appears that many white Americans found it easier to mourn a post–September 11 wounded state than to mourn black bodies, which signals a limited capacity for democratic community; if we cannot mourn the deaths of fellow citizens caused by our own state apparatus, the Constitution's "we the people" will continue to mean "we the white people." More profoundly, it suggests that many whites do not see blacks *as people*. BLM, then, is a democratic movement calling us to revisit the contours of American identity and our responsibility to one another.

In this chapter, I first argue that activism in response to the deaths of Trayvon Martin, Mike Brown, George Floyd, and so many others are an example of political mourning, while noting some important differences between the deaths of Martin and Brown. Second, I address how white responses to these deaths and the activism that followed signal a democratic deficit that BLM is working to expose and repair. Finally, returning to Dewey, I argue that BLM is challenging the rest of America to realize Dewey's democracy, not as institutional arrangements but as embodied relations that take inequality of vulnerability seriously.

Black Lives Matter as Political Mourning

Several works have traced how Trayvon Martin's death in 2012 and Mike Brown's in 2014, along with several other young black men killed by police officers who were not held accountable, generated the Black Lives Matter movement. Keeanga-Yamahtta Taylor's *From #BlackLivesMatter to Black Liberation* provides an overview of five key parts of the social context in 2012. First, Taylor argues that the dialectic relationship between "American exceptionalism" and a "culture of poverty" have created poverty-stricken black communities "where people have failed to succeed and cash in on the abundance that American ingenuity has apparently created, [and] their personal failures or deficiencies serve as the explanation."[3] Second, color blindness has become an accepted norm; rather than ameliorate harm, it has served to justify withdrawal of state support for those only recently, and formally rather than substantively, included as part of the "we the people."[4] Third, Taylor asserts that the rise of a black elite has served to fracture the black community and distanced those who have gained some forms of power from those who remain disempowered.[5] Fourth, Taylor describes the long history of police brutality against black people in the United States, interconnected with the history of slavery, the war on drugs, and mass incarceration.[6] Finally, Taylor argues that while Barack Obama's candidacy and election in 2008 drove black participation and hope for change in positive directions, disappointment soon followed.[7] Taylor argues that while candidate Obama's March 2008 "race speech" was groundbreaking, it also served to establish

> the terms upon which he would engage race matters—with dubious evenhandedness, even in response to events that required decisive action on behalf of the racially aggrieved. He spoke quite eloquently about the nation's "original sin" and "dark history," but has repeatedly failed to connect the sins of the past to the crimes of the present, where racism—albeit it without epithet or insult—thrives when police stop-and-frisk, when subprime loans are reserved for Black buyers, when public schools are denied resources, and when double-digit unemployment has become so normal that it barely registers a ripple of recognition.[8]

Obama's focus on unity around higher American ideals persisted, while for many who opposed him, his race was the most salient part of their opposition.[9] Driving black frustration was the growing sense that while Obama might be a black president, he either chose not to act or was constrained from acting. Given that the ideology of color blindness ruled, and Obama's election signaled to some the advent of a postracial era, the persistent disparity between white and black America stung even more.

In *The Making of Black Lives Matter*, Christopher Lebron traces the rise of Black Lives Matter through an intellectual history, demonstrating that black Americans have long asserted that black lives matter; while the slogan may be new, the sentiment is not. Through "shameful publicity" of the distance between asserted ideals and reality; black-centered art that seeks to "countercoloniz[e] the white imagination" with images of complex, wise, and funny people of color; "unconditional self-possession" demonstrating that while black lives may not matter to white people, blacks are nevertheless morally owed equal standing; and "unfragmented compassion" that seeks not revenge but the strength of a democratic love, black thinkers and activists have long known and asserted their equality, even if whites refuse to acknowledge it.[10]

Barbara Ransby, in *Making All Black Lives Matter*, provides a combination of context, ethnographic accounts of various actors, and organizational genealogies within the BLM constellation of movements. Ransby argues that BLM specifically grew out of black feminist thought: "a tradition that embraces an intersectional analysis while insisting on the interlocking and interconnected nature of different systems of oppression; advocates the importance of women's group-centered leadership; supports LGBTQIA issues; and seeks to center the most marginalized and vulnerable members of the Black community in terms of the language and priorities of the movement."[11] This movement takes power, identity, and positionality seriously. Black feminist thought—intersectional, grounded, radical, and democratic—prepared future BLM leaders to break out of traditional elite models of political power and reimagine democratic potential.

These scholars offer accounts of how Trayvon Martin's and Mike Brown's deaths—as well as the seeming endless reports of other deaths, including those of Eric Garner, Laquan McDonald, Tamir Rice, Sandra Bland, John Crawford, Freddie Gray, George Floyd, and others—gave rise to Black Lives Matter. While there are important differences between the accounts offered by Taylor, Lebron, and Ransby, I leave those aside for now. In arguments running sometimes as text and sometimes as subtext, all claim that near the middle of Obama's presidency in 2012, there was a context in which the status of blacks in the United States as full citizens was contested, particular actors took their grief public in the wake of black deaths, these deaths raised questions about political responsibility and identity, and the legal responses to these deaths showed the limits of law to address injustice. From this, I suggest that Martin's and Brown's deaths, together, have the components of political mourning I lay out: a context in which identity questions matter, a highly visible event or series of events, actors taking grief public to call for change, the failure of law to hold anyone accountable, and political change. The first four components are readily obvious, but the last—political change—is of a different kind than we see in other events addressed in this book. I return to the question of what kind of political change BLM calls for in a later section.

Before moving on, though, I want to briefly consider how the deaths of Martin and Brown differ. Recall that Trayvon Martin, a seventeen-year-old black male, was killed by George Zimmerman, a twenty-eight-year-old Hispanic male, on the evening of February 26, 2012, when Martin was returning to his father's fiancée's house from a nearby convenience store. Zimmerman, a member of a community watch group, called 911 to report a suspicious person. Although instructed by the 911 dispatcher to leave this matter to the police, Zimmerman pursued Martin on foot. A few minutes later, after a scuffle and a gunshot, Martin lay dead. The police questioned Zimmerman and then released him several hours later. After the governor appointed a special prosecutor, a month and a half after Martin's death, Zimmerman was charged and indicted.[12] In 2013, he was tried and acquitted.

Although at the time of his death Martin was doing nothing to indicate he was engaged in criminal behavior, he was denied the status of an innocent victim. Having not spoken directly about Martin's death, President Obama, in a Rose Garden press conference on March 23, 2012, said, "If I had a son, he'd look like Trayvon." As Monica Potts wrote in *Vogue*, "Before Obama said these words, the conservative press had joined in the condemnation of Zimmerman: Now they seemed to rise in his defense."[13] Two days after Obama's comments, a conservative blogger falsely reported that Martin had been a drug dealer. This claim quickly spread through the right-wing blogosphere and news media, leading to the release of an image of Martin smoking a joint and the release of a school suspension report resulting from Martin's possession of a baggy with marijuana residue.[14] Martin had been made into a thug, the readily available stereotype of dangerous young black men that circulates in the United States in the wake of the war on drugs, rather than a young man walking to and from a convenience store to buy snacks.

While it seemed obvious based on witness accounts that Zimmerman would be arrested and indicted, Florida was a "stand your ground" state. The stand-your-ground law not only did away with the duty to retreat in the face of threat but also provided immunity from civil charges resulting from a death (meaning that Martin's family had no recourse to sue for damages in a civil trial).[15] These laws—sponsored by the American Legislative Exchange Council (ALEC), itself heavily funded by the libertarian brothers Charles and David Koch, who have donated millions of dollars to the National Rifle Association (NRA)—have been successfully implemented in twenty-seven states. Stand-your-ground laws seem to encourage vigilantism by doing away with a duty to retreat, and they have disproportionately been used to justify the murders of people of color. The race of the victim is highly significant: when whites kill blacks, prosecutors are 281 percent less likely to charge the perpetrator with a crime than when whites kill other whites.[16]

Perhaps because of racial bias, perhaps the result of stand-your-ground laws, or more likely a combination of both, Zimmerman was not immediately arrested or indicted. He was taken into custody after Martin's death but released several hours later. He was not charged until April 11—a month and a half after Martin's death. In a nuanced reading of how race, prosecutorial discretion, and stand-your-ground laws interacted in the state's response to Martin's death, Tamara Lawson uses Derrick Bell's "interest convergence dilemma" to suggest that in that interval,

> the facts did not change, but the perception of the facts changed. Or even the motivation to view the same facts differently changed. It was not just in the best interest of the upset and protesting minority group . . . but it was more importantly in the interest of the majority

group to promote the appearance of race-neutral impartiality, fairness, and justice in the exercise of prosecutorial discretion. . . . It was the collective fear of potential riots that also compelled the special prosecutor to do something to counter the growing view that law enforcement's inaction or its perceived racially biased application of justice was acceptable. . . . The charges confirmed for the public that the killing was allegedly criminal, which is how many already viewed it. The decision to charge murder, as opposed to manslaughter, did much to calm the flames of discontent. Murder . . . projected that the prosecution was serious about its allegation. There were no riots. Protests were cancelled and the public's outcry quieted.[17]

The evening Zimmerman was acquitted, protesters gathered at the courthouse and in other cities across the United States, but protests were relatively peaceful and short-lived, perhaps respecting Martin's parents' calls for calm and reference to scriptures.[18] President Obama, too, asked for calm, saying, "We are a nation of laws, and a jury has spoken. I now ask every American to respect the call for calm reflection from two parents who lost their young son."[19]

Trayvon Martin had been killed by a private citizen, but it seems fair to conclude that George Zimmerman thought of his community watch work as an extension of the police. Consider the many recently publicized calls to the police by white citizens, reporting black people for barbecuing in the park, black parents for yelling instructions at their children during a soccer game, or a black child for selling water without a permit.[20] These are all significant overreactions, premised on white fear of black people doing things that white people do all the time, which disregard the likelihood that calling police to confront black people may result in disproportionate violence or even death. As Charles Mills argued in *The Racial Contract*, in the age of de jure segregation, whites were actually deputized to enforce the racial order, keeping black people in black spaces and out of white spaces, violently punishing those who were in the wrong spaces; in the age of de facto segregation, that deputization continues tacitly.[21] Zimmerman, along with the various Beckys and Chads who call the police when they see a black person in what they imagine as a white space, enforced a racial order that no longer legally exists.

While Martin was killed by a white-appearing Hispanic man acting on behalf of a racial state, Mike Brown was killed by a white police officer on August 9, 2014.[22] Brown, an eighteen-year-old black male, was shot several times by Officer Darren Wilson of the Ferguson Police Department around noon on August 9, 2014. Wilson told Brown and a friend to move to the sidewalk, drove off, and then backed up to stop near the two men again, at which point Brown and Wilson engaged in a physical confrontation. Wilson fired twice from inside the car and then ten more times as he chased Brown, though witness reports differ as to whether Brown was charging Wilson or fleeing when he was fatally shot. The *New Yorker* reports that once Brown lay on the ground, bleeding, "as far as one can tell from the disjointed details released by the Ferguson and St. Louis County authorities, Wilson did not immediately call the shooting in or try to resuscitate Brown, and no E.M.T.s rushed him to the hospital. That raises the question of whether he might possibly have survived."[23] (On the basis of autopsy reports, it is unlikely that Brown could have survived.) Brown's corpse lay in the summer sun for more than four hours on the neighborhood street where he died, facedown, in a pool of his own blood. According to Julie Bosman and Joseph Goldstein in the *New York Times*:

> Local officials say that the image of Mr. Brown's corpse in the open set the scene for what would become a combustible worldwide story of police tactics and race in America, and left some of the officials asking why.
>
> "The delay helped fuel the outrage," said Patricia Bynes, a committeewoman in Ferguson. "It was very disrespectful to the community and the people who live there. It also sent the message from law enforcement that 'we can do this to you any day, any time, in broad daylight, and there's nothing you can do about it."[24]

That the body remained on the street and somewhat visible—covered by a sheet first and then surrounded with privacy screens after about an hour and a half—is another significant difference between Trayvon's death and Mike Brown's. The street where Brown died is surrounded by apartment complexes, several facing the street. The school year had not yet started, and many children were home; parents reported that they had to keep their children away from the windows so they would not see Brown's body. This very visible instance of police violence visited on a young black body shook the citizens of Ferguson and the nation.

The prosecutor convened a grand jury in late November to determine whether Wilson would be indicted. The grand jury declined to indict, and Wilson was not charged. That night, protesting the grand jury's decision, citizens of Ferguson gathered to confront police in riot gear. Protesters threw objects, the police responded with tear gas, and soon a police cruiser and about a dozen structures in Ferguson were on fire. Demonstrations lasted for weeks and were leading news in many national news sources. The Missouri National Guard was called in to "restore order," leading to less violent confrontations and dwindling numbers of demonstrators.

A U.S. Department of Justice report, issued in March 2015, declared "that the city had engaged in so many constitutional violations that they could be corrected only by abandoning its entire approach to policing, retraining its employees and establishing new oversight. The report described a city that used its police and courts as moneymaking ventures, a place where officers stopped and handcuffed people without probable cause, hurled racial slurs, used stun guns without provocation, and treated anyone as suspicious merely for questioning police tactics."[25] In essence, the police in Ferguson ruled over the residents like Hobbesian subjects rather than policing their fellow citizens. It was truly sovereign power: arbitrary, hierarchical, and without recourse.

Brown's death was preceded and followed by a growing list of black men and women whose lives ended because minor encounters with police spiraled out of control. Barely a month before Brown's death, Eric Garner had been choked to death by a police officer in Staten Island, New York, on July 17. Garner's last minutes, including him repeating, "I can't breathe" eleven times while in a headlock, were captured on a cell phone and immediately became headline news. The officer whose chokehold led to Garner's death was not indicted.[26] Laquan McDonald, holding a knife, was shot sixteen times while moving away from police officers in Chicago on October 20. In an unusual twist, the officer was found guilty of second-degree murder and sentenced to eighty-one months of jail time.[27] Twelve-year-old Tamir Rice was shot and killed on November 22 by Cleveland police officers while at a playground, because they thought he had a gun. Neither officer involved in Rice's death was indicted.[28] Sandra Bland was pulled over for a minor traffic violation and then arrested and detained by a domineering state trooper in July 2015. Her lifeless body was found hanging in her jail cell three days later. The officer was indicted for perjury for lying about what happened during the stop, but the prosecutors declined to prosecute. After agreeing never to work in law enforcement again, the officer was cleared of charges.[29] These instances of disregard for black lives, the willingness of police to kill black people for minor infractions, and the (white) public's seeming lack of interest in demanding police accountability for black deaths sent a clear signal to black citizens: your lives *do not* matter.[30]

In the wake of Brown's death, the other deaths at the hands of police that followed, and the general inability of the legal system to hold police accountable, Black Lives Matter exploded into the American consciousness. As with Martin's killing, defenders of Wilson's actions immediately sought to portray Brown as a thug; a few days after his death, the police department released video of Brown allegedly stealing a handful of cigarillos from a convenience store, released the name of the officer who killed Brown, and clarified that Wilson did not know that Brown was a potential suspect for robbery.[31] The disconnect between Brown stealing something worth a few dollars and being gunned down by a police officer in the middle of the street drove much of the protesters' outrage. Barbara Ransby notes that "Michael Brown was not a saint. However, in the resistance that followed his death, organizers insisted he did not have to be. There did not have to be a correlation between 'sainthood' and Black citizenship. This is an important shift in the discourse about who is or is not a sympathetic victim of injustice. Brown did not have to be a church-going, law-abiding, proper-speaking embodiment of respectability in order for his life to matter."[32] This is a crucial shift that lays the groundwork for the radically democratic politics of the Black Lives Matter movement and the networks it has spawned.

To sum up, the deaths of Trayvon Martin and Mike Brown together—along with the several other unarmed black people killed by police—served as the basis for the response of Black Lives Matter. While the tragic deaths of Martin and Brown are often linked, there are two significant differences. First, Martin was killed by a civilian (albeit one who functioned as an extension of state power), while Brown was killed by a police officer. Second, the public did not see Martin's body, while Brown's remained in view—if partially covered—for several hours. These differences, as well as the additional black people killed by police before and after Brown's death, help explain the explosion of black protest after Brown's death. If Martin's death and the response of white America demonstrate a lack of empathy for black suffering, Brown's death and the lack of an indictment suggest a state actively arrayed against black life. This interpretation of reality was further bolstered when George Floyd's murder by police was captured on camera in the summer of 2020, sparking massive demonstrations across the country.[33] And yet the overall response by white people was to suggest that the call for black lives to matter did harm to whites. I suggest, as I argue below, that the white response to black deaths signals a democratic deficit.

The Democratic Deficit of All Lives Matter .

In the wake of the lack of indictment of Officer Wilson in Mike Brown's death and of Officer Daniel Pantaleo in Eric Garner's death, #BlackLivesMatter trended on Twitter to call attention to police violence against black citizens and support demonstrations occurring in Ferguson and elsewhere. #AllLivesMatter appeared in an immediate response. In this section, I draw on James Baldwin and Keeanga-Yamahtta Taylor to argue that the "All Lives Matter" (ALM) response can be best characterized as an example of the racial innocence and color blindness that have defined white responses to black demands for racial justice.

More than half a century ago—not long after Emmett Till's brutalized body helped spark the civil rights movement—James Baldwin shared, first with his nephew and then with the world, his haunting reflections on the racial situation in America. Baldwin wrote:

> I know what the world has done to my brother and how narrowly he has survived it. And I know, which is much worse, and this is the crime of which I accuse my country and my countrymen, and for which neither I nor time nor history will ever forgive them, that they have destroyed and are destroying thousands of lives and do not know it and do not want to know it. One can be, indeed one must strive to become, tough and philosophical concerning destruction and death, for this is what most of mankind has been best at since we have heard of men. (But remember: *most* of mankind is not *all* of mankind.) But it is not permissible that the authors of devastation should also be innocent. It is the innocence which constitutes the crime.[34]

The innocence Baldwin finds rightly horrifying is that his fellow (white) Americans deny responsibility, not just in a moral or legal sense, but in a *political* sense, and still more specifically, in a *democratic* sense. Baldwin not only calls out his fellow Americans for failing to act to remedy the racial inequity that is plain to see; he calls them out for failing to acknowledge that racial inequity—in particular, disproportionate black "destruction and death"—results from their actions. The crime is not merely that whites do not know what they are doing (mere ignorance); it is that they do not want to know what they are doing and actively avoid responsibility for the conditions they have created (a far worse innocence). White Americans actively engage in self-deception about race and its terrible effects. Charles Mills calls this blindness to the obvious effects of race "the epistemology of ignorance."[35]

Baldwin accomplishes this in part by using the language of "we" ambivalently; as Lawrie Balfour deftly illustrates, when Baldwin writes "we," he sometimes means blacks, sometimes whites, and sometimes all Americans.[36] Baldwin pushes us to question who the "we" of our democracy-in-name is, while constantly urging us to imagine a more inclusive we. This is a fundamental question for democracy. Who among this "we the people" rule, and who are ruled? For whites in America, "we" has long meant whites only. As the epigraph to Charles Mills's *The Racial Contract* puts it, "When white people say 'Justice,' they mean 'Just us.'"[37] The question, then, is whether whites in America want an actual democracy or a white democracy—that is, whether whites can genuinely embrace a nonwhite we. Our current political climate suggests that this is as important a question as ever for the American polity.

Baldwin believed that whites may be able to lose their innocence, but writing in the 1960s and 1970s, he seemed to believe that moment was still generations away. Whites in America continue to mistakenly cling to innocently white aspirations of democratic inclusion and equality while doing their best to ignore the actually existing reality of racial tyranny; this disconnect between the innocence and the harmful actions it enables is what Baldwin wants whites to recognize.

The racial innocence Baldwin identified has fueled the rise of contemporary color blindness, which Keeanga-Yamahtta Taylor calls out as an important precursor to the rise of BLM. In *From #BlackLivesMatter to Black Liberation*, Taylor argues that the ideology of color blindness has served to make blacks solely responsible for their own failure in the United States. In a culture built around white domination and superiority,

> explanations for Black inequality that blame Black people for their own oppression transform material causes into subjective causes. The problem is not racial discrimination in the workplace or residential segregation; it is Black irresponsibility, erroneous social mores, and general bad behavior. Ultimately this transformation is not about "race" or even "white supremacy" but about "making sense" of and rationalizing poverty and inequality in ways that absolve the state and capital of any culpability.[38]

In its embrace of color blindness—a reactive response to the proactive demands of affirmative action—the American people have increasingly refused to take responsibility for negative effects of American state institutions on people of color in the United States, including wealth generated by whites at the expense of blacks through redlining and restrictive covenants, exclusion from high-paying jobs, and limited educational options.[39]

Worryingly, this color blindness increasingly has a partisan edge. A 2017 Pew Research report found that while "41% of Americans say racial discrimination is the main reason many blacks cannot get ahead . . . when the racial discrimination question was first asked in 1994, the partisan difference was 13 points. . . . But today, the gap in opinions between Republicans and Democrats about racial discrimination and black advancement has increased to 50 points."[40] Even in 2009, the partisan difference was only 19 points; the jump from 19 points of difference to 50 in less than a decade implies a significant shift in perception of white understandings of political responsibility toward blacks in the United States—one that has had powerful political effects.

This echoes many whites' response to the black deaths that served as the foundation of BLM. If color blindness makes it difficult for whites to see inequality in the domain of economics, it surely also obscures the differences in types and kinds of black and white deaths. Having benefited from state protection of both white property and identity,[41] whites are more disposed to trust the police as protectors, leading them to view black victims as having invited the harm they experienced. White people's comments such as "Why were the police there if he wasn't doing anything wrong?" or "The police wouldn't have shot him if he hadn't been doing something stupid" signal a fundamental misunderstanding of the conditions of black life in the United States. They also ignore the violence of sovereign power—violence that initially targets the excluded and marginalized, but has a dangerous way of exposing all citizens to increased state violence.[42] Taylor argues that while the police are undoubtedly killing proportionally more black men and women than their white counterparts, the police—increasingly imagined as foot soldiers in the war on terror—have also killed "hundreds of Latinos and thousands of white people." While this might serve as the basis of a "multiracial movement against police terrorism," white people have not responded this way.[43] Thinking through the response of ALM helps us consider why.

The combination of white racial innocence and color blindness is exemplified in the response to #BlackLivesMatter with #AllLivesMatter on social media. In her analysis of social media in the days after the grand juries declined to indict, Nikita Carney found that

> the #BlackLivesMatter slogan met a great deal of resistance in the wake of the killings of Michael Brown and Eric Garner. On social media, one of the primary ways in which people resisted the #BlackLivesMatter movement came in the form of using #AllLivesMatter as a counterslogan to undermine the purpose and message of the #BlackLivesMatter call to action. Many social media users deployed #AllLivesMatter as a way to deny the specific and prominent violence against Blacks by appealing to a larger universal. Thus, in the guise of presumably broader politics, it depoliticized and deracialized the specificity of #BlackLivesMatter.[44]

Over the course of five days in December 2014, Carney found that the "#BlackLivesMatter hashtag was deployed as a way to draw attention to systemic racism faced by Black people in the United States. . . . #BlackLivesMatter tweets represent[ed] the call to action at the heart of the movement by highlighting the ways in which Black bodies are disproportionately targeted for violence by the police."[45] In response to these calls for fellow citizens to recognize the highly disproportionate and violent deaths of black people at the hands of police, Carney's analysis shows that "well over half of those arguing against the #BlackLivesMatter movement on Twitter in my sample appeared to be young white women. The argument generally centered on a color-blind politic, accusing #BlackLivesMatter protesters of being exclusive and privileging Black lives over any other lives."[46] Twitter users challenging #AllLivesMatter tended to be young, black women, but Carney finds that those organizing to protest eventually abandoned the debate over semantics, prioritizing instead protest in real life.[47]

Similarly, in a quantitative analysis of more than eight hundred thousand tweets, Ryan Gallagher, Andrew Reagan, Christopher Danforth, and Peter Dodds found that "#AllLivesMatter diverges from #BlackLivesMatter through support of pro-law-enforcement sentiments. This places #BlackLivesMatter and hashtags such as #PoliceLivesMatter and #BlueLivesMatter in opposition, a framing that is in line with the theoretical understanding of #AllLivesMatter and that mimics how relationships between black protesters and law enforcement have been historically depicted." In addition, they find that "#AllLivesMatter experiences significant hijacking from #BlackLivesMatter, while #BlackLivesMatter exhibits rich and informationally diverse conversations, of which hijacking is a much smaller portion."[48] In contrast, they conclude that within #AllLivesMatter, "we do not find evidence of significant discussion of 'all lives.'"[49]

If, as the data seem to indicate, those using the hashtag #AllLivesMatter are generally white and pro-law-enforcement, #AllLivesMatter seeks to equalize the risk of being a police officer with being a black citizen. This is telling. While police officers of all races make a choice to work in law enforcement, black citizens did not choose to be born black; yet both groups are in harm's way by virtue of their social identities. It also disregards the long history of law enforcement's purpose: to protect both property and whiteness. After all, it was not that long ago that blacks in the United States *were* property.[50] In equating the two, #AllLivesMatter erases the hundreds of years of violence, dispossession, and exclusion experienced by blacks in the United States and supported by the state.

Public opinion about BLM reflects a similar pattern of white disinterest in the harms visited on black bodies in the United States. According to a Harvard-Harris poll in August 2017, a clear majority of American voters (57 percent) had a negative view of BLM. When the data are disaggregated on the basis of race, the differences are stark: "Only 35 percent of whites have a favorable view of the movement, while 83 percent of blacks have a favorable view."[51] Party differences are also sharp. Jonathan Easley writes for the *Hill* that only "twenty-one percent of Republicans have a positive view of the movement. That figure dips to 18 percent among those who voted for

President Trump. Meanwhile, 65 percent of Democrats and 66 percent of those who voted for Democratic presidential nominee Hillary Clinton support the movement."[52]

In a context framed by of white racial innocence and color blindness, it should perhaps not be surprising that the white response to BLM is to interpret that call as a weapon meant to wound or exclude white people. The universalized white response of ALM as a response to the specific, located, embodied grievance captured by BLM seems, on its face, to be a broader category, but the analysis of social media posts above suggests that the alliance of "all" is with police rather than black lives and with a white, sovereign state rather than the multiracial demos. The wounded sovereignty of American post–September 11 mourning has been taken up by the (white) demos as a weapon to further obscure sovereignty's violence against people of color.

The Black Lives Matter hashtag and movement, then, seek to push Americans to recognize and repair our thin conception of democracy, replacing faith in the sovereign state and its violent force with the power of the demos. The white response of "All Lives Matter" suggests that, as has long been the case, when whites say democracy, they mean *white* democracy. As Gallagher and colleagues note, the discussions on Twitter under #BlackLivesMatter exhibited "rich and informationally diverse conversations" in ways that conversations under #AllLivesMatter did not. This reflects the broad diversity of the movement itself. As Taylor and Ransby point out in their tracing of the various radical, democratic, black feminist, and social justice organizations that have shaped the movement, Black Lives Matter might well be the antidote for the sovereign mourning that took hold after September 11.[53] The inability or refusal of whites to see clearly the consequences of their actions draws us back to Dewey's insights about the formation of a public, which I turn to as a way to make sense of the rise and potential reach of "Black-led mass struggle" in the movements that have come out of Black Lives Matter activism.[54]

The Embodied Democracy of Black Lives Matter

I suggest in Chapter 1 that Dewey's insights in *The Public and Its Problems* can help us identify four obstacles that prevent a democratic public from coalescing: apathy, indirect effects, the problem of presentation, and the development of judgment.[55] As argued earlier, mourning may help overcome these obstacles. First, by providing a single event that helps a public toward solidarity to solve *this* problem, mourning helps overcome the obstacle of apathy. In working to fix one problem, we build a shared platform on which to stand to better see and address the next problem. Second, witnessing a death that might have been avoided can inspire us to think about structures and institutions in a more complicated fashion; this is what Dewey refers to as learning to apprehend "indirect effects" of our actions and to understand that we can change course. If the problem is sufficiently collective and broad, a public can begin to form around this particular harm that should be mitigated. Third, the visceral nature of images of the dead—often graphic—illustrates that presentation matters. While not all depictions of death must be visceral to move us, a captured image serves to distill the loss; it seems as though descriptions of the event move us less than images of the dead. Finally, to form the judgment needed to act in an informed way, Dewey argues, "the essential need . . . is the improvement of the methods and conditions of debate, discussion and persuasion. That is *the* problem of the public. We have asserted that this improvement depends essentially upon freeing and perfecting the processes of inquiry and of dissemination of their conditions."[56] Those affected and those drawn into inquiry by its pathos can come together to debate causes and effects, whether there are differential effects, and what needs to be done to ensure that the negative effects can be mitigated in the future. This process, then, is part of how a public is aroused into knowing itself as a public. We can see this process in the rapid dissemination of the hashtag #BlackLivesMatter, which led to real-world, in-person movements working to make the slogan true.

Dewey is clear throughout his political works that the state is not *above* the people. Rather, the state is an expression of a public's desire to address particular problems and to make life predictable more generally. The government is not the same as the public, but the public is organized through officers of the government.[57] We, as members of mass society, may be fooled into seeing the state as above us, as a power that exists beyond our control, but Dewey argues that that happens only because we are having a hard time imagining ourselves *as a public*. As Melvin Rogers writes in his introduction to Dewey's work, "Who constitutes the people is the result of individuals fighting to give direction to their lives, rather than something determined by the governing nation."[58] Rather than see the state as a divine instrument, a social contract, a stable set of institutions, or a focus on legal procedures, we should, according to Dewey, understand that the state is *our* tool, that its agencies and institutions are expressions of *our* needs. Thus, the state exists to serve the needs of the people rather than to preserve its own power; a democratic state should express broader democratic relations among citizens.

But once established, the political forms born from a coalesced public become bound by institutional inertia that resists changed conditions. This gap between institutions set up to address particular problems and new problems that may have arisen (often as a result of those institutions, new technologies, or changed circumstances) creates new publics, which are often excluded from power. As a result, "to form itself, the public has to break existing political forms."[59] Taken-for-granted agencies, institutions, bases for solidarity, distribution of goods, and so on—all the things that provide stability—may have to be disturbed to account for new challenges. In a good state, Dewey argues, where

> the officers of the public genuinely serve the public interests, this reflex effect [of modifying our wants, beliefs, and work to engage in shared action] is of great importance. It renders the desirable associations solider and more coherent; indirectly it clarifies their aims and purges their activities. It places a discount upon injurious groupings and renders their tenure of life precarious. In performing these services, it gives the individual members of valued [nongovernmental] associations great liberty and security: it relieves them of hampering conditions which if they had to cope with personally would absorb their energies in mere negative struggle against evils. It enables individual members to count with reasonable certainty upon what others will do, and thus facilitates mutually helpful coöperations. It creates respect for others and for one's self. A measure of the goodness of a state is the degree in which it relieves individuals from the waste of negative struggle and needless conflict and confers upon him positive assurance and reinforcement in what he undertakes.[60]

In essence, while holding a private space for individuals to thrive ("for the state is a distinctive and secondary form of association"[61]), Dewey's ideal state evolves to address new problems even as it provides a container of stability; these two urges are often in conflict, of course, as new publics have to "break existing political forms" to have their shared problems addressed. But at its best, the state is an expression of our collective desire to share our problems, then creatively imagine and enact collective solutions.

The image of democracy that Dewey gives us—centering on humans rather than gods, the people rather than the Constitution, citizens rather than politicians, lawyers, or judges—is a provocative pragmatist challenge to both classical liberalism and modern democracy.[62] Nonetheless, it has some serious flaws. In his critique of Dewey, Melvin Rogers writes, "The integrity of democracy hinges on the extent to which the minority never feels permanently alienated from the process of decision-making. Because the status of the minority is not perpetual, and as a result, the minority does not exist under the weight of a tyrannical majority, the idea of political loss becomes an institutionalized reciprocal practice of decision-making," which fosters "habits of reciprocity and mutual trust amongst citizens and between citizens and their representatives."[63] If there *is* a permanent minority that is permanently alienated, democracy is in trouble. Thus, according to Rogers, Dewey never offers a good means for resolving conflict in a context in which some have experienced long-standing exclusion. Losing well, as Danielle Allen and Juliet Hooker have pointed out, is a central requirement of democratic politics.[64] Rogers's point is that Dewey's argument imagines a state in which race or some other deep divide can be overcome through deliberation. But we live in a state purposefully organized to support a tyrannical white public at the expense of subjected and excluded people of color.

And it seems increasingly true that no amount of Deweyan deliberation will overcome this exclusion, in part because one cannot argue one's way to being seen as equal. Using the work of Frederick Douglass from before the Civil War, Christopher Lebron argues that one way to break through this logjam is to use "shameful publicity." Lebron argues that the shameful publicity exemplified by the work of Douglass and Ida B. Wells served to highlight existing inequalities, demanded moral realignment consistent with stated values, and, together with a demand for reinvigorated civic virtue, helped Americans reimagine democracy.[65] Shameful publicity, Lebron argues, is not a defensive strategy but an offensive one; it mobilizes a vision of America as it ought to be and demands "correspondence between politics and polity."[66] Whites who respond to demands that black lives matter with fear that their white lives might matter less are engaging in zero-sum thinking, and, as Lebron notes, "No one who looks at the world this way can be prepared to sacrifice. And here, by sacrifice, I do not mean to lose. Rather, I mean, to make oneself vulnerable to new political possibilities and personal relationships."[67] Similarly, Juliet Hooker's *Race and the Politics of Solidarity* argues that white racial solidarity has prevented an inclusive and robust democratic solidarity in the United States.[68] This difficulty of forming a cross-racial public is a problem for Dewey's pragmatic, experience-based, evolving state; there is, in fact, a permanent and tyrannical majority and an equally permanent and excluded-from-power minority. The public whose interests the state reflects and whose interactions become predictably "canalized" is a *white* public, who has rejected both logical and emotive calls to recognize the humanity of blacks and other people of color in the United States.[69]

And yet blacks (and other excluded groups) regularly challenge the undemocratic institutional arrangements that define our white democracy. In doing so, they are acting exactly as Dewey argues publics do: seeking to overcome apathy or paralysis, identifying indirect effects, mobilizing forms of presentation that draw others in, and opening space for deliberation and debate that is central to democratic life. Using this framework, Black Lives

Matter is the kernel of an evolving Deweyan public that seeks to "break with existing political forms":[70] in this instance, the existing political form is specifically law enforcement that routinely kills people of color without repercussions or legal constraint. But it is not limited to this aspect of existing political forms, which is the genius of the phrase. The movements may not yet have succeeded in canalizing the state's actions to better match racially inclusive aspirations, and yet it has disrupted the taken-for-granted exclusion of the permanent minority, opening this condition up for deliberation and debate. Putting Dewey, mourning, and Black Lives Matter together helps demonstrate how mourning can play an important role in forming a public that sees itself as such: as a collective that faces a problem that can and should be mitigated and that demands that the state evolve to address the problem. While the zero-sum thinking of the white response helped lodge President Donald Trump in the White House, the promise of Black Lives Matter is that it poses opposition to the promise of a strongman savior. No *one* can save us; we must instead save ourselves.

Further, differently focused organizations and avenues of advocating for change that have come out of many organizations making up what Ransby calls the "Black Lives Matters Movement" (BLMM) or later the "Movement for Black Lives" (M4BL) have an expanded understanding of democracy that is not necessarily bound by institutions. Ransby writes:

> BLMM/M4BL includes an assemblage of dozens of organizations and individuals that are actively in one another's orbit, having collaborated, debated, and collectively employed an array of tactics together: from bold direct actions to lobbying politicians and creating detailed policy documents . . . It also includes a mass base of followers and supporters, who may not be formally affiliated with any of the lead organizations but are supportive of and sympathetic toward the spirit of the movement and are angered by the practices, policies, and events that sparked it. The different sectors don't always agree, and there have been some partings of the ways, but for the most part there is a sense of camaraderie—that they are a political family with a critical core holding them together.[71]

This sense of shared fate—that we are as well off as the least among us—is a fundamentally democratic response. Working to build coalitions, trying to raise consciousness, and responding to shared problems with collective solutions rather than making those problems the responsibility of individuals are all in line with Dewey's vision of democracy. Like all movements, Black Lives Matter has struggled to attain its goal of inclusion, but as Taylor, Lebron, and Ransby all point out, the self-conscious effort to err on the side of inclusion is radical.[72]

Dewey, then, gives us democracy as an active verb, one realized through being in community: coming to understand that we have shared vulnerabilities that can be addressed by coming together to mitigate them. BLM takes this a step further by demonstrating that democracy is also *embodied*. BLM points our democratic attention to bodies—their vulnerability, their suffering—but in particular to the disparate experiences of black vulnerability in a state whose interests have been largely defined by white vulnerability rather than black.[73] White refusal to stand in solidarity with black lives and to stand up against state-sponsored violence directed toward black bodies starkly illustrates the existing limits of American democracy.

BLM directly challenges white Americans to give up their racial innocence. Those who are not black have generally responded in one of two ways. First, many have come to recognize the particular vulnerability of people of color to state violence. Simon Stow argues that this willingness to see the humanity of those unlike ourselves is the necessary precursor to democratic politics.[74] Many white people took up this call. The color blindness and false universal of ALM, however, demonstrates a second response: refusal. The "All" of ALM means "me and people who look like me": respectable white people—people who are not shot by community watch captains, who are not arrested after being pulled over for failing to use a turn signal, who are not killed by police for selling loose cigarettes. We might interpret white efforts to incorporate black lives into all lives as a way of redirecting just, black mourning toward falsely universalized and symbolic *white* injury: the injury, ironically, of being excluded by the modifier "black" from a harm particularly experienced by those who are black.

ALM seems to deny the claims of BLM because BLM has refused the politics of respectability by publicly demonstrating, disrupting white lives, or talking about race in impolite ways. But Ransby suggests that it is a fantasy to assume that the politics of respectability will work for blacks in the United States, "as if proper behavior and politeness have ever protected Black people from discrimination or racial violence." The politics of respectability assumes that good people who ask politely will get a fair hearing from those in power. But Ransby notes that this response to injustice serves to "advocate individual solutions to systemic problems and, conversely, to blame individual 'bad' behavior and mistakes for system-wide conditions of racism and poverty."[75] BLM, on the other hand, comes at the question of black vulnerability to state violence via "a radical politics of intersectionality" that demands "not only that marginalized sectors of oppressed communities be included in any political calculus for liberation but that their suffering, interests, and aspirations be at the very center of any movement concerned with social transformation."[76] Rather than being moved to consider collective bodily vulnerability—our vulnerability to sovereign power seems to be only increasing when a president seeks to denaturalize immigrants and cage children—white Americans imagine that if they follow the rules and do not dissent, they will remain safe. The failure of respectability politics to secure safety for black Americans suggests that white confidence in limited sovereign power is misplaced.

Conclusion

As W.E.B. Du Bois suggested at the start of the twentieth century, we cannot reconstruct American democracy without realizing that American democracy has always been black.[77] The question is not whether that is true; the question is whether white Americans are willing to disavow their innocence in order to acknowledge it. Similarly, in his intellectual history of the ideas culminating in the Black Lives Matter moment and movements, Christopher Lebron writes:

> Taken together, [Frederick Douglass, Ida B. Wells, Langston Hughes, Zora Neal Hurston, Anna Julia Cooper, Audre Lorde, James Baldwin, and Martin Luther King Jr.] recommend a political ethical comportment to America that suggests an endorsement of the ideals of democracy while soundly and roundly rejecting the distortions and corruptions of *American* democracy without compromise— black humanity will be respected or blacks will no longer endorse the centuries-old asymmetrical project Audre Lorde famously spelled as "america" to demote the idea from grandness and properness to an immature and unformed state of a union.[78]

This refusal by white Americans to take the demands of Black Lives Matter seriously is not unlike the American response to September 11: a denial that the American state bore any responsibility for creating conditions in which a movement like al-Qaeda might rise. This is the problem with sovereign mourning; it attends not to the *people*, not to all its *citizens*, but to the needs of the state and the citizens the state was established to represent. Our state was never set up to address the needs of all its people. Though the aspirations of the Declaration have inspired many toward inclusion, the institutions established by the Constitution have long worked to contain the expansion of the boundaries of belonging. Brief and meaningful moments of expansion are often followed by legal containment that maintains institutional inertia, leaving those who relied on the state for rights again exposed and betrayed by a government never meant to represent them.

The various organizations that have rallied around the slogan Black Lives Matter have not fallen into this trap; they have not been fooled by the institutions and illusions of sovereignty. They instead demand actual democracy in a Deweyan sense. That kind of democracy is not only about state-overseen procedures or processes but also about relations of equality between persons to enable deliberation about how to address collective problems, which should manifest as a democratic state. In that sense, the movements gathering people together under the rubric of Black Lives Matter are laying the groundwork necessary to transform the American state.

David McIvor, in the afterword of *Mourning in America*, argues that part of the power of the mourning-inspired Black Lives Matter is a realization that

> the spaces and practices of political engagement are insufficient and untrusted, that there are few options for pursuing redress for grievances, and that the formal institutions of law and justice are normatively bankrupt or part of the problem. . . . One detects within these scenes of public grieving a genuine sense of impasse: a shared sentiment of injustice, disrespect, or misrecognition alongside a palpable confusion over how best to respond to such injustices.[79]

McIvor rightly holds up the example of the Greensboro Truth and Reconciliation Commission (GTRC) as an example of how "the democratic work of mourning [can help] locate and cultivate spaces and norms of public interaction that might erode some of the projections and pathologies attendant to ongoing relations of misrecognition."[80] Through their own initiative and without state support, the citizens of Greensboro organized to hold hearings to learn about what actually happened on a dark day in their past. The result helped "break down not only a simplified account of history but also simplified accounts of group (and individual) identity."[81] In acting outside the institutions of a state not meant to serve them, "by acknowledging the broader social patterns—living legacies of racial discrimination and durable patterns of poverty, police abuse, and social distrust—the GTRC problematized bystander innocence and identified sins of omission as well as commission."[82]

But as McIvor argues in the section "Freddie Gray, Citizen?," it is an open question whether American democracy more broadly can recognize people of color *as citizens*, given that "the history of American democracy is undeniably ambivalent: it is replete with murder *and* repair, brutality *and* sacrifice, oppression *and* emancipation—and neither side of those terms can fully cancel out the other."[83] To answer that question, McIvor turns to contemporary writers Ta-Nehisi Coates and Claudia Rankine, who urge us to embrace the ideals of democracy while recognizing the flaws of our actually existing one.[84] McIvor writes, "The challenge issuing from [Coates and Rankine] is the location of particular settings and viable practices of historical acknowledgement and social repair."[85] These locations, which may mitigate "the inherent cruelty of democratic stuckness . . . require[] building civic relationships that can simultaneously address concrete social problems while extending relations of mutual recognition across intransigent social divides, and to do so *from within* cultures and customs of misrecognition."[86] For McIvor, the GTRC provides an example of exactly this kind of "civic bridge building."[87] This is the most challenging part, of course; while the GTRC is one example, we need hundreds or even thousands of similar instances to reach enough people to fundamentally re-form the public as antiracist. The many movements mobilizing under the umbrella claim that black lives matter are doing this important work.

In the wake of the September 11 attacks, many Americans were drawn into sovereign mourning; fearing for the security of our state, we gave our leaders broad powers designed to protect us. The sense of vulnerability in the wake of the attacks in New York and Washington, D.C., led many to demand greater protections. This is reasonable, though recall that Americans were divided regarding whether they should fear the government or terrorists more. We mourned the state's sense of lost power, which served to obscure the foundation of that power in violence. Because the security of the state itself felt so connected to our own security, many Americans supported efforts to expand the state's powers.

But those very powers are now being used against fellow, black citizens. And instead of responding with affirmations of our shared stake in a safer future for all, white Americans have innocently denied responsibility for the losses experienced by the black community. If it was easier to mourn the loss of the state's power after September 11, ALM suggests that it is more difficult for whites to mourn those whose lack of security props up our own.

Juliet Hooker's analysis in "Black Protest, White Grievance" provides a compelling argument for why Black Lives Matter has divided white and black America rather than brought them together. Hooker "interrogates how white grievance, particularly the inability to accept loss (both material and symbolic), continues to be the dominant force shaping contemporary racial politics."[88] Her argument is that "the political imagination of white citizens has been shaped not by the experience of loss but rather by different forms of white supremacy and that this results in a distorted form of racial political math that sees black gains as white losses, and not simply losses but defeats."[89] As a 2017 Pew Research report shows, Americans' political orientation and their response to Black Lives Matter strongly correlate.[90] The result is that racial justice—or even recognizing that race is a political question—has become a firmly partisan issue. White Americans, in Baldwin's words, are doubling down on their innocence. Words and taunts by President Trump in 2019 that four elected members of Congress should "go back" to their countries if they do not love America in the way he does signal the ugly expression of open hostility toward immigrants and people of color. The Republican Party's tortured efforts to deny the racism of those words signal the ascension of a major party's support (and thus institutional support) for raw racism.

We are at a perilous moment in American democracy; as perilous as the founding, the Civil War, and the civil rights era. The fundamental question is whether we will continue as a white democracy or transform into a democracy for all. The adage that for those accustomed to privilege, equality feels like oppression has never been more true. The rise of Donald Trump—whom Arlie Hochschild calls "the identity politics candidate for white men"—suggests that a majority of white Americans are more invested in preserving whiteness than they are in building democracy.[91] Those whom the state has long represented—white people—are threatened by the possibility of actual democracy. Black Lives Matter has forced this question into public deliberation, but which public the state will represent in the coming years remains unclear at the start of the 2020s. It is an open question whether the United States will survive the transformation from white democracy to actual democracy.

Conclusion

The focus of this book is instances when the deaths of everyday citizens have generated political change. Why do some deaths move us to act while others do not? Political mourning is a thorny site of inquiry in part because of its unpredictability. There are countless deaths each day, some of which could, in theory, serve as mournable moments like the ones described here. And yet few do. In a similar vein, it seems clear that political mourning can be a powerful motivator for political change, and yet the changes that occur are also unpredictable. Sometimes political mourning moves the polity toward democratic inclusion and an acknowledgment of political responsibility. But other times, it leads the polity toward sovereign mourning that supports the state, marked exclusion of those deemed not American enough, a hardening of traditional identity categories, and an eschewal of complex political responsibility. One goal of this book is to establish a way to normatively assess our responses to political mourning. Can mourning serve democracy rather than sovereignty? I believe it can, though the events of September 11 and the still unfolding American response to Black Lives Matter suggest that such an outcome is perhaps rarer than we would like. In essence, what are the possibilities and limitations of mobilizing political mourning to call for political change?

Identity and responsibility are crucial conceptual tools to understand political mourning. Without a sense of how political identities shape the public's response to any particular death, it is difficult to make sense of why some instances generate political change while others do not. And our understanding of the extent of our responsibility to fellow citizens or humans is integrally connected to identity. Once a "we" has been imagined, we owe one another equal protection. But the makeup of that "we" and the content of equal protection is not a given; the boundaries of both fluctuate. Identity fundamentally shapes the visibility of deaths, but identity categories can be transformed as a result of mournable moments. Similarly, the bounds of collective, properly political responsibility can also expand or contract with that "we."

The processual model of political mourning I lay out in the Introduction and in the case studies shows similarities even when the events under consideration differ in era, location, numbers of dead, and normatively desirable outcomes. The model suggests that the four events I discuss, though quite different, are still comparable. Each includes contested identities, a highly visible event, the inadequacy of legal stories about responsibility, actors using mourning about particular deaths to support calls for political action, and political change. Why is locating this process that threads through all these cases important? Recall Peter Verovšek's argument about the need to determine what actually comprises a "politics of memory"; while scholars in many fields of inquiry use the language of a politics of memory, without some shared criteria to judge inclusion in or exclusion from the set of instances, comparing them becomes difficult if not impossible.[1] I seek here to do something similar for mournable moments, so that we can better compare instances when death is used to mobilize calls for political change; even if we cannot predict in advance the outcome, there are patterns in the events. Acknowledging the unpredictability provides ways for us to better analyze and respond to mournable moments when they occur.

The (Normatively Desirable) Possibilities of Political Mourning

A visible death can be a powerful site around which mobilization for democratic political change can occur. The response to Till's murder and a public demanding an end to white democracy through the calls for black lives to matter are the most obvious examples of this possibility. Though a more complicated example, the Triangle Fire also exposed the dangerous plight of industrial workers and helped incorporate workplace regulation as a fundamental duty of government. All three events contributed to expansions of the boundaries of belonging and an enlarged sense of political responsibility in the polity. Thus, it is fair to claim that political mourning can play a role in *expanding the boundaries of belonging*. This is true even if that expansion is temporary. Being confronted with the consequences of events can make visible the inequalities we know exist but have failed to remedy. When a death occurs because of these taken-for-granted inequalities, we are more likely to see and understand the connection between the previously existing inequalities and the death; we are able to see connections more easily than when the harms are more quotidian and less severe.

A related point is that political mourning can *expose everyday violence and open it up to critique*. When a fatal event exposes the distance between American ideals of equal protection of law and practices that fail to realize those goals, we may begin to interrogate the practices in ways we did not before the fatal event. Clarissa Hayward argues that ordinary stories about "who we are" frame our collective and individual identity stories. But these ordinary stories often obscure how the taken-for-granted present was produced through the institutionalization and objectification of some narratives rather than others.[2] Shootings or factory fires may prompt us to consider whether the story of who we are matches the world we live in. The past is filled with instances when the state has responded to a newly realized collective threat; it has adapted to address newly identified problems and serve the publics that coalesced around them to demand change. John Dewey's vision of a state not above a public but reflecting it helps make sense of how this happens.

Political mourning can also contribute to *expansions in our understanding of the extent of political responsibility*. When confronted with bodies produced by legal but unjust conditions, we may come to realize that legal responsibility is not enough and take up political responsibility.[3] Consider, for instance, Stuart Scheingold's arguments about the politics of law.[4] Scheingold argues that most Americans adhere to what he calls the "myth of rights," where law is above and contains the messiness and disorder of politics. But the political power that created legal systems tends to preserve the status quo (including a focus on property rights, individuals, and limited government). Thus, the legal system tends to be conservative, focusing on individuals rather than structures. Scheingold argues instead for a "politics of rights" that draws on the myth of rights to fuel political mobilization beyond legal institutions and frameworks. When a death occurs and the legal system proves incapable of locating responsibility in a single actor, it may prompt us to consider whether legal responsibility is sufficient, potentially pushing us to expand political responsibility to include broader conditions of justice rather than maintaining a too-narrow focus on procedural due process and individual guilt.

Political mourning may *generate in-group solidarity and draw outsiders in* (or at least make them friendly rather than hostile to a group's demands). While those most directly affected—say factory workers after the Triangle Fire or young black men after Emmett Till's death—may be those most likely to politically mobilize to demand a change in conditions, the impact of a visible death can draw into action even those who are not directly affected. It can also motivate fence-sitters to engage in more active ways. In general, then, a death can spur people to engage in the collective action at the heart of democratic politics. Similarly, political mourning can *make the stakes clear* to those in similar situations. When a young man is killed for whistling at a white woman or refusing to obey a police officer's directive to walk on the sidewalk, or when workers die on the job, an individual's calculus regarding the costs of political activism may shift. In conditions so dire, those most likely to be affected may determine that they may as well do something worth dying for rather than simply waiting to die.

In sum, political mourning can serve as a powerful resource to demand Deweyan democracy: a state that reflects and works to solve the problems faced by the public. By exposing the political nature of responsibility and showing the distance between stated ideals and practices, political mourning can generate a productive perplexity that moves us to act. Dewey's fellow traveler, Jane Addams, considered perplexity one of the great educators of a democratic populace.[5] Addams argued that when we encounter others who have different values or experiences, who come from different contexts and have different skills, we are faced with a choice: we may choose to think about the problem from their perspective, learning the empathy and insight necessary for democratic life, or we may reject their point of view out of hand. The former orientation toward our experiences is an essential democratic character trait, because it leads us to begin to question why we do things the way we do. Yet this is not always how things turn out. For a variety of reasons, political mourning may also lead the polity down dark roads of xenophobia and the denial of our own role in shaping the world. Thus, while political mourning may serve to help us identify collective problems that we can join together to solve through politics, it may also serve to unite us around undemocratic ones.

The (Normatively Undesirable) Limitations of Political Mourning

While political mourning sometimes helps move the polity toward democratic inclusion and justice, this is not always the case. Because visible deaths can generate a tremendous emotional response from the watching public, the deaths can be used to move the polity toward unjust rather than just ends. While I only offer four instances here, the one that most obviously led to normatively suspect outcomes is September 11. Likewise, the white majority's All Lives Matter in response to the mournable moments that led to the creation of Black Lives Matter has been markedly undemocratic; rather than a multiracial democratic public forming, a white public has. The response to the Triangle Fire was more mixed; while the response moved the United States in the direction of including not-quite-whites into the "we" and expanding the role of the state in regulating industrial workplaces, it also worked to make black losses and employment spaces less visible. It thus serves as a cautionary tale of the unpredictability of political mourning. There are many potential losses that have contributed to similarly problematic processes of contracting the boundaries of belonging and eschewing complex and political responsibility, but I leave those for others to explore.

If either the events or the changes required to address them are *extraordinary in scope*, the threat is perceived to be so great that the reflective response that should be prompted is essentially short-circuited. Overwhelmed, shocked, and dismayed by the events of September 11, Americans quickly settled on a framing of this event as existential rather than political in nature. The result is Simon Stow's description of the dangers of *mênis*—the grief-wrath that blinds us to the humanity of those deemed enemies and to our responsibility to treat ourselves and others with democratic respect.[6] In *Emergency Politics*, Bonnie Honig asks how a polity can respond to tragic situations in ways that do not destroy the demos. She writes, "For [Bernard] Williams, the question posed to the moral agent by the tragic situation is not simply what should we do in a tragic situation but what does the tragic situation do to us and how can we best survive with our moral integrity intact?"[7] Rather than focus on our responsibility, Americans instead claimed innocent victimhood and turned our anger outward. The American response to September 11 has exposed massive rifts between our stated ideals of being a nation bound together by aspirations of rights, liberties, freedom, and equality, and our actual practices of imperialism, forced democratization abroad, torture, indefinite detention, and racial scapegoating.

Likewise, the white response to Black Lives Matter has involved a turning away from a commitment toward democracy and instead a turning toward an image of sovereign protection of "real" Americans: white, Christian, straight, and able to work. White Americans have chosen to deny responsibility to help create a world where all lives matter by focusing on symbolic white losses rather than addressing the material losses of people of color.[8] Given an untenable situation revealed by a tragedy, we could accept responsibility for the damage caused through our support for authoritarians abroad and for white democracy at home that whites have long found satisfactory. Honig argues that our responses to such crises should lead us to consider "the conditions of a democracy's survival"; the question is whether "we are . . . committed . . . to national unity . . . [or] the preservation of a regime's identity as democratic."[9]

September 11 and the white response of All Lives Matter have illuminated how weak our commitment to actual democracy is. The search for enemies abroad and now within our borders has morphed into the pursuit of and beratement of those with whom we disagree at home. No one better illustrates this than Donald Trump. As Elisabeth Anker argues in *Orgies of Feeling*, the oversimplified narrative plot of political melodrama demands victims, villains, and heroes.[10] But these stark divides of good and evil leave little space for the agonistic nature of democratic life and complex engagement with political responsibility. The search for clear divides abroad has led to battle lines at home. The outcome has been to *contract the boundaries of belonging*; those who disagree are not our fellow citizens but our enemies, not to mention all those seeking refuge from the chaos the United States has created in their homelands, now imagined as feral animals or natural disasters rather than humans.[11]

Alongside this contraction of identity has come a similar *contraction in a sense of complex responsibility*. When we imagine ourselves as pure victims rather than actors in a complex world where none have clean hands, it is easier to turn those we disagree with into monsters than it is to sit with the possibility that we may bear some responsibility for enabling conditions in which fallible humans believe terrible actions are the only reasonable response. Simon Stow's call for a tragic response rather than a wrathful one—his argument that Americans, too, should mourn bin Laden—is a call to recognize the humanity of those we oppose.[12] Stow argues that "it is the acknowledgement of this shared humanity that makes politics possible."[13] When we see those who oppose us not as humans but as something less than, the only proper response is annihilation.

Those who mobilize grief to call for change play a large role regarding how the issue will be framed and interpreted by the public. Much depends on *who speaks for the dead* and whether we listen to those affected or whether the meaning of the event is overtaken by other actors or speakers with agendas potentially unrelated to the event at hand. We should be particularly wary of how easily political mourning can be used to justify *calls for change that target members of entire racial groups as a threat*. Consider, for example, the 2018 murder of eighteen-year-old Mollie Tibbetts by an undocumented immigrant,[14] a group characterized by Donald Trump in his 2015 campaign announcement as criminals and rapists.[15] Tibbetts's tragic death became a political football, used by Republicans as a campaign issue meant to increase support for the law-and-order party.[16] Yet Tibbetts's father consistently asked that she be left out of such efforts. In an op-ed in the *Des Moines Register*, he wrote, "Mollie was nobody's victim. Nor is she a pawn in others' debate. She may not be able to speak for herself, but I can and will. Please leave us out of your debate. Allow us to grieve in privacy and with dignity."[17] (That this sad death has become about race and immigration rather than violence against women boggles the mind.) And yet in part because the family chose to grieve privately rather than grasp the opportunity to shed light on the conditions in which women die at severely disproportionate rates from sexual assault and gender-based violence, Mollie's death was essentially captured by those who wished to advance anti-immigration policy rather than being a resource for other demands for political change.

Charges of *politicizing death* can serve to dampen calls for political reflection, as well. In *American Mourning*, Simon Stow carefully reads criticism of politicizing Coretta Scott King's funeral.[18] Two African American speakers at the funeral used the pulpit to condemn racism in American politics, a response Mrs. King, no doubt, would have looked on favorably. Though several former presidents and political leaders were in attendance, the critical tone of the speakers was condemned as improper politicization. As Stow points out, however, this disregards the long tradition in African American funerary practices that draw on grief to motivate action for justice. Charges of politicization of a death are often an effort to particularize and depoliticize critique of ideals or ideologies, serving to limit our reflection on the relation between identity and political responsibility.

Political mourning is also *unpredictable*. It is difficult to say in advance how the meaning and signification of the event will unfold. This is both a strength and a weakness, however. Because mourning can rupture our taken-for-granted narratives of how the world works, it can open us to new interpretations or reflection. But as shown by the example of September 11, this is not always what occurs. To be clear, the portrait of political mourning I offer here is not a causal story. However, future work might be done on the effects of particular actors accessing media to frame a death as a call for justice and expanded responsibility or as a call for the contraction of responsibility. For mourners seeking to move the needle toward justice, it might be worth attending to the effect of targeted media outlets that provide space for those affected to share their stories.

Perhaps most alarming, however, is when the state and its leaders mobilize mourning to increase invasive state power rather than understanding the state as an expression of the collective needs of the demos. This *sovereign mourning* interprets dialogue, debate, and dissent as fundamental threats to security. Like Hobbes's sovereign who frees his subjects from the demands of politics by assuming the status of a mortal god, leaders relying on sovereign mourning use the losses of citizens to assert a clarity of purpose and imagine a low bar for the legitimacy of the state: security. Anything that threatens or is perceived to threaten the security of the *state* (and not of the citizens, who eventually become mere subjects) must be destroyed.

While mourning may help us better realize an inclusive, more perfect democracy, it can also serve deeply undemocratic ends. When used to harden and contract identity boundaries on the basis of race; to stunt reflection on our collective responsibility to others, to fellow citizens, and to ourselves; and to target outsiders while absolving ourselves of responsibility, mobilizing political mourning is a high-risk move.

Unanswered Questions

This project is a beginning. While the framework laid out relies on a fundamental commitment to democracy as relations among persons that result in institutional arrangements, it is unclear whether regime type or cultural differences affect the processes I lay out here. My hope is that those with knowledge of other regime types and cultures can determine whether this framework works in other settings. Examples might include instances like the 2013 Rana Plaza fire in Bangladesh (sadly similar to the Triangle Fire in circumstances but with ten times more deaths) or infrastructure collapse as a result of corruption in authoritarian regimes. What is similar and what is different? Future research and evaluation of the claims made here could yield important modifications to this framework.

Another unanswered question is whether other identity categories, such as gender, sexuality, or disability, are mobilized in similar ways. Matthew Shepard's 1998 murder seems to fit well as an instance of political mourning. And yet even today, the steadily rising number of murders of trans people barely attains visibility. Why have the overwhelming number of women murdered by their partners not generated massive political mourning? Given the example of Mollie Tibbetts's murder, why do we so quickly jump to race rather than gender? Do other kinds of deaths do something similar? Why or why not?

Also unclear is what happens when those most affected speak and are accused of inappropriately politicizing deaths. Charges of politicization usually seek to preserve the status quo (whatever it may be), while calls for political change often require fundamental shifts. Instances such as the school shootings at Sandy Hook Elementary School in Newtown, Connecticut, and Marjory Stoneman Douglas High School in Parkland, Florida, have opened conversations about gun violence but have failed to yield much change. Why have they not succeeded? Second Amendment advocates have successfully made "gun owner" synonymous with "real American"; is this an identity category that is simply too powerful for political mourning to challenge? Are the challenged practices too fundamental to our sense of identity? Are the ideals being upheld too abstract? The ongoing evolution of the calls of Black Lives Matter suggests that when deaths mobilize a public whose calls for change are fundamental, the backlash is intense. It might be that there are some foundationally undemocratic institutions that cannot be changed unless we literally re-form the polity.

It is also unclear whether the new media landscape of the twenty-first century has changed our ability to see and reflect on losses like the ones outlined here. The bombardment of terrible news from around the world may be desensitizing us to the suffering of others. That said, the rise of Black Lives Matter suggests that mobilization of political mourning for justice is still possible.

In sum, I hope that this work contributes to an already existing series of texts that address the power of mourning in politics: works like Judith Butler's *Precarious Life*, Bonnie Honig's *Antigone, Interrupted*, Simon Stow's *American Mourning*, and David McIvor's *Mourning in America*. I have also entered into debates about how to make sense of each of the events I consider here, because I believe that understanding how mourning becomes political helps make sense of the particular responses to those deaths. Attending not only to social movement building but also to the trigger of a particular death at a particular time provides a way to think about how movements come into being at particular moments. At the same time, the theory I lay out here opens up productive new avenues of research: different identity categories, different cultures and regime types, more sustained attention to mournable moments that have not yielded results, and inquiries into how transformations in the media landscape will enable or stymie similar efforts in the future.

Final Thoughts

In *Emergency Politics*, Bonnie Honig writes:

> The irresolvable paradox of politics commits us to a view of the people, democratic actors and subjects, as also always a multitude. The paradox of politics posits democracy as always embedded in the problem of origins and survival: how to (re)shape a multitude into a people, daily. From the perspective of this paradox, we see democracy as a form of politics that is always in emergence in response to everyday emergencies of maintenance. The assumed antagonisms between democracy and emergency is to some extent undone from this angle of vision and new sightlines are opened up. The work of democratic politics can be seen to entail not just rupture but maintenance, not just new beginnings but preparation, receptivity, and orientation.[19]

Honig's keen insights—that democratic politics is always about both ruptures and maintenance, the people are always both citizens and multitude, that beginnings and maintenance are bound together—are at the heart of the accounts I offer here. When we engage in political mourning, the depth of our courage, the quality of our integrity, and the democratic valence of our priorities are exposed. Thus, it is a valuable site to consider the distance between our ideals and our practices—a site that can move us to lessen the distance between practices and aspirations or that can lead to a refusal to interrogate the practices. It is a process in which the political "we" reveals itself. When faced with the body, we have a choice; we can turn away from the questions it prompts, or we can dig in to understand what happened and how we can prevent it from happening again. It is a moment of reflection. While our responses to the bodies of the dead say something about who *they* were, our responses say even more about *us*. "Who are we?" can be partially answered by considering who counts as, and how we respond to, our dead.

Afterword

The COVID-19 Pandemic of 2020

I sent what I hoped would be the final manuscript of this book to my editor at Temple University Press on March 9, 2020, the same day the state of Ohio—where I live and teach—announced its first positive tests for COVID-19 (the disease caused by the novel coronavirus SARS-CoV-2). First reported by China to the World Health Organization on December 31, 2019, the virus had rapidly spread across the globe, from China to Europe and then around the world. It was surreal to have completed a manuscript on political mourning just as our nation and the world was poised to face suffering and loss of life on a massive scale.

One morning in late April, while working on this Afterword, I checked the statistics, which had been updated at 8:03 A.M.: the global number of reported positive cases was roughly 2.7 million, with about 190,000 deaths. By the update at 2:07 P.M. that same day, the global case count had risen to more than 2.8 million, with 195,000 deaths.[1] That is 100,000 new reports of positive tests and 5,000 more deaths reported in six hours on a Saturday. In the eight days since, the totals have risen to about 3.4 million cases and around 245,000 deaths.[2] Although the United States is the hardest hit as I write this, with more than 1.1 million cases and more than 67,000 deaths (New York City alone has about one in three of both cases and fatalities in the United States),[3] humanity as a whole will suffer unthinkable losses in the coming months and years. Until a vaccine or an effective treatment is found, the virus will continue to spread, killing as it goes, even if we are able to sustain the massive social distancing efforts that many states have implemented. The numbers are grim, but it is obvious that the actual counts are much higher than the reported number of cases because of the lack of capacity to test suspected infections, limitations on who qualifies to be given one of the few tests, and our still-evolving knowledge of the many vicious ways the virus weakens and kills the human body.[4]

Attempting to be analytical about this now, in the spring of 2020, feels impossible. The sheer horror and scale of this pandemic are too vast to comprehend. The number of lives that will be lost, the lives that will persist but be irrevocably damaged by the permanent effects of serious illness, the economic toll of looming unemployment, homelessness, and hunger; all are staggering to imagine. And these do not even account for the various mental health effects of prolonged social distancing—so many lost opportunities to celebrate loved ones' birthdays, weddings, graduations. We ache to see and hug our friends and families.

Perhaps most gutting is knowing that those dying from this disease do not have the opportunity for a "good death," surrounded by loved ones who can hold their hand and say the things that need to be said; because of the threat of contagion, those who go to a hospital are dying alone, surrounded not by family and friends but by nurses and doctors in full protective gear doing their best not to get sick themselves. Compounding the grief of losing a loved one is that end-of-life celebrations and funerals cannot happen right now, because social distancing demands that to stay safe, we not gather. In the hardest-hit places, there are too many bodies for funeral homes to deal with. The overwhelming number of dead in localized hotspots has led to bodies being stacked in morgues and churches in Italy, while in New York City, refrigerated trucks line the streets outside hospitals to receive the dead, and interments of unclaimed dead in mass graves on Hart Island have "risen fivefold."[5] It is all so devastatingly inhumane and inhuman. Despair, fear, and anticipatory mourning are pervasive, even as the majority of us do our best to keep ourselves and others healthy by staying home as much as possible, wearing masks, and not visiting friends and family.

Alongside the human toll of the pandemic, the global economy has cratered as nations have closed nonessential businesses, sports events, theaters: anywhere large groups of people might congregate. While national, regional, state, and local governments have adopted vastly different strategies to "flatten the curve" of case rates (in the hopes of not overwhelming healthcare systems), by the last day of April, unemployment in the United States reached epic proportions, with more than 30 million claims in six weeks, which, when combined with already existing claims, yielded a real unemployment level of about 23 percent.[6] As billions of people sheltered in place and demand for oil and gas plummeted, the price of oil went negative for the first time in history in late April, meaning that there was more oil in production than there were places to put it.[7] Thus far, the U.S. federal government has spent more than $3 trillion in various stimulus and response efforts.[8] Experts predict the global economy in 2020 will contract at levels not seen since the Great Depression.

The virus itself is apolitical; it is an unthinking lump of RNA that mutated to infect and be spread among humans. Previous coronaviruses that became epidemics, including SARS (severe acute respiratory syndrome) in 2002–2003 and MERS (Middle East respiratory syndrome) in 2012, were far more deadly than SARS-CoV-2; the fatality rate of SARS is estimated to be about 15 percent, while for MERS it is about 35 percent. Solid information regarding transmission, incidence, symptoms, actual cases, and case fatality rates is still unfolding, but early reports show that "SARS-CoV-2 seems to be more infectious than other coronaviruses—such as those that cause SARS and MERS—but less likely to lead to death."[9] It does appear, however, that elderly people (those older than sixty-five, and particularly those older than eighty-five) are at much higher risk of death if they contract the virus; by early April in the United States, about 75 percent of deaths had occurred in those over the age of sixty-five.[10] Those with preexisting conditions (such as hypertension, diabetes, or cancer) also appear more likely to be felled by SARS-CoV-2.

While the virus itself may be mutating, the mutations alone seem unlikely to fully explain the considerable differences in fatality rates across the globe. Different cities, regions, and countries have emerged as hot spots where new cases, and then fatalities, double in two or three days. Some variation can be explained by population density, which, paired with rapid and wide transmission of the disease, led to huge numbers of hospitalizations in very local areas; New York City has been devastated. Some, too, can be explained by cultural artifacts, such as how integrated elderly people are into society as a whole; Italy has the second-oldest population in the world and beloved elders regularly interact with their younger family members, which meant massive community spread before social distancing was implemented.[11] Certainly, the capacity and quality of the health-care system affect mortality rates as well; high-quality health care plausibly helps reduce the death rate, which is concerning given the low availability of health care in rural America and other parts of the world. These variations will be exhaustively analyzed in the years ahead, as we analyze this pandemic and prepare for the next.

As many news reports and analyses have suggested, the American response has been uniquely awful. There is no question that we knew well in advance that another pandemic would happen, and the president was warned in early January that it would be arriving in the United States soon.[12]

Instead of using the two months between identification of the first case in the world and the virus's arrival in the United States to build capacity—for example, by invoking the Defense Production Act to compel private corporations to begin making protective gear and tests—the American government sat idly by. Many Republican congressional leaders and the president himself consistently downplayed the threat, even as intelligence services and the World Health Organization sounded alarms and Italy descended into a nightmare.

While no country has been spared suffering and death in this pandemic, it seems increasingly clear that effective government helps lower the number of infections and deaths. For example, while the sheer size differences between New Zealand and the United States preclude meaningful comparison, Prime Minister Jacinda Ardern's calm, honest, and empathetic leadership has yielded a much lower per capita rate of infection and death. On April 26, 2020, the United States' rates of infection and death, respectively, were 237 and 15 per 100,000 people, while New Zealand's rates were 30 and less than 1 per 100,000.[13] New Zealand declared the virus "eliminated" by April 27.[14] Germany, perhaps the developed nation most comparable to the United States because it is not an island, has a large population, and has reliable data, had 186 cases and 7 deaths per 100,000 people on April 26. These variations suggest that the actions of effective leaders who took science seriously and mobilized political and institutional resources reduced the number of cases and deaths. The failures of the American executive to respond well has cost American lives.

One clear trend emerging forcefully in the United States is that people of color are falling seriously ill and dying at highly disproportionate rates. In its analysis of the report of April 8, 2020, from the U.S. Centers for Disease Control and Prevention (CDC), the *New York Times* notes:

> While the highest overall percentage of hospitalized patients were white (45 percent), the percentage of black patients (33 percent) was much higher than the percentage of African-Americans in the population as a whole. In the geographical areas covered by the study, 59 percent of the population is white, the report said, and 18 percent is black, "suggesting that black populations might be disproportionately affected by Covid-19."[15]

In its own analysis of hospitalizations and deaths two days later, the *Washington Post* determined that "majority black counties ha[d] three times the rate of infections and nearly six times the rate of deaths as majority white counties."[16] As the Associated Press reported on April 18, "On Friday, the

Centers for Disease Control and Prevention released its first breakdown of COVID-19 case data by race, showing that 30% of patients whose race was known were black. . . . The latest Associated Press analysis of available state and local data shows that nearly one-third of those who have died are African American, with black people representing about 14% of the population in the areas covered in the analysis."[17] Though blacks make up 30 percent of the population of Chicago, as of late April, blacks make up 56 percent of COVID-19 deaths.[18] These numbers do not account for the devastating effects of the virus once it reaches prisons—places where social distancing is impossible and where the population is disproportionately black and brown. While the overall number of cases in the United States as a whole—237 cases and 15 deaths per 100,000—is dreadful, the number of cases among the prison population is catastrophic: for example, 7,977 cases and 59 deaths per 100,000 among prisoners in Ohio, as of May 1, 2020.[19]

Shortly after the demographic data were released showing that people of color were dying disproportionately, largely white protesters in several states demanded that the economy be reopened. As historian Heather Cox Richardson notes, these protests largely align with groups seeking the reelection of President Donald Trump, who apparently believed that his reelection chances hung on how well the economy was doing.[20] Many such calls challenging government power, ironically, have been coming from those holding elected positions, as Republicans from the president down argue that shuttering businesses in the name of safety is a symptom of tyranny.[21] An unknown internet user referred to these protestors as the "Flu Klux Klan," while journalist Michael Harriot argued on April 22 that "Open the Economy" is another incarnation of "All Lives Matter."[22] Harriot writes:

> Every bit of available data shows that black and brown people are the ones who are suffering the most from COVID-19. And it's not just in urban areas like New York and Chicago. It's doing the same thing in rural black communities like Allendale, S.C., St. John the Baptist Parish, La. and Albany, Ga. Black residents outnumber whites in eight of the 10 cities with the highest coronavirus death rates per capita. Only one, Greensburg, Ind. is majority white. Even in Vermont, the whitest state in the union, the percentage of black people infected with COVID-19 is *10 times* the black population percentage.
>
> The suffering is not restricted to those infected. According to CBS News, black workers are less likely to be able to work from home and The Guardian reports that black employees are more likely to be employed as "essential workers." As the unemployment rate skyrockets, the percentage of black people losing jobs nearly

doubles the white unemployment rate. There is no doubt that black people are bearing the brunt of this pathogen's deadly attack.[23]

Protests by those demanding that the economy open regardless of the death toll have grown increasingly menacing, with armed protesters at numerous state capitols and death threats to elected officials. While these antigovernment protesters are loud, they are currently a minority. Public opinion polls in late April show that a clear majority of Americans were in favor of prioritizing public health, and a CBS poll shows that "sixty-three percent of Americans are more worried about restrictions lifting too fast and worsening the outbreak than worry about lifting restrictions too slowly and worsening the economy."[24]

But whether this rare moment of bipartisan agreement about staying home to limit the spread of the disease holds is unclear. By early May, states like Texas and Georgia had defied CDC recommendations to open the economy only after fourteen days of a decrease in the reported number of cases, instead choosing to open businesses even as the number of confirmed cases grew.[25] It seems plausible that the decision to prioritize the economy over public health will cost a significant number of lives and that those losses will occur primarily among the poor, the elderly, and people of color. Is this who we Americans are? Is it who we Americans want to be? Whose lives matter enough for us to protect them by remaining at home? What is our collective responsibility to one another?

There is no question that this event is highly visible and that the mourning is widespread and public. But is it yet *political* mourning in the ways I describe it? Will it spur political change in ways comparable to the other events I consider here? If so, how? Will these deaths lead us toward justice— to expand the boundaries of belonging and accept our responsibility for one another? This disease has shown that individual actions alone are not enough to keep any one of us safe; it is in our interests for the most vulnerable to have safe homes, adequate food, and available health care. Countless community and neighborhood groups have sprung into action to help those who need it, even as mutual aid societies have formed to coordinate aid for strangers in larger cities.

Our interdependence has been exposed by illuminating which kinds of work are actually essential—health care, grocery stores, food production, sanitation, gas and electricity production, and childcare and education, among others. These jobs, as Harriot notes, are often held by people of color and the working poor. Society as a whole works because people do these jobs that allow all of us to have ordered and safe lives, and yet those who do this important work are most vulnerable to the virus. My hope is that this terrible plague will help us realize the true worth of these workers and drive us to build a stronger safety net able to catch all of us—all workers, as well as the elderly and disabled who cannot work. I hope we can return to the ideals regarding the proper balance between capitalism and democracy laid out in 1933 by Franklin Delano Roosevelt in his Commonwealth Club Address; there is no reason anyone should go hungry in a country as abundantly blessed as the United States. It could be that this is the start of a new understanding of what it means to be a citizen in this democracy, enabling us to come together to build a better future, lay aside the divisive politics of the past, and focus on what we *all* need.

But these deaths might lead us further down the rabbit hole of individualism, too: the rejection of the truth that in a democracy, we rise and fall together. Here in the United States, the deep current of individualism and the increasingly libertarian penchant to fetishize economic choice as the only meaning of "freedom" has led many to attribute poverty or illness to failures of individual responsibility rather than evidence of structural inequality. It is telling that protests regarding state-ordered closures of nonessential businesses have not demanded that the government do more to help workers; they have instead demanded that businesses open up so they can return to work and risk infection and death. Freedom in this vein is the right to sell one's labor, not the responsibility to work together to ensure a good life for all.

This trend may have larger implications, too, as states vie for scarcer resources. Senate Majority Leader Mitch McConnell's suggestion on April 22 that states should go into bankruptcy if they run out of funds angered wealthier states with large urban centers, such as California, Illinois, and New York; the states hardest hit by the virus are those whose taxes subsidize federal spending in less populated and more rural states.[26] In the worst-case scenario, a series of conflicts might emerge as the now-weakened federal government abandons states and they begin to compete and cooperate among themselves, making the federal government increasingly irrelevant. State-level and regional agreements, such as the Western States Pact (among California, Oregon, Washington, Nevada, and Colorado in April[27]), not to open for business until they reach shared health markers serve to build institutional frameworks and intrastate cooperation—typically a function of the federal government. Given high levels of partisanship that have divided the country into red states and blue states, the election looming over 2020, the economic inequality that preceded the pandemic, and the starkly different life prospects for people of color, the United States is in a precarious position.

The United States is one of the wealthiest countries in the world, with vast resources, and people are dying here as though it is a failed state. George

Packer of the *Atlantic* went as far as to argue that the United States is a failed state. Packer describes the context into which this pandemic burst:

> This was the American landscape that lay open to the virus: in pros-
> perous cities, a class of globally connected desk workers dependent
> on a class of precarious and invisible service workers; in the coun-
> tryside, decaying communities in revolt against the modern world;
> on social media, mutual hatred and endless vituperation among dif-
> ferent camps; in the economy, even with full employment, a large
> and growing gap between triumphant capital and beleaguered labor;
> in Washington, an empty government led by a con man and his in-
> tellectually bankrupt party; around the country, a mood of cynical
> exhaustion, with no vision of a shared identity or future.[28]

The United States has always had the resources to address this crisis. What it lacks is the political vision and will to do so effectively. At this point, it is anyone's guess regarding how the United States and the world will change as a result of this pandemic; this is part of why political mourning is worth studying. As of early May 2020, we are not even sure about the science and data of this virus: rate of reproduction, rates of infection, case fatality rates, not to mention why some fall severely ill while others remain asymptomatic or whether those who have recovered will gain immunity. It seems plausible that essential workers will suffer higher death rates, but there is no way to know that now. While the death toll is already consider-able, estimates about its final death count or end date are speculative. Given our lack of knowledge and the dynamic context, to offer predictions would be folly.

While the virus itself is apolitical, the *response* to the virus is deeply connected to our understandings of the purpose, possibilities, and limita-tions of politics. It has illuminated how institutional arrangements, political commitments, and leadership matter when it comes to preserving human flourishing and reducing harms to human health and well-being. Govern-ments exist to coordinate responses to events like this: events that single persons, communities, or states cannot hope to address effectively on their own. John Dewey's idea of a public whose identified problems lead to the formations of governments once again seems apt; most of us want a capable, effective government response, particularly in times of crisis such as this. What Americans are getting in 2020 at the federal level is anything but that, as the Trump administration first denied the threat and then tragically bungled the response. At the state level, there is far more variation, as gov-ernors' responses can best be sorted not on the basis of party but on the basis of whether they attend to science and data. The apolitical virus has shown how politics matters.

It has also exposed the vast inequalities within and between countries. The virus—like the Triangle Fire and Emmett Till's and Trayvon Martin's murders—has illuminated the precarity and violence of everyday life for the poor, the elderly, and people of color in the United States. Internationally, it seems likely that poorer countries with less infrastructure and fewer resources will suffer even more than those in developed countries. Without an equitable social safety net to catch those harmed by the excesses of capitalism; without universal health care to provide support for the most vulnerable; and without affirmative action to repair centuries of discrimination, expropriation, and violence . . . without these in place, our country and the world will continue to sacrifice its most vulnerable to the gods of (white) economic well-being rather than attending to (everyone's) human well-being. As George Packer concluded in the *Atlantic*:

> We're faced with a choice that the crisis makes inescapably clear. We can stay hunkered down in self-isolation, fearing and shunning one another, letting our common bond wear away to nothing. Or we can use this pause in our normal lives to pay attention to the hospital workers holding up cellphones so their patients can say goodbye to loved ones; the planeload of medical workers flying from Atlanta to help in New York; the aerospace workers in Massachusetts demanding that their factory be converted to ventilator production; the Floridians standing in long lines because they couldn't get through by phone to the skeletal unemployment office; the residents of Milwaukee braving endless waits, hail, and contagion to vote in an election forced on them by partisan justices. We can learn from these dreadful days that stupidity and injustice are lethal; that, in a democracy, being a citizen is essential work; that the alternative to solidarity is death. After we've come out of hiding and taken off our masks, we should not forget what it was like to be alone.[29]

When we can once again gather, we must do better. We must ask for more than the right to labor and seek only our own ends; we must invoke the names of the unnecessarily dead to demand the rights and resources so that the demos *and* democracy can flourish.

Notes

INTRODUCTION

1. For journalistic timelines of events, see Grew Botelho and Holly Yan, "George Zimmerman Found Not Guilty of Murder in Trayvon Martin's Death," *CNN*, July 14, 2013, https://edition.cnn.com/2013/07/13/justice/zimmerman-trial/index.html; and Sara Sidner and Mallory Simon, "The Rise of Black Lives Matter," *CNN*, December 28, 2015, http://edition.cnn.com/2015/12/28/us/black-lives-matter-evolution/index.html. For more scholarly takes on the rise of Black Lives Matter and the movement's connection to contemporary events, see Keeanga-Yamahtta Taylor, *From #BlackLivesMatter to Black Liberation* (Chicago: Haymarket Books, 2016); Chris Lebron, *The Making of Black Lives Matter: A Brief History of an Idea* (Oxford: Oxford University Press, 2017); and Barbara Ransby, *Making All Black Lives Matter: Reimagining Freedom in the 21st Century* (Berkeley: University of California Press, 2018).

2. Lebron, *Making of Black Lives Matter*.

3. Joel Olson, *Abolition of White Democracy* (Minneapolis: University of Minnesota Press, 2004).

4. Lebron, *Making of Black Lives Matter*, 81–82, 95. See also Nikita Carney, "All Lives Matter, but So Does Race: Black Lives Matter and the Evolving Role of Social Media," *Humanity and Society* 40, no. 2 (2016): 180–199; and Ryan J. Gallagher et al., "Divergent Discourse between Protests and Counter-protests: #BlackLivesMatter and #AllLivesMatter," *PLoS ONE* 13, no. 4 (2018), https://doi.org/10.1371/journal.pone.0195644.

5. Anne Barnard, "Beirut, Also the Site of Deadly Attacks, Feels Forgotten," *New York Times*, November 15, 2015, https://www.nytimes.com/2015/11/16/world/middleeast/beirut-lebanon-attacks-paris.html.

6. Michael Walzer suggests that this preference for those who share our membership in a group is unavoidable and serves as the basis of the concept of political membership.

Walzer persuasively argues that any given political community has a right to determine who can enter and the terms of membership. I tend to agree with Walzer's position here, although I remain certain that the American state has consistently failed to apply those rules fairly and equitably. See Michael Walzer, *Spheres of Justice* (New York: Basic Books, 1983).

7. Amartya Sen, *The Idea of Justice* (Cambridge, MA: Harvard University Press, 2004); Martha Nussbaum, *Creating Capabilities: The Human Development Approach* (Cambridge, MA: Harvard University Press, 2013).

8. David McIvor, *Mourning in America: Race and the Politics of Loss* (Ithaca, NY: Cornell University Press, 2016), 161–166.

9. Juliet Hooker, *Race and the Politics of Solidarity* (Oxford: Oxford University Press, 2009), 4.

10. Judith Butler, *Precarious Life: The Powers of Mourning and Violence* (New York: Verso, 2004).

11. For example, missing adults receive more media coverage if they are white women. See Gene Demby, "What We Know (and Don't Know) about 'Missing White Women Syndrome,'" *NPR*, April 13, 2017, https://www.npr.org/sections/codeswitch/ 2017/04/13/523769303/what-we-know-and-dont-know-about-missing-white-women -syndrome. The discrepancy is even more pronounced when multiple minority catego- ries coalesce in one body—for instance, with black lesbians or trans people. See Casey Quinlan, "Four Black Lesbians Were Killed in One Week, and the Media Still Isn't Pay- ing Attention," *ThinkProgress*, January 10, 2018, https://archive.thinkprogress.org/black -lesbians-murdered-393925aa7af1/.

12. Marc Galanter, "Why the 'Haves' Come Out Ahead: Speculations on the Limits of Legal Change," *Law and Society Review* 9, no. 1 (1974): 95–160.

13. Sheldon Wolin, *Politics and Vision: Continuity and Innovation in Western Politi- cal Thought*, expanded ed. (Princeton, NJ: Princeton University Press, 2006), 18.

14. Wolin, *Politics and Vision*, 6.

15. Wolin, *Politics and Vision*, 7.

16. As I clarify in Chapter 1, it might be true that political mourning need not be restricted to institutional politics; the mourning after a loss may help build what John Dewey calls a "public" that is broadly political without its demands having been institu- tionalized or codified. See John Dewey, *The Public and Its Problems* (1927; repr., Athens: University of Ohio Press, 1991). Nonetheless, in an effort to illustrate the possibilities and limitations of political mourning, three of my cases focus on deaths that led to po- litical action within political institutions, while the outcomes of the most contemporary instance—Black Lives Matter—are still unfolding.

17. My use of "unremarkable" here is meant to signify that women disproportion- ately die at the hands of men and that it appears that this long-standing pattern makes such deaths not particularly newsworthy. The racial identities of the murdered and the murderer clearly played a role in driving media coverage and political salience of the Tibbetts story.

18. Rob Tibbetts, "From Mollie Tibbetts' Father: Don't Distort Her Death to Advance Racist Views," *Des Moines Register*, September 1, 2018, https://www.desmoinesregister .com/story/opinion/columnists/2018/09/01/mollie-tibbetts-father-common-decency -immigration-heartless-despicable-donald-trump-jr-column/1163131002.

19. John Seery, *Political Theory for Mortals: Shades of Justice, Images of Death* (Ithaca, NY: Cornell University Press, 1996), 6.

CHAPTER 1

1. Sheldon Wolin, *Politics and Vision: Continuity and Innovation in Western Political Thought*, expanded ed. (Princeton, NJ: Princeton University Press, 2006), 6.

2. Bonnie Honig, *Antigone, Interrupted* (Cambridge: Cambridge University Press, 2013), 2.

3. Honig, *Antigone, Interrupted*, xii.

4. Peter J. Verovšek, "Collective Memory, Politics, and the Influence of the Past: The Politics of Memory as a Research Paradigm," *Politics, Groups, and Identities* 4, no. 3 (2016): 529–543.

5. Verovšek, "Collective Memory."

6. This is a truncated version of the primary definition in the *Oxford English Dictionary* for the word "mourn." The entire definition is as follows: "Mourn: *I. Intransitive* 1. To feel sorrow, grief, or regret (often with added notion of expressing one's grief); to sorrow, grieve, or lament. 2. To lament the death of some one. 3. To have a painful longing. 4. To make a low, inarticulate sound indicative of pain or grief. In literary use only of a dove. *II. Transitive* 5. To grieve or sorrow for (something); to lament, deplore, bewail, bemoan. 6. To lament, grieve, or sorrow for, to express grief for (some one dead, or some one's death). 7. To utter in a sorrowful manner." See *The Compact Edition of the Oxford English Dictionary*, vol. 1 (Oxford: Oxford University Press, 1971), s.v. "mourn."

7. Anne Norton, *Reflections on Political Identity* (Baltimore: Johns Hopkins University Press, 1988); David McIvor, *Mourning in America: Race and the Politics of Loss* (Ithaca, NY: Cornell University Press, 2016).

8. Honig, *Antigone, Interrupted*; William E. Connolly, *Identity\Difference: Democratic Negotiations of Political Paradox*, expanded ed. (Minneapolis: University of Minnesota Press, 2002); Simon Stow, *American Mourning: Tragedy, Democracy, Resilience* (Cambridge: Cambridge University Press, 2017); Danielle Allen, *Talking to Strangers: Anxieties of Citizenship since Brown v. Board of Education* (Chicago: University of Chicago Press, 2006); Melvin Rogers, "Introduction," in *The Public and Its Problems: An Essay in Political Inquiry*, by John Dewey, ed. Melvin Rogers (Athens, OH: Swallow Press, 2016), 1–30.

9. Stow, *American Mourning*.

10. Freud provided this definition of mourning in "Mourning and Melancholia": mourning is "the reaction to the loss of a beloved person or an abstraction taking the place of the person, such as fatherland, freedom, and ideal and so on." Sigmund Freud, "Mourning and Melancholia," in *On Murder, Mourning and Melancholia*, ed. Adam Phillips, trans. Shaun Whiteside (New York: Penguin, 2005), 203. There is a small cottage industry within the humanities on the distinction between mourning and melancholia. I do not engage that debate because it moves too far away from how mourning plays a part in building shared political identities. The therapeutic literature offers two potentially helpful descriptions: "disenfranchised grief" and "complicated grief."

Disenfranchised grief occurs when a community does not acknowledge one's loss; without this external acknowledgment, it is difficult for people to recover from the loss. The prime example of disenfranchised grief is when someone in a same-sex partnership loses a partner but is not out. As a result, the person is mourning a spouse while others think the mourning is for a friend. See Kenneth Doka, "Death, Loss, and Disenfranchised Grief," in *Disenfranchised Grief: Recognizing Hidden Sorrow*, ed. Kenneth Doka (Lexington, MA: Lexington Books, 1989), 13–24; and generally, Kenneth Doka, ed.,

Disenfranchised Grief: New Directions, Challenges, and Strategies for Practice (Champaign, IL: Research Press, 2002). The therapeutic language of "complicated grief" refers to those bereaved who are unable to move on. See Robert A. Neimeyer, Holly Prigerson, and Betty Davies, "Mourning and Meaning," *American Behavioral Scientist* 46 (2002): 235–251.

11. McIvor, *Mourning in America*, 13–14.

12. One indicator of the ordering nature of mourning is the fact that people tend to discount the loss of friends or pets as relatively insignificant. Why the loss of an aunt one barely knows (or even dislikes) would be more difficult to bear than the loss of a dear and daily friend is perplexing without this sense of ordering losses based on social or familial positions. Judith Butler considers and troubles this tie between structural familial positions and mourning in *Antigone's Claim* (New York: Columbia University Press, 2002).

13. Freud's discussion of the psychic work necessary to overcome loss is instructive here; see Freud, "Mourning and Melancholia," 204–205. David McIvor explicitly links Melanie Klein's object relations theory to political mourning, too, recognizing the tremendous "protopolitical" skills gained in the process of individuation. See McIvor, *Mourning in America*, 14.

14. Judith Butler, *Precarious Life: The Powers of Mourning and Violence* (New York: Verso, 2004), 23.

15. Judith Butler, *Undoing Gender* (New York: Routledge, 2004), 19. See also Butler, *Precarious Life*, 20, where her claim is restated as "each of us is constituted politically in part by virtue of the social vulnerability of our bodies—as a site of desire and physical vulnerability, as a site of a publicity at once assertive and exposed." While the referenced chapter in *Undoing Gender* ("Beside Oneself: On the Limits of Sexual Autonomy") focuses more on gay and lesbian loss and the question of sexual autonomy, "Violence, Mourning, and Politics" in *Precarious Life* is more amenable to broader questions of loss and politics in both a national and an international context.

16. For example, an analysis of Matthew Shepard's 1998 murder using a framework of political mourning might show that political mourning after this event helped shift the trajectory of the gay rights movement and move queers from excluded to included in the "we" at the heart of American citizenship.

17. Though I might argue that all persons should be provided a dignified communal parting ceremony, such as the one held yearly by Los Angeles County for those whose bodies are unclaimed or who lack family able to pay for private burial. See Julia Wick, "This Is How Los Angeles Buries Their Unclaimed Dead," *LAist*, December 1, 2016, http://laist.com/2016/12/01/unclaimed.php. This accords with Butler's conception and Stow's defense of a shared recognition of mortalist humanism as a necessary precursor to Honig's agonistic democracy.

18. Anne Norton's and David McIvor's use of Klein's object relations theory suggests that at the heart of identity is the experience of loss. Like them, I am suggesting that loss can be a foundational experience of collective identity formation. Norton, *Reflections on Political Identity*; McIvor, *Mourning in America*.

19. Benedict Anderson, *Imagined Communities: Reflections on the Origin and Spread of Nationalism*, rev. ed. (New York: Verso, 2003).

20. Juliet Hooker, *Race and the Politics of Solidarity* (Oxford: Oxford University Press, 2009), 4.

21. As Norton and McIvor argue, object relations theory gives us a sense of how the experience of loss at the start of our lives provides us with what McIvor calls "protopo-

litical" skills. Learning how to go on, wounded and fragmented yet still alive, is a crucial step in establishing identity. See Norton, *Reflections on Political Identity*, and McIvor, *Mourning in America*.

22. While only sitting presidents, former presidents, and presidents-elect are automatically granted state funerals, the president may choose to honor anyone with a state funeral. Others may be honored by Congress with open public mourning in recognition of their service to the nation (Rosa Parks, for example). According to Donald Ritchie, associate historian at the Senate's Historical Office, "when a member of government dies, if his casket is on display in a government building—including the Capitol—he lies in state. If his casket is in any other building, he lies in repose. If the person is *not* a member of government, he lies in honor." The language of "lying in state" is explicitly political: the state itself is surrounding one's body. See David Gura, "'Lying in Repose' vs. 'Lying in State' vs. 'Lying in Honor': What's the Difference?," *NPR*, August 26, 2009, https://www.npr.org/sections/thetwo-way/2009/08/lying_in_repose_v_lying_in_sta.html.

23. John Dewey, *The Public and Its Problems* (1927; repr., Athens: University of Ohio Press, 1991).

24. Dewey, *Public and Its Problems*, 134–135.

25. Dewey, *Public and Its Problems*, 131.

26. Dewey, *Public and Its Problems*, 183–184.

27. Dewey, *Public and Its Problems*, 208.

28. The best example of this trend is David L. Eng and David Kazanjian, eds., *Loss: The Politics of Mourning* (Berkeley: University of California Press, 2002). While there are some explicitly political pieces, many of the chapters are more focused on literary efforts to communicate loss rather than the political causes of those losses. William Haver's *The Body of This Death: Historicity and Sociality in the Time of AIDS* (Stanford, CA: Stanford University Press, 1996) does something similar by carefully documenting the impossibility of survivors sharing their suffering. To be clear, these are important contributions to understanding how mourning works in a social sense. However, focusing on the communicative impossibility and creating literary echoes of loss are not the same thing as coming to terms with how politics produced that loss.

29. Jenny Edkins, *Trauma and the Memory of Politics* (Cambridge: Cambridge University Press, 2003); Wendy Brown, *Walled States, Waning Sovereignty* (New York: Zone Books, 2014).

30. Honig, *Antigone, Interrupted*, 2.

31. Honig critiques Butler and others in the "ethical turn" for what Honig terms *mortalist* humanism; Honig's concern is that the elevation of suffering and loss inappropriately prioritizes the universal equality found in death and suffering rather than the striving and contest for equality in life that is demanded by a more agonistic democratic politics. Thus, rather than a recognition of universal fragility that leads us to mourn the agonistic realities of political life (potentially even to seek to limit the reach of politics and reduce it to ethics), we should instead consider how to generate the resilience that will enable us to survive, even thrive, in an agonistic political space. See Honig, *Antigone, Interrupted*, 17, 10, 31. Honig thus reads in Sophocles's *Antigone*—a tragedy often interpreted as about mourning, burial, and loss in the vein of kinship—a deeply political strain that many commenters have overlooked. While Antigone the character may be mourning father/brother and two brothers/uncles (losses typically considered private in nature), those family members—like Antigone herself—are members of the former

royal house of Thebes (thus very much political). Antigone contests sovereign power, conspires with others, refuses to be silenced or made inactive; in short, she acts like a political agent rather than a private one. Antigone, though she is mourning, is doing so in heretofore overlooked *political* ways as she asserts her political agency. Because of these other, explicitly political acts, Honig reads Antigone as engaging not in the politics of *lamentation* but in the *politics* of lamentation. The question is not whether to mourn losses but how and to what ends. See Honig, *Antigone, Interrupted*, 2.

32. Stow, *American Mourning*.

33. Like Butler, Stow seeks to hold onto the valuable insights of shared vulnerability and dignity of each life; but like Honig, Stow wants to keep our eyes on the prize of this *life* rather than the looming universal reality of death. Death happens, but life here is what we make of it. How we approach death and how we respond to the deaths of others, then, serves as a means to refract our views on political life. For example, Stow suggests that when Americans celebrate the death of Osama bin Laden, we refuse to take democracy seriously by making him something other than human; when we separate the deaths of American soldiers in the Middle East from the politics that put them in harm's way, we fail to take political responsibility for the decisions that put them in that space; when a eulogy for a civil rights leader calls out the party that is most guilty of obstructing racial justice and the eulogist is then condemned for being partisan, we fail to understand that equality in death does not depend on equality in life. See Stow, *American Mourning*, chap. 3, 4, and 2, respectively.

34. For example, see Jay Winter, *Sites of Memory, Sites of Mourning* (Cambridge: Cambridge University Press, 2014).

35. See Marita Sturken, *Tangled Memories: The Vietnam War, the AIDS Epidemic, and the Politics of Remembering* (Berkeley: University of California Press, 1997); and Edkins, *Trauma and the Memory of Politics*.

36. Among the historians who consider how mourning shapes politics, Drew Gilpin Faust's work is more closely aligned with my goals. Faust's careful examination of how the Union's treatment of soldiers changed over the course of the Civil War, leading to a changed relationship between citizen and state itself and a much more robust federal bureaucracy, is closest to the kind of policy-focused rather than memorial-focused inquiry I suggest is more obviously political. Drew Gilpin Faust, *This Republic of Suffering: Death and the American Civil War* (New York: Alfred A. Knopf, 2008).

37. The passage continues: "Is the suffering of others also our own? In thinking that it might in fact be, societies expand the circle of the we. By the same token, social groups can, and often do, refuse to recognize the existence of others' trauma, and because of their failure they cannot achieve a moral stance. By denying the reality of others' suffering, people not only diffuse their own responsibility for suffering but often project the responsibility for their own suffering onto these others. In other words, by refusing to participate in what I will describe as the process of trauma creation, social groups restrict solidarity, leaving others to suffer alone." Jeffrey C. Alexander, *Trauma: A Social Theory* (Malden, MA: Polity Press, 2012), 6.

38. Alexander, *Trauma*, 13.

39. Alexander, *Trauma*, 15–28.

40. Verovšek, "Collective Memory."

41. John Kingdon, *Agendas, Alternatives, and Public Policies* (Boston: Longman, 2003), 94–100.

42. Kingdon, *Agendas*, 98.

43. Peter May, *Recovering from Catastrophes: Federal Disaster Relief Policy and Politics* (Westport, CT: Greenwood Press, 1985); Tom Birkland, *Lessons of Disaster: Policy Change after Catastrophic Events* (Washington, DC: Georgetown University Press, 2006).

44. Birkland, *Lessons of Disaster*, 2, referencing Tom Birkland, *After Disaster: Agenda Setting, Public Policy, and Focusing Events* (Washington, DC: Georgetown University Press, 1997).

45. Birkland, *Lessons of Disaster*, 3.

46. Stow, *American Mourning*; McIvor, *Mourning in America*.

47. Stow, for example, uses the Greeks to great effect to argue for a tragic response to death, a response that eschews certainty, hubris, and the endless tears of mourning that have marked the postplanes years. I draw on Stow, but my project is differently situated within an American political development framework rather than turning to the Greeks as a guide for better mourning practices. Nonetheless, Stow's typology of mourning is helpful for showing how political mourning can move the polity toward or away from justice.

Similarly, David McIvor's work turns to psychoanalytic theory—particularly Melanie Klein's object relations theory—to lay out the protopolitical as well as explicitly political aspects of mourning. McIvor argues that psychoanalytic accounts serve as complements to material and institutional ones, because while psychoanalysis can never fully explain political events, "political life cannot be adequately interpreted without an understanding of psychological defenses and dramas." McIvor, *Mourning in America*, 23, citing Alford and then Habermas. McIvor is absolutely correct. His deep consideration of how we come to understand ourselves in relation to our earliest experiences of loss illuminates the tenuous and fragile achievement that is subjectivity and how the subject may remain immature and certain (remaining in what Klein calls the "paranoid-schizoid position," where the world is divided into good and evil) or may mature and learn to negotiate ambivalence and uncertainty (the "depressive position"). See McIvor, *Mourning in America*, 22–29, citing Melanie Klein, "Notes on Some Schizoid Mechanisms," in *Envy and Gratitude: And Other Works, 1946–1963* (New York: Free Press, 1975). Stow and McIvor, then, come to the question of the significance of political mourning differently than I do, but their goal of honest, tragic, and humbled mourning is complementary rather than antagonistic.

48. Stow, *American Mourning*, 215, 217.

49. I take "borders of belonging" in this section's title from the title of Barbara Young Welke's book, *Law and Borders of Belonging in the Long Nineteenth-Century United States* (Cambridge: Cambridge University Press, 2008).

50. Norton, *Reflections on Political Identity*; McIvor, *Mourning in America*.

51. Connolly, *Identity\Difference*.

52. For discussion of how citizenship is not a unified category, see Elizabeth Cohen, *Semi-citizenship in Democratic Politics* (Cambridge: Cambridge University Press, 2008). For a discussion of multiple traditions of citizenship that draw on liberal, republican, and ascriptive identities, see Rogers Smith, *Civic Ideals: Conflicting Visions of Citizenship in U.S. History*. (New Haven, CT: Yale University Press, 1997).

53. Welke, *Law and the Borders of Belonging*.

54. Judith Shklar, *American Citizenship: The Quest for Inclusion* (Cambridge, MA: Harvard University Press, 1991).

55. Clarissa Rile Hayward, *How Americans Make Race: Stories, Institutions, Spaces* (Cambridge: Cambridge University Press, 2013).

56. Hayward, *How Americans Make Race*, 123.

57. Norton, *Reflections on Political Identity*, 53.

58. Norton, *Reflections on Political Identity*, 76.

59. Norton, *Reflections on Political Identity*, 89.

60. Doug McAdam, *Political Process and the Development of Black Insurgency, 1930–1970*, 2nd ed. (Chicago: University of Chicago Press, 1999), chap. 3.

61. Norton, *Reflections on Political Identity*, 89.

62. For critiques of the limits of liberal and legal accounts of responsibility, see Chad Lavin, *The Politics of Responsibility* (Champaign: University of Illinois Press, 2008); and Iris Marion Young, *Responsibility for Justice* (New York: Oxford University Press, 2011). For a critique of responsibility as calculable in advance and thus irreducible to moralism, see Shalini Satkunanandan, *Extraordinary Responsibility: Politics beyond the Moral Calculus* (Cambridge: Cambridge University Press, 2015). For a critique of the conflation of ethical and political responsibility, see Antonio Vázquez-Arroyo, *Political Responsibility: Responding to Predicaments of Power* (New York: Columbia University Press, 2016).

63. Jade Larissa Schiff, *Burdens of Political Responsibility: Narrative and the Cultivation of Responsiveness* (Cambridge: Cambridge University Press, 2014), 2.

64. Schiff, *Burdens of Political Responsibility*, 16.

65. Schiff, *Burdens of Political Responsibility*, 17–19.

66. Vázquez-Arroyo, *Political Responsibility*, ix.

67. Vázquez-Arroyo, *Political Responsibility*, 242–251.

68. Rogers Smith, "Identities, Interests, and the Future of Political Science," *Perspectives on Politics* 2 (2004): 301.

69. Kerwin Lee Klein, "On the Emergence of Memory in Historical Discourse," *Representations* 69 (2000): 127–150.

70. In *Race and the Politics of Solidarity*, Juliet Hooker suggests that the solidarity needed for democracy to function is disrupted by racial lines. As a result, before the larger polity can act in solidarity responsibly, the dominant white majority must develop the ability to see "themselves 'seeing whitely.'" See Hooker, *Race and the Politics of Solidarity*, 115.

71. McAdam, *Political Process*; Keeanga-Yamahtta Taylor, *From #BlackLivesMatter to Black Liberation* (Chicago: Haymarket Books, 2016); Francesca Polletta and James Jasper, "Collective Identity and Social Movements," *Annual Review of Sociology* 27 (2001): 283–305; Francesca Polletta, *Freedom Is an Endless Meeting: Democracy in American Social Movements* (Chicago: University of Chicago Press, 2004).

72. Recent examples of authors who assert that we should reconsider political practices in light of universal mortality include John Seery, *Political Theory for Mortals: Shades of Justice, Images of Death* (Ithaca, NY: Cornell University Press, 1996); Ruth Miller, *Law in Crisis: The Ecstatic Subject of Natural Disaster* (Stanford, CA: Stanford University Press, 2009); and Jacqueline Stevens, *States without Nations: Citizenship for Mortals* (New York: Columbia University Press, 2010). I am particularly indebted to Simon Stow, whose argument that mourning should lead to reflection has fundamentally shaped this project; see Stow, *American Mourning*.

73. A few examples of how war memorials function include Sturken, *Tangled Memories*; Edkins, *Trauma and the Memory of Politics*; and Winter, *Sites of Memory*.

74. Examples of the vast literature on the politics of memory and collective memory include John Gillis, ed., *Commemorations: The Politics of National Identity* (Princeton, NJ: Princeton University Press, 1994); Maurice Halbwachs, *On Collective Memory* (Chi-

cago: University of Chicago Press, 1992); and Katherine Verdery, *The Political Lives of Dead Bodies: Reburial and Postsocialist Change* (New York: Columbia University Press, 1999).

75. Francesca Polletta and James Jasper define collective identity as "an individual's cognitive, moral, and emotional connection with a broader community, category, practice, or institution. It is a perception of a shared status or relation, which may be imagined rather than experienced directly, and it is distinct from personal identities, although it may form part of a personal identity." Polletta and Jasper, "Collective Identity," 285.

76. See, for example, Jeffrey Alexander et al., *Cultural Trauma and Collective Identity* (Berkeley: University of California Press, 2004).

77. See Cohen, *Semi-citizenship in Democratic Politics*; and Norton, *Reflections on Political Identity*.

78. See, for example, Simon Stow's discussion of the condemnation of President Jimmy Carter's and Rev. Dr. Joseph Lowery's remarks at Coretta Scott King's funeral. Though several former presidents and other elected officials were present, some pundits argued that the funeral of a civil rights icon was not an appropriate place to demand racial justice. Stow vehemently disagrees. See Stow, *American Mourning*, chap. 2.

79. Lawrie Balfour, *The Evidence of Things Not Said: James Baldwin and the Promise of American Democracy* (Ithaca, NY: Cornell University Press, 2001).

80. Balfour, *Evidence of Things Not Said*, 36.

81. Hooker, *Race and the Politics of Solidarity*, 115.

82. Juliet Hooker, "Black Protest/White Grievance: On the Problem of White Political Imaginations Not Shaped by Loss," *South Atlantic Quarterly* 116, no. 3 (2017): 483–504.

83. Hooker, *Race and the Politics of Solidarity*, 115.

84. Lavin, *Politics of Responsibility*; Young, *Responsibility for Justice*.

85. Miriam Ticktin, "A World without Innocence," *American Ethnologist* 44, no. 4 (2017): 577–590.

86. Ticktin, "World without Innocence," 579.

87. Ticktin, "World without Innocence," 587.

88. Dora Apel, *Imagery of Lynching: Black Men, White Women, and the Mob* (New Brunswick, NJ: Rutgers University Press, 2004), 83–131.

89. Michael W. McCann, *Rights at Work: Pay Equity Reform and the Politics of Legal Mobilization* (Chicago: University of Chicago Press, 1994).

90. Butler, *Precarious Life*, chap. 1.

CHAPTER 2

1. Clarissa Rile Hayward makes a distinction between "good stories" and "bad stories." Good stories are ones that are credible, legitimate, and coherent; they are widely believed to be true. This is not to say that these good stories actually have all those characteristics, however, and as her work shows, the stories Americans tell about race regularly violate all those aspects. The good story (widely believed to be true) about the role of government at this time was that regulation of workplaces was an illegitimate use of state power. After the fire, however, this story became a bad story such that political intervention into the workplace became widely acceptable. The change in stories, Hayward suggests, is most effective when it is institutionalized and objectified through

agencies such as the Factory Investigating Commission. See Clarissa Rile Hayward, *How American Make Race: Stories, Institutions, Spaces* (Cambridge: Cambridge University Press, 2013), 29–30.

2. Matthew Guterl, *The Color of Race in America, 1900–1940* (Cambridge, MA: Harvard University Press, 2001).

3. This claim is aligned with the work of Iris Marion Young, who argues that we should incorporate different ways of communicating (she specifies greeting, rhetoric, and storytelling) to realize a truly democratic politics. See Iris Marion Young, "Communication and the Other: Beyond Deliberative Democracy," in *Intersecting Voices: Dilemmas of Gender, Political Philosophy, and Policy* (Princeton, NJ: Princeton University Press, 1997), 60–74.

4. Several scholarly works analyze the 1909 strike in terms of class, gender, and Progressive politics. For an outstanding discussion of labor history and the resultant Progressive political order, see Richard Greenwald, *The Triangle Fire, the Protocols of Peace, and Industrial Democracy in Progressive Era New York* (Philadelphia: Temple University Press, 2005). See also Leon Stein, *The Triangle Fire* (Ithaca, NY: Cornell University Press, 2001); David von Drehle, *Triangle: The Fire That Changed America* (New York: Atlantic Monthly Press, 2003); and Jo Ann Argersinger, *The Triangle Fire: A Brief History with Documents* (New York: Bedford/St. Martin's Press, 2009). Additional resources from a feminist perspective include Nancy Schrom Dye, *As Equals and As Sisters: Feminism, the Labor Movement, and the Women's Trade Union League of New York* (Columbia: University of Missouri Press, 1980); Susan Lehrer, *Origins of Protective Labor Legislation for Women, 1905–1925* (Albany: State University of New York Press, 1987); Annelise Orleck, *Common Sense and a Little Fire: Women and Working-Class Politics in the United States, 1900–1965* (Chapel Hill: University of North Carolina Press, 1995); and Meredith Tax, *The Rising of the Women: Feminist Solidarity and Class Conflict, 1880–1917* (Champaign: University of Illinois Press, 2001).

5. Intersectionality is an apt description for the type of analysis adopted in this study. Because of space constraints, I cannot fully address the complex intersections between race, class, and gender here. My point is not that these forces do not influence each other in complicated ways, but that other scholars have already discussed in detail the relationships between gender and class in the case of the Triangle Fire. However, scholars have not paid adequate attention to the role race played in constructing events before and after the fire. Thus this inquiry, while not truly intersectional, contributes to the literature on intersectionality by considering the role of a previously overlooked category in this case.

6. Von Drehle, *Triangle*, 108.

7. Women were the lowest-paid workers in the ladies' garment industry. See Dye, *As Equals*, 19–20, 23.

8. Dye, *As Equals*, 8.

9. Dye, *As Equals*, 9–12.

10. The AFL's exclusionary tendencies have been well documented by David Roediger, *Working toward Whiteness: How America's Immigrants Became White* (New York: Basic Books, 2005); Dye, *As Equals*; and Greenwald, *Triangle Fire*.

11. Roediger, *Working toward Whiteness*, 91.

12. For a discussion of the complex interplay between racial classification, immigration, political identity, and class politics in the United States at this time, see Roediger, *Working toward Whiteness*; Theodore Allen, *The Invention of the White Race*, vol. 1,

Racial Oppression and Social Control (New York: Verso, 1994); Noel Ignatiev, *How the Irish Became White* (New York: Routledge, 2009); Ian Haney López, *White by Law: The Legal Construction of Race* (New York: New York University Press: 1996); and Alexander Saxton, *The Rise and Fall of the White Republic: Class Politics and Mass Culture in Nineteenth-Century America* (New York: Verso, 2003).

13. This process calls to mind Claire Jean Kim's work on racial triangulation in *Bitter Fruit: The Politics of Black-Korean Conflict in New York City* (New Haven, CT: Yale University Press, 2000). Kim demonstrates how conflict between nonwhites results from white privilege rather than their own inherent differences. White power constructs clashes between nonwhites as natural, but does not disturb the racial hierarchy that keeps whites on top.

14. The litany of factory abuses is long. Argersinger offers a concise discussion in *Triangle Fire*, 8–9 and 56–57 (excerpting Clara Lemlich, "Life in the Shop," *New York Evening Journal*, November 26, 1909).

15. For additional information on the Newark High Street Fire, see Mary Alden Hopkins, "1910 Newark Factory Fire," *McClure's Magazine*, April 1911, http://old newark.com/histories/factoryfirearticle.php.

16. Stein, *Triangle Fire*, 26–27.

17. Von Drehle, *Triangle*, 52.

18. For an overview of the grim conditions workers faced, as well as workers' goals, see Greenwald, *Triangle Fire*, 26–48.

19. Argersinger, *Triangle Fire*, 12.

20. Argersinger, *Triangle Fire*, 14.

21. Argersinger, *Triangle Fire*, 14.

22. The strike could never have gotten off the ground without the financial and organizational support of the WTUL. But the more socialist leanings of the ILGWU and the more liberal leanings of the WTUL eventually led to conflict over what kind of agreement was satisfactory: the union wanted union recognition and the right to collectively bargain, while many of the wealthy members of the WTUL focused on improving employment conditions and wages. As a result, when the Triangle owners offered better terms without union recognition, the union refused the offer while wealthy patrons in the WTUL urged the union to accept. Similarly, although both suffragists and socialist women wanted the vote, the tension over an alliance based on class or on gender made any cross-class endeavor fraught. See, for example, "Women Socialists Rebuff Suffragists," *New York Times*, December 20, 1909, p. 5.

23. Elizabeth Anne Payne, *Reform, Labor, and Feminism: Margaret Dreier Robins and the Women's Trade Union League* (Urbana: University of Illinois Press, 1988).

24. Von Drehle, *Triangle*, 52.

25. "College Girls as Pickets in a Strike," *New York Times Magazine*, December 19, 1909, p. 5. See also von Drehle, *Triangle*, 75. Von Drehle asserts that there was an explicit decision to keep union leaders off the picket lines while putting middle-class reformers front and center. See von Drehle, *Triangle*, 52.

26. "Girl Strikers Tell the Rich Their Woes," *New York Times*, December 16, 1909, p. 3.

27. Miss Milholland, along with her escort, Lt. Henry Torney (formerly of West Point), was later arrested merely for following officers to the Mercer Street station and inquiring why fourteen strikers were arrested. "Inez Milholland Held in Strike Case," *New York Times*, January 18, 1910, p. 1.

28. For proposals about how advocates might better deal with these social cleavages by addressing them head-on, see Cathy Cohen, *The Boundaries of Blackness: AIDS and the Breakdown of Black Politics* (Chicago: University of Chicago Press, 1999); Sharon Kurtz, *Workplace Justice: Organizing Multi-identity Movements* (Minneapolis: University of Minnesota Press, 2002); and Dara Strolovitch, *Affirmative Advocacy: Race, Class, and Gender in Interest Group Politics* (Chicago: University of Chicago Press, 2007). All of these authors discuss how crosscutting identities can trouble advocacy efforts when they are not explicitly addressed.

29. See Roediger, *Working toward Whiteness*, 72–78.

30. "Girl Strikers Tell the Rich Their Woes," 3.

31. Von Drehle, *Triangle*, 60.

32. Von Drehle, *Triangle*, 61. While some Italian immigrant and native-born workers joined with the primarily Jewish strikers, the numbers did not entirely match the percentages of employees. This is another indication that perceptions about race played a significant role in the strike.

33. "Girl Strikers Tell," 3.

34. "Photos and Illustrations: Shirtwaist Strike and Other Strikes," *Remembering the 1911 Triangle Fire*, image 5780pb32f27d, https://trianglefire.ilr.cornell.edu/slides/277.html#screen (accessed November 5, 2020). It is remarkably difficult to discern what, precisely, the strikers' priorities were. Greenwald reports that at the meeting before the big walkout in November, Samuel Gompers (who, as head of the AFL, supported unionism in general but was reluctant to support strikes and even more reluctant to support strikes by these workers) suggested that strikers limit their focus to a 10 percent wage increase, union recognition, and an end to police violence against strikers. Greenwald, *Triangle Fire*, 32. During the Uprising of 20,000, the ILGWU settled with several shops for "union recognition; shop-committee arbitration for piece-rates; a union shop, or at least union preferences when hiring; and an end to charges for thread, needles, and electricity." Greenwald, *Triangle Fire*, 33.

35. Argersinger, *Triangle Fire*, 14.

36. Elizabeth Mensch, "The History of Mainstream Legal Thought," in *The Politics of Law: A Progressive Critique*, 3rd ed., ed. David Kairys (New York: Basic Books, 1998), 32.

37. Greenwald, *Triangle Fire*, 15–16.

38. This follows from Michael Frazer's argument that sympathy with *particular* others, rather than generalized sympathy, helps generate justice. See Michael Frazer, *The Enlightenment of Sympathy: Justice and the Moral Sentiments in the Eighteenth Century and Today* (New York: Oxford University Press, 2010), 110–111.

39. In her introduction to a *Chicago Sunday Tribune* story about the fire, Argersinger writes, "According to newspapers in small towns and large cities, popular interest in the fire was unusually intense, and readers pored over every detail of the tragedy." See Argersinger, *Triangle Fire*, 76.

40. Stein, *Triangle Fire*, 73.

41. Stein, *Triangle Fire*, 22–23.

42. See William Shepherd, "Eyewitness at the Triangle," *Remembering the 1911 Triangle Fire*, http://trianglefire.ilr.cornell.edu/primary/testimonials/ootss_WilliamShepherd.html (accessed November 5, 2020).

43. Von Drehle, *Triangle*, 1.

44. Stein, *Triangle Fire*, 107–108.

45. Argersinger, *Triangle Fire*, 22–23.

46. Greenwald, *Triangle Fire*, 141–145. Eight caskets were buried that day: seven with unidentified bodies and an eighth with remains that could not be matched to bodies: see Stein, *Triangle Fire*, 155. Only recently were the final victims identified. See Joseph Berger, "100 Years Later, the Roll of the Dead in a Factory Fire Is Complete," *New York Times*, February 20, 2011, https://www.nytimes.com/2011/02/21/nyregion/21triangle.html.

47. Greenwald, *Triangle Fire*, 138–141; Stein, *Triangle Fire*, 148.

48. Stein, *Triangle Fire*, 151.

49. "120,000 Pay Tribute to the Fire Victims," *New York Times*, April 6, 1911, p. 1.

50. There is no consensus regarding how many people watched or participated in the ILGWU procession, but somewhere between 300,000 and 400,000 seems reasonable. Argersinger writes that 350,000 people participated (*Triangle Fire*, 87–88); Stein writes that "the final police estimate was that about 400,000 had seen the parade and of these about one-third had marched in it" (*Triangle Fire*, 156); and von Drehle notes that "some 350,000 people participated in a funeral march for the Triangle dead" (*Triangle*, 193). Other processions with thousands in attendance accompanied the bodies from the Manhattan morgue to Cypress Hills Cemetery. "120,000 Pay Tribute."

51. "120,000 Pay Tribute," 1.

52. Stein, *Triangle Fire*, 154.

53. See Argersinger, *Triangle Fire*, cover. See also Stein, *Triangle Fire*, 150.

54. Stein, *Triangle Fire*, 149–157.

55. Stein, *Triangle Fire*, 152–153.

56. Anne Norton, *Reflections on Political Identity* (Baltimore: Johns Hopkins University Press, 1988), 89.

57. Judith Butler, *Undoing Gender* (New York: Routledge, 2004), 19. See also Butler, *Precarious Life: The Powers of Mourning and Violence* (New York: Verso, 2004), 20, where her claim is restated as "each of us is constituted politically in part by virtue of the social vulnerability of our bodies—as a site of desire and physical vulnerability, as a site of a publicity at once assertive and exposed." Stow seeks to rebut Bonnie Honig's claim in *Antigone, Interrupted* that such mortalist humanism constrains the political by arguing that this kind of embodied equality is an achievement rather than natural (a stance he attributes to Butler) and a necessary precursor to any democratic politics. See Bonnie Honig, *Antigone, Interrupted* (Cambridge: Cambridge University Press, 2013); and Simon Stow, *American Mourning: Tragedy, Democracy, Resilience* (Cambridge: Cambridge University Press, 2017), 101.

58. Sharon Krause, *Civil Passions: Moral Sentiments and Democratic Deliberation* (Princeton, NJ: Princeton University Press, 2008), 3.

59. John Dewey, *The Public and Its Problems* (1927; repr., Athens: University of Ohio Press, 1991), 131, 134–135.

60. See William Graham Sumner, *What Social Classes Owe Each Other* (1883; repr., Caldwell, ID: Caxton Press, 1983); and John Locke, *Second Treatise on Government* (1690; repr., Indianapolis, IN: Hackett, 1980).

61. Jane Addams, *Democracy and Social Ethics* (1902; repr., Champaign: University of Illinois Press, 2002).

62. Argersinger, *Triangle Fire*, 39–42, excerpting Arthur McFarlane, "Fire and the Skyscraper: The Problem of Protecting Workers in New York's Tower Factories," *McClure's Magazine*, September 1911, pp. 466–472.

63. Ken Kersch argues that analogizing business owners to criminals was a common tactic used by Progressive reformers to gain access to "private" business records. See Ken Kersch, "The Reconstruction of Constitutional Privacy Rights and the New American State," *Studies in American Political Development* 16 (2002): 61–87.

64. Stein, *Triangle Fire*, 121.

65. It is worth asking if Blanck's and Harris's status as Jewish immigrants mattered. Both emigrated in the late 1880s and, after working their way up from sweatshops, came to own several successful factories along the East Coast. Von Drehle, *Triangle*, 48–54. Having arrived in the United States with nothing thirty years before the fire, their identities were surely complicated. They were emblematically American in terms of their success in business. Still, it is likely that the wider public viewed them as foreign. The *New York Times*, which had supported owners during the 1909 strike, interviewed Blanck after the fire and described him as "an average type of successful business man— short, stocky, and unemotional." Argersinger, *Triangle Fire*, 79, excerpting "Partners' Account of the Disaster," *New York Times*, March 26, 1911. While the indictment may have been linked to their foreignness, the acquittal may have been linked to their Americanness and to the stark contrast between their material success and the poverty of the more recent, poorer immigrants testifying against them. All twelve men of the jury were "from business and the trades," and many appear to have been immigrants, too. Von Drehle, *Triangle*, 254.

66. For a discussion of how contemporary legal understandings prevented the conviction of Blanck and Harris, see Arthur McEvoy, "The Triangle Shirtwaist Fire of 1911: Social Change, Industrial Accidents, and the Evolution of Common-Sense Causality," *Law and Social Inquiry* 20 (Spring 1995): 621–651.

67. See Argersinger, *Triangle Fire*, 110–111, excerpting "147 Dead, Nobody Guilty," *Literary Digest*, January 6, 1912.

68. Stein, *Triangle Fire*, 135.

69. Stein, *Triangle Fire*, 39 (emphasis added).

70. Al Smith was a New York street kid who, at thirty-eight, became the leader of the New York State Assembly, thanks to his Tammany Hall connections. Smith was also an adept politician who cared about the working class, and the Triangle Factory was in his district. He visited families of the deceased and accompanied some families to the morgue to identify their kin. According to Frances Perkins, Smith transformed the reformist-but-ineffective Committee of Safety into an effective legislative committee. See von Drehle, *Triangle*, 200–218.

71. Greenwald, *Triangle Fire*, 71. The committee received not only public support but also support from the influential Tammany Hall machine. Greenwald, *Triangle Fire*, 213.

72. See Greenwald, *Triangle Fire*, chap. 5–7, for a discussion of the FIC's expanding mandate. Also see Stein, *Triangle Fire*, 207–210; von Drehle, *Triangle*, 212–218, 259, 267; and Argersinger, *Triangle Fire*, 31–33.

73. Frances Perkins delivered a speech in 1964 recalling the fire and its effects on the public of New York. She said that the fire "made a terrible impression on the people of the State of New York. I can't begin to tell you how disturbed the people were everywhere. It was as though we had all done something wrong. It shouldn't have been. We were sorry. Mea culpa! Mea culpa! We didn't want it that way. We hadn't intended to have 147 girls and boys killed in a factory. It was a terrible thing for the people of the City of New York and the State of New York to face." The fire also made a great impression on then assemblyman Al Smith. When Perkins and her friends approached Smith to recommend the

formation of a government committee, he argued that if left to the governor, a committee would be formed but it would not have the power to do anything. Smith instead suggested a legislative committee, because it could propose laws. By the time the FIC completed its report, Smith was speaker of the house and ensured that the FIC's recommendations were turned into law. Frances Perkins, lecture at Cornell University School of Industrial and Labor Relations, September 20, 1964, https://trianglefire.ilr.cornell.edu/primary/lectures/FrancesPerkinsLecture.html?CFID=5042574&CFTOKEN=23588311.

74. Greenwald, *Triangle Fire*, 153.

75. Arthur McEvoy argues that the trial of Triangle's owners led to a new distinction between public and private space. As a result, what had been seen as solely a private contracting situation became subject to government regulation. See McEvoy, "Triangle Shirtwaist Fire."

76. Greenwald argues that Triangle contributed to the institutionalization and bureaucratization of government oversight of industry, which ended the push toward participation that previously had characterized industrial labor unions. See Greenwald, *Triangle Fire*.

77. In *The Color of Race in America, 1900–1940* (Cambridge, MA: Harvard University Press, 2001), Matthew Guterl analyzes the shift from fear of immigrants to Negrophobia. He argues that fears in the United States about race were very different in 1900 than they were in 1940. Guterl traces this shift through discursive analysis of several leading commentators, including nativist Madison Grant and African American scholar W.E.B. DuBois. For another discussion about how racial discourse in America shifted over time and increasingly focused on the poles of white and black, see Matthew Frye Jacobson, *Whiteness of a Different Color: European Immigrants and the Alchemy of Race* (Cambridge, MA: Harvard University Press, 1998).

78. For a much deeper tracing of the rise of the language of ethnicity as opposed to race, see Roediger, *Working toward Whiteness*, chap. 1.

79. Argersinger, *Triangle Fire*, 5; Orleck, *Common Sense*, 58.

80. Von Drehle, *Triangle*, 193; Argersinger, *Triangle Fire*, 24.

81. Quoted in Stein, *Triangle Fire*, x.

82. Roediger, for one, argues that it is important to preserve an awareness of the "messiness" of intra-white contests about race as this contributes to our awareness of how whiteness is also a social construction. His project is aligned with this book, as I am trying to expose how intra-white conflict was erased from the history of Triangle. See Roediger, *Working toward Whiteness*, chap. 2.

83. See Guterl, *Color of Race*, 11–12, 122. According to census data, the population of African Americans in New York City had stayed remarkably stable between 1810 and 1870 (hovering between 10,000 and 12,000) and then increased rapidly. Between 1880 and 1900, the number of African Americans in New York City tripled (from 19,663 to 60,666), and the African American population increased considerably each year thereafter—to 91,709 in 1910 (1.9%) and 152,467 by 1920 (2.7%). See U.S. Census Bureau, "Table 33: New York—Race and Hispanic Origin for Selected Large Cities and Other Places: Earliest Census to 1990," in "Historical Census Statistics on Population Totals by Race, 1790 to 1990, and by Hispanic Origin, 1790 to 1990, for Large Cities and Other Urban Places in the United States," by Campbell Gibson and Kay Jung, U.S. Census Bureau Working Paper no. 76, February 2005, https://www.census.gov/content/dam/Census/library/working-papers/2005/demo/POP-twps0076.pdf.

84. Hayward, *How Americans Make Race*, chap. 2.

85. Roediger notes that the language of ethnicity began in close proximity to this event. As a result, from the beginning to the middle of the twentieth century, "Irish" shifted from a racial category to an ethnic one. See Roediger, *Working toward Whiteness*, chap.1, esp. 10–13.

86. McEvoy, "Triangle Shirtwaist Fire," 644.

87. See, for example, Karen Brodkin, *How Jews Became White Folks and What That Says about Race in America* (New Brunswick, NJ: Rutgers University Press, 1998).

88. Janet Abu-Lughod also argues that while the Triangle Fire achieved significant gains for white workers, it did not benefit African Americans, who were and continue to be excluded from the garment trades. See Janet Abu-Lughod, *Race, Space, and Riots in Chicago, New York, and Los Angeles* (New York: Oxford University Press, 2007), 16, 36n38.

89. See Butler, *Undoing Gender*, 17–39.

90. Lipsitz and Katznelson both point out the deeply racialized exclusions from the benefits of the New Deal. See George Lipsitz, *The Possessive Investment in Whiteness: How White People Profit from Identity Politics*, rev. and expanded ed. (Philadelphia: Temple University Press, 2006); and Ira Katznelson, *When Affirmative Action Was White: An Untold History of Racial Inequality in Twentieth-Century America* (New York: W. W. Norton, 2005).

CHAPTER 3

1. For movement building in the civil rights movement, see Doug McAdam, *Political Process and the Development of Black Insurgency, 1930–1970*, 2nd ed. (Chicago: University of Chicago Press, 1999); Aldon Morris, *The Origins of the Civil Rights Movement: Black Communities Organizing for Change* (New York: Free Press, 1984); and Francesca Polletta, *Freedom Is an Endless Meeting: Democracy in American Social Movements* (Chicago: University of Chicago Press, 2004). For legal tactics, see Mark Tushnet, *The NAACP's Legal Strategy against Segregated Education, 1925–1950* (Chapel Hill: University of North Carolina Press, 2004). For the international relations aspect, see Derrick A. Bell Jr., "*Brown v. Board of Education* and the Interest-Convergence Dilemma," *Harvard Law Review*, 93, no. 3 (January 1980): 518–533; Mary L. Dudziak, *Cold War Civil Rights: Race and the Image of American Democracy* (Princeton, NJ: Princeton University Press, 2000); Azza Salama Layton, *International Political and Civil Rights Policies in the United States, 1941–1960* (New York: Cambridge University Press, 2000); and Carol Anderson, *Eyes Off the Prize: The United Nations and the African American Struggle for Human Rights, 1944–1955* (New York: Cambridge University Press, 2003).

2. Here, I follow McAdam's exhortation in the introduction to the reissue of *Political Process* to take seriously the effects of interpretive processes on constructions of collective identities, a call similar to the one made by Rogers Smith in "Identities, Interests, and the Future of Political Science," *Perspectives on Politics* 2 (2004): 301–312.

3. I am not arguing that Till's death was the true start of the civil rights movement, as Clenora Hudson-Weems does in *Emmett Till: The Sacrificial Lamb of the Civil Rights Movement* (Troy, MI: Bedford, 1994); nor am I claiming that without Till's death, the civil rights movement would never have happened. Instead, I am suggesting that the mourning after Till's death enabled white Americans to see the circumstances of African Americans in new ways. It also, of course, helped create in-group solidarity.

4. McAdam, *Political Process*, intro.

5. Both Dudziak, in *Cold War Civil Rights*, and Layton, in *International Political and Civil Rights Policies*, argue that elites saw the "race problem" as a significant problem for American foreign policy. The perception of vulnerability to Communism overlays with the bodily vulnerability to racial violence in interesting ways depending on one's place in the fight about white supremacy.

6. For an explanation of white innocence, see James Baldwin, "My Dungeon Shook: Letter to My Nephew on the One Hundredth Anniversary of Emancipation," in *The Fire Next Time* (New York: Vintage International, 1993), 1–11. For the argument that we live in a white democracy, see Joel Olson, *The Abolition of White Democracy* (Minneapolis: University of Minnesota Press, 2004). There, Olson argues that American democracy is a white democracy, where "whiteness . . . functions as a norm in which racial privilege is sedimented into the background of social life as the 'natural outcome' of ordinary practices and individual choices" (74).

7. Gene Roberts and Hank Klibanoff, *The Race Beat: The Press, the Civil Rights Struggle, and the Awakening of a Nation* (New York: Alfred A. Knopf, 2006), 86. This is not to dismiss the long-standing important work done by heroic members of the African American press to highlight white violence against blacks, coverage such as was called for and celebrated by Ida B. Wells in *Southern Horrors and Other Writings: The Anti-lynching Campaign of Ida B. Wells, 1892-1900*, ed. Jacqueline Jones Royster (New York: Bedford/St. Martin's Press, 1996).

8. McAdam, *Political Process.*

9. Frederick C. Harris uses public opinion polls to demonstrate that Till's death had a greater effect on black organizing than any other event prior to 1966. Harris's work powerfully demonstrates how the black community was affected. This book differs slightly in that it is trying to trace how a white majority that had been uninterested in black oppression became at least sympathetic, if not enthusiastic, about civil rights claims. Frederick C. Harris, "It Takes a Tragedy to Arouse Them: Collective Memory and Collective Action during the Civil Rights Movement," *Social Movement Studies* 5 (2006): 19–43.

10. Jane Addams, *Democracy and Social Ethics* (1902; repr., Champaign: University of Illinois Press, 2001).

11. For insightful discussions of the power of lynching images and succinct discussions of lynching practices, see James Allen et al., *Without Sanctuary: Lynching Photography in America* (Santa Fe: Twin Palms, 2000); Dora Apel, *Imagery of Lynching: Black Men, White Women, and the Mob* (New Brunswick, NJ: Rutgers University Press, 2004); and Michal Belknap, *Federal Law and Southern Order: Racial Violence and Constitutional Conflict in the Post-Brown South* (Athens: University of Georgia Press, 1987). In relation to Till's lynching, see also Jacqueline Goldsby, "The High and Low Tech of It: The Meaning of Lynching and the Death of Emmett Till," *Yale Journal of Criticism* 9 (1996): 245–282, as well as the more recent work by Timothy B. Tyson, *The Blood of Emmett Till* (New York: Simon and Schuster, 2017).

12. Robert Cover, *Narrative, Violence, and the Law: The Essays of Robert Cover*, ed. Martha Minow, Michael Ryan, and Austin Sarat (Ann Arbor: University of Michigan Press, 1995), 203–238.

13. Northern law was perhaps subtler but often equally violent and targeting. See, for example, Matthew D. Lassiter and Joseph Crespino, "Introduction: The End of Southern History," in *The Myth of Southern Exceptionalism*, ed. Matthew D. Lassiter and Joseph Crespino (New York: Oxford University Press, 2010), 3–22.

14. David Blight argues that to "heal" from the wounds of the Civil War, white northerners chose not to challenge white supremacy in the South. See David Blight, *Race and Reunion: The Civil War in American Memory* (Cambridge, MA: Harvard University Press, 2001). Michal Belknap argues that while Congress initially provided means for federal intervention, the Supreme Court shut down that avenue of redress beginning with *United States v. Cruikshank* in 1876 and culminating in *United States v. Harris* in 1883; Congress itself then proved stubbornly resistant to legislative campaigns by the NAACP and other groups. See Belknap, *Federal Law and Southern Order*, 1–26.

15. Wells, *Southern Horrors*.

16. William Bradford Huie, "The Shocking Story of Approved Killing in Mississippi," *Look*, January 24, 1956, https://www.pbs.org/wgbh/americanexperience/features/till -killers-confession/.

17. Hugh Stephen Whitaker, "A Case Study in Southern Justice: The Emmett Till Case" (master's thesis, Florida State University, 1963), 2–16.

18. Stephen Whitfield, *A Death in the Delta: The Story of Emmett Till* (New York: Free Press, 1988), 1–14.

19. Wells, *Southern Horrors*.

20. Christine Harold and Kevin Michael DeLuca, "Behold the Corpse: Violent Images and the Case of Emmett Till," *Rhetoric and Public Affairs* 8 (2005): 263–286; see also James Allen et al., *Without Sanctuary*.

21. Harold and DeLuca, "Behold the Corpse," 269.

22. The number of registered black voters in Mississippi had fallen precipitously in the first half of the 1950s. Smith and Lee were both actively working to register black voters and were having moderate success in their work. Their murders are clearly related to their voter registration and mobilization efforts. See Roberts and Klibanoff, *The Race Beat*, 80–83.

23. The *Chicago Defender* ran images of Lee's open casket funeral and reported that over one thousand people attended his funeral in Belzoni, Mississippi. I have not been able to locate any similar images or even many reports of Lee's death in mainstream media. See "Exclusive Pictures of Lynch Victim's Funeral," *Chicago Defender*, May 28, 1955, p. 5.

24. Roberts and Klibanoff report that southern press coverage focused more on the "questionable" legality of Smith's efforts to use absentee ballots for African American voters rather than questioning the circumstances of his death and the unwillingness of witnesses to identify the shooter. See Roberts and Klibanoff, *Race Beat*, 81.

25. Belknap, *Federal Law and Southern Order*, 32.

26. Tushnet, *The NAACP's Legal Strategy*.

27. See, for example, the inflammatory anti-*Brown* booklet *Black Monday* (Winona, MS: Association of Citizens' Councils, 1955), penned by Mississippi circuit court judge Tom Brady in 1955 and printed with the support of the White Citizen's Councils of Mississippi. Brady argues that segregation is a breach of citizens' rights to free association. Brady won a seat on the Mississippi Supreme Court in 1963.

28. See James Patterson, *Brown v. Board of Education: A Civil Rights Milestone and Its Troubled Legacy* (Oxford: Oxford University Press, 2001); and George Lewis, *Massive Resistance: The White Response to the Civil Rights Movement* (New York: Hodder Arnold/Oxford, 2006), 27–69.

29. Morris, *Origins of the Civil Rights Movement*, 15.

30. Gerald Rosenberg argues that *Brown v. Board* and the delay between decision and implementation exemplifies his "constrained court" view that courts are not the dynamic policy makers some have claimed, while George Lovell and Michael McCann argue that courts are a part of the complex political context at any point, a context that sometimes empowers courts and sometimes ignores their decrees. My argument is more in line with Lovell and McCann's constitutive view. My argument is not about the efficacy of courts, but about a larger view of law as it relates to conceptions of political belonging. See Gerald Rosenberg, *The Hollow Hope: Can Courts Bring about Social Change?* (Chicago: University of Chicago Press, 1991); and George Lovell and Michael McCann, "A Tangled Legacy: Federal Courts and Democratic Inclusion," in *The Politics of Democratic Inclusion*, ed. Christina Wolbrecht and Rodney E. Hero (Philadelphia: Temple University Press, 2005), 257–280.

31. Mamie Till-Mobley and Christopher Benson, *Death of Innocence: The Story of the Hate Crime That Changed America* (Newark, NJ: One World/Ballantine Books, 2003).

32. See interviews with Till's seventh-grade classmates in *American Experience: The Murder of Emmett Till*, directed by Stanley Nelson, written by Marcia Smith (WGBH Educational Foundation, 2003), DVD, 11:45–12:30.

33. Till-Mobley and Benson, *Death of Innocence*, 19.

34. *American Experience*; Till-Mobley and Benson, *Death of Innocence*, 19–25.

35. Tyson notes that by the trial a few weeks later, this interaction had morphed into an assault, although numerous witnesses focus primarily on "ugly remarks" or "smart talk" as the real issue. Tyson, *Blood of Emmett Till*, 53.

36. Tyson, *Blood of Emmett Till*, 53–54.

37. Numerous texts take up the question of what may or may not have happened between Carolyn Bryant and Emmett Till. The best account of the circumstances are found in Whitfield's *A Death in the Delta*, but there are numerous other sources, including, among others, Till-Mobley and Benson's *Death of Innocence*; Henry Hampton and Stephen Fayer's *Voices of Freedom: An Oral History of the Civil Rights Movement from the 1950s through the 1980s* (New York: Bantam Books, 1990); and the excellent compilation of contemporary news accounts in Christopher Metress, ed., *The Lynching of Emmett Till: A Documentary Narrative* (Charlottesville: University of Virginia Press, 2002). The makers of two documentaries try to determine what exactly happened by interviewing some of Till's friends and relatives who were present that day. Even after one views these interviews, however, the circumstances remain unclear. See *The Untold Story of Emmett Louis Till*, directed by Keith Beauchamp (New York: ThinkFilm, 2005), DVD; and *American Experience*.

38. *Untold Story*, 8:45–9:00. An alternate reading is that he whistled in appreciation of a move in a game of checkers, and given his earlier impudence toward Bryant, everyone present interpreted the whistle as directed at her. See Till-Mobley and Benson, *Death of Innocence*, 122, for a review of the various stories about "the whistle."

39. *American Experience*, 19:30.

40. Tyson, *Blood of Emmett Till*, 54.

41. Whitfield, *Death in the Delta*, 19.

42. Till-Mobley and Benson, *Death of Innocence*, 123.

43. Both of the authoritative documentaries on the Till case include interview footage with Moses Wright to this effect. See *American Experience*, and *Eyes on the Prize: America's Civil Rights Years*, episode 1, "Awakenings, 1954–1956," directed by Judith Vecchione, created by Henry Hampton (Los Angeles: Pacific Arts, 1992), DVD.

44. Murray Kempton, "He Went All the Way," in *Reporting Civil Rights, Part I: American Journalism, 1941–1963*, ed. Clayborne Carson, David J. Garrow, Bill Kovach, and Carol Polsgrove (New York: Library of America, 2003), 214–216.

45. President Eisenhower never responded. Whitfield, *Death in the Delta*, 74–75. Till-Bradley's telegraph to the White House reads as follows: "I the mother of Emmett Louis Still [*sic*] am pleading that you personally see that justice is meted out to all persons involved in the beastly lynching of my son in Money Miss. Awaiting a direct reply from you." See the Eisenhower Library's online archives for a scanned image of this telegraph, at https://www.eisenhowerlibrary.gov/sites/default/files/research/online -documents/civil-rights-emmett-till-case/1955-09-02-bradley-to-dde.pdf (accessed March 9, 2020).

46. Till-Mobley and Benson, *Death of Innocence*, 118–121.

47. Till-Mobley and Benson, *Death of Innocence*, 120.

48. Till-Mobley and Benson, *Death of Innocence*, 138–148.

49. Till-Mobley and Benson, *Death of Innocence*, 130.

50. *Untold Story*, 23:30.

51. Till-Mobley and Benson, *Death of Innocence*, 130.

52. Goldsby, "The High and Low Tech of It," 256.

53. "Homecoming of a Lynch Victim," *Life*, September 12, 1955, p. 47.

54. Till-Mobley and Benson, *Death of Innocence*, 132 (emphasis in original).

55. Till-Mobley and Benson, *Death of Innocence*, 132.

56. Till-Mobley and Benson, *Death of Innocence*, 133.

57. Till-Mobley and Benson, *Death of Innocence*, 134–136.

58. Till-Mobley and Benson, *Death of Innocence*, 136.

59. Till-Mobley and Benson, *Death of Innocence*, 139.

60. Like all crowd estimates, there is wild variation regarding how many people viewed Till's body. The *Chicago Defender*, probably the most reliable, estimates that fifty thousand streamed by the casket at the funeral on Saturday, September 10, while over the four days that followed, 250,000 viewed the body, first at the A. A. Rayner and Sons Funeral Home and then at the funeral service at Chicago's Roberts Temple Church of God in Christ. See Robert Elliott, "Thousands at Rites for Till," *Chicago Defender*, September 10, 1955, p. 1; and "Hundreds Weep, Faint at Sight," *Chicago Defender*, September 17, 1955, p. 2. *Jet Magazine*, the popular-interest African American weekly of the period, gives an estimate of 600,000 who viewed the body "in an unending stream." See "Nation Horrified by Murder of Kidnaped Youth," *Jet*, September 15, 1955, p. 8. Vecchione and Hampton's *Eyes on the Prize* includes footage of viewers passing by the open casket. They are moving quickly and without pause, giving each person only two or three strides in which to view the body. Given that evidence and the claims of local media, the larger numbers are plausible.

61. "Hundreds Weep." Nurses and ushers stood near the casket to assist viewers who became distraught, as seen in footage provided of the funeral service in *Eyes on the Prize*, *American Experience*, and *Untold Story*. While there is no way to empirically confirm that actually viewing a body was more significant than viewing pictures of a body or reading accounts of a death, it does seem plausible that the—always uncanny—experience of being in a room with a corpse is different and more affectively intense than the more distant experience of viewing an image or reading an account.

62. For an overview of coverage by both African American and mainstream media, see Michael Randolph Oby, "Black Press Coverage of the Emmett Till Lynching as a Catalyst to the Civil Rights Movement" (master's thesis, Georgia State University, 2007).

63. *Jet* was ubiquitous in most African American–owned or frequented places of business where one waited, barbershops and beauty parlors in particular. Thus, while the figure of 425,000 may not seem that high, each copy was likely read by several people not themselves subscribers. The accounts of several civil rights activists discuss the extraordinary staying power that Till's death had in terms of community discussion. For weeks after the death and again after the trial, African American communities across the nation continued to discuss Till's death. See Whitfield, *Death in the Delta*, 90–100, for several examples. For a discussion of black counterpublics that clarifies the importance of "everyday talk" to ideology and political identities, see Melissa Victoria Harris-Lacewell, *Barbershops, Bibles, and BET: Everyday Talk and Black Political Thought* (Princeton, NJ: Princeton University Press, 2004). For a brief outline of the importance of places like barbershops and beauty parlors and magazines like *Jet*, see Harris-Lacewell, *Barbershops*, 1–11.

64. Vicki Goldberg, *The Power of Photography: How Photographs Changed Our Lives* (New York: Abbeville, 1991), 201.

65. Goldsby, "High and Low Tech of It," 250.

66. Goldberg, *Power of Photography*, 201. This finding is also supported by Oby, "Black Press Coverage," 56–58.

67. Sara Ahmed, "Affective Economies," *Social Text* 79 (2004): 117.

68. *Eyes on the Prize*, 17:05; *Untold Story*, 30:22.

69. In his discussion of Coretta Scott King's funeral and the outcry when two black ministers dared to mention race at the funeral of a civil rights icon, Simon Stow argues that black funerals have long connected despair at American race relations with hope of a better tomorrow: "part celebration, part jeremiad." See Simon Stow, *American Mourning: Tragedy, Democracy, Resilience* (Cambridge: Cambridge University Press, 2017), 85.

70. See Goldsby, "High and Low Tech of It," 264–269.

71. Roberts and Klibanoff, *Race Beat*, 89.

72. Ahmed, "Affective Economies," 119.

73. For an overview of early strong southern condemnation, quickly followed by accusations that northerners were using Till's death as a means of humiliating southerners, see Whitfield, *Death in the Delta*, 15–31. See Stow, *American Mourning*, chap. 2, for another example of white Americans calling the discussion of race too political, in this case after the death of Coretta Scott King.

74. Jesse Jackson, "Foreword," in Till-Mobley and Benson, *Death of Innocence*, xii.

75. Joy James points out how rare it is to say such things aloud, and that they are often confined to funeral or memorial services. See Joy James, *Resisting State Violence: Radicalism, Gender, and Race in U.S. Culture* (Minneapolis: University of Minnesota Press, 1996), 46.

76. For example, Amzie Moore, Charles Diggs, Myrlie Evers, Anne Moody, Eldridge Cleaver, Cleveland Sellers, Ruby Hurley, Shelby Steele, Michael Eric Dyson, Kareem Abdul-Jabbar, and Muhammad Ali all reference Till's death in their memoirs as a turning point. For the best overview of a wide variety of references in memoirs, see Metress, *Lynching of Emmett Till*, 226–288; see also Whitfield, *Death in the Delta*, 145; Hampton and Fayer, *Voices of Freedom*, 1–15, 321–334; and Goldsby, "The High and Low Tech of It," 276n4.

77. Till-Mobley, *Death of Innocence*, 142.

78. Whitfield, *Death in the Delta*, 25–27; Apel, *Imagery of Lynching*, 181; Metress, *Lynching of Emmett Till*, 16–43.

79. This is terribly ironic given the long history of white southerners' public displays of lynched black bodies. See James Allen et al., *Without Sanctuary*; and Apel, *Imagery of Lynching*. Regarding the specific charges about displaying Till's body, see *American Experience*, 35:54–36:30. The first sentiment is voiced by a white man in his mid-thirties, the second by an older white woman in her fifties or sixties.

80. Whitaker, "A Case Study in Southern Justice," viii. Roberts and Klibanoff report fifty journalists at the start of the trial; see *Race Beat*, 89.

81. Roberts and Klibanoff, *Race Beat*, 90–94.

82. Actually, he is quoted by several witnesses as saying "thar he," but that seems a stretch considering how well spoken he is in footage in *Eyes on the Prize*; *American Experience*; and *Untold Story*. See also Roberts and Klibanoff, *Race Beat*, 99; Metress, *Lynching of Emmett Till*, 68; and Whitfield, *Death in the Delta*, 38–39.

83. Kempton, "He Went All the Way," 215.

84. Whitfield, *Death in the Delta*, 39.

85. Till-Mobley and Benson, *Death of Innocence*, 140.

86. Till-Mobley and Benson, *Death of Innocence*, 196.

87. Whitfield, *Death in the Delta*, 39, quoting Dan Wakefield.

88. Till-Mobley and Benson, *Death of Innocence*, 153–154, 168–169.

89. Whitfield, *Death in the Delta*, 40, 55–56; *Untold Story*, 57:20–59:00.

90. Metress, *Lynching of Emmett Till*, 97–103.

91. For an overview of press reactions to the prosecution, including many that praise the district attorneys and the judge for their impartiality, see Metress, *Lynching of Emmett Till*, 115–151. The fact that impartiality was praiseworthy is notable.

92. Till-Mobley and Benson, *Death of Innocence*, 189.

93. See footage to this effect in *Eyes on the Prize*; *American Experience*; and *Untold Story*. See also Till-Mobley and Benson, *Death of Innocence*, 188–190.

94. Till-Mobley and Benson, *Death of Innocence*, 188.

95. The work of Baldus, Woodworth, and Pulaski in 1990 demonstrated that when blacks kill whites, they are far more likely to be sentenced to death than when blacks kill other blacks, whites kill blacks, or whites kill other whites. See David C. Baldus, George Woodworth, and Charles A. Pulaski, *Equal Justice and the Death Penalty: A Legal and Empirical Analysis* (Boston: Northeastern University Press, 1990).

96. For a quick review of international headlines about Till's murder and the acquittal of his killers, see Whitfield, *Death in the Delta*, 46. For additional discussions of international reactions to Till's murder, see Layton, *International Politics and Civil Rights Policies*, 20, 95, 164–165nn90–91; and Dudziak, *Cold War Civil Rights*, 113.

97. Matthew D. Lassiter, "De Jure/De Facto Segregation: The Long Shadow of a National Myth," in *The Myth of Southern Exceptionalism*, ed. Matthew D. Lassiter and Joseph Crespino (New York: Oxford University Press, 2010), 25–48.

98. Whitfield, *Death in the Delta*, 48; Apel, *Imagery of Lynching*, 185–186.

99. Apel, *Imagery of Lynching*, 185.

100. Whitfield, *Death in the Delta*, 86–87.

101. See Metress, *Lynching of Emmett Till*, 226–288. See also Whitfield, *Death in the Delta*, 145; Hampton and Fayer, *Voices of Freedom*, 1–15, 321–334; and Goldsby, "The High and Low Tech of It," 276n4.

102. Belknap, *Federal Law and Southern Order*, 37.

103. Till-Mobley and Benson, *Death of Innocence*, 285.

104. The social movements literature argues that there are a host of other reasons why the civil rights movement succeeded in 1955 in ways it could not before, and I am persuaded by those claims. See McAdam, *Political Process*; and Polletta, *Freedom Is an Endless Meeting*. But I think it is still worthwhile to trace how the affective impact of Till's death helped prime the pump for the explosion of activism shortly thereafter.

105. Whitfield, *Death in the Delta*, 106.

106. Harris, "It Takes a Tragedy to Arouse Them."

107. Harris, "It Takes a Tragedy to Arouse Them," 32–38.

108. Harris, "It Takes a Tragedy to Arouse Them," 23.

109. While this is true, as shown in Lassiter and Crespino's *Myth of Southern Exceptionalism*, another way to interpret the North's interest in forcing southern whites to integrate was simply to push off any white northern responsibility to address its own racism. See Matthew D. Lassiter and Joseph Crespino, eds., *The Myth of Southern Exceptionalism* (New York: Oxford University Press, 2010).

110. See Layton, *International Politics and Civil Rights Policies*; and Dudziak, *Cold War Civil Rights*. See also Whitfield, *Death in the Delta*, 71–84.

111. See Metress, *Lynching of Emmett Till*, 139, excerpting "Memorandum from the Paris Office of the American Jewish Committee on European Reaction to the Emmett Till Case," October 13, 1955.

112. "Survey Finds U.S. Hurt by Till Case," *New York Times*, October 22, 1955, p. 40.

113. The place of African Americans in the electoral strategies of both major parties in 1950s America has been documented by, among others, Edward Carmines and James Stimson, *Issue Evolution: Race and the Transformation of American Politics* (Princeton, NJ: Princeton University Press, 1989); Paul Frymer, *Uneasy Alliances: Race and Party Competition in America* (Princeton, NJ: Princeton University Press, 1999); and Donald Jackson and James Riddlesperger Jr., "The Eisenhower Administration and the 1957 Civil Rights Act," in *Reexamining the Eisenhower Presidency*, ed. Shirley Anne Warshaw (Westport, CT: Greenwood Press, 1993), 85–101.

114. Belknap, *Federal Law and Southern Order*, 40.

115. "New Drive Set in Congress," *New York Times*, October 22, 1955, p. 40.

116. "New Drive Set in Congress," 40.

117. In other areas of law enforcement, the lack of federal jurisdiction rarely hampered J. Edgar Hoover's FBI. Whitfield offers an example of a bomb planted by a labor activist in Minnesota that sparked FBI involvement, even though no federal law was broken. See Whitfield, *Death in the Delta*, 75–76.

118. David Allen Nichols, *A Matter of Justice: Eisenhower and the Beginning of the Civil Rights Revolution* (New York: Simon and Schuster, 2007), 117.

119. Belknap, *Federal Law and Southern Order*, 40.

120. Belknap, *Federal Law and Southern Order*, 40.

121. President Eisenhower mentioned mostly civil rights gains, including the "elimination of discrimination and segregation" in the executive branch and the District of Columbia's voluntary moves to desegregate. Eisenhower also stated, "It is disturbing that in some localities allegations persist that Negro citizens are being deprived of their right to vote and are likewise being subjected to unwarranted economic pressures." His response was not to call for vigorous enforcement of civil rights laws and federal oversight of state legal functions but to call for a bipartisan commission. Dwight D. Eisenhower, "Annual Message to the Congress on the State of the Union," January 5, 1956, https://www.presidency

.ucsb.edu/documents/annual-message-the-congress-the-state-the-union-11. Ironically, as demonstrated by Jackson and Riddlesperger, although it was one of the less controversial proposals at the time, the Civil Rights Commission established by the Civil Rights Act of the 1957 ended up being quite important. See Jackson and Riddlesperger, "Eisenhower Administration," 86.

122. Belknap, *Federal Law and Southern Order*, 40.

123. Belknap, *Federal Law and Southern Order*, 44.

124. Whitfield, *Death in the Delta*, 82–83.

125. Belknap, *Federal Law and Southern Order*, 44.

126. Patterson, *Brown v. Board of Education*, 87.

127. Till-Mobley and Benson, *Death of Innocence*, 19.

CHAPTER 4

1. "September 11 Terror Attacks Fast Facts," *CNN*, September 18, 2020, https://www.cnn.com/2013/07/27/us/september-11-anniversary-fast-facts/index.html.

2. According to Stefaan Walgrave and Dieter Rucht, these protests were the largest in recorded history. See Stefaan Walgrave and Dieter Rucht, "Introduction," in *The World Says No to War: Demonstrations against the War in Iraq*, edited by Stefaan Walgrave and Dieter Rucht (Minneapolis: University of Minnesota Press, 2010), xiii.

3. Andrew Buncombe, "America Has No Idea How Many Innocent People It's Killing in the Middle East," *The Independent*, November 20, 2017, https://www.independent.co.uk/voices/us-isis-air-strikes-civilian-deaths-syria-iraq-america-no-idea-how-many-dead-the-uncounted-a8066266.html.

4. Physicians for Social Responsibility, *Body Count: Casualty Figures after 10 Years of the "War on Terror"* (Washington, DC: Physicians for Social Responsibility, 2015), 15, https://www.psr.org/wp-content/uploads/2018/05/body-count.pdf. This source includes a significantly higher number than the source in the next note, because Physicians for Social Responsibility attempted to estimate not just direct but also indirect loss of life (that is, to include those who died not because of military action but from malnutrition occasioned by destroyed infrastructure, treatable illnesses that became fatal because of lack of medical help, and so on).

5. Neta C. Crawford, "Human Cost of the Post-9/11 Wars: Lethality and the Need for Transparency," Brown University Watson Institute International and Public Affairs, November 2018, https://watson.brown.edu/costsofwar/files/cow/imce/papers/2018/Human%20Costs%2C%20Nov%208%202018%20CoW.pdf.

6. Simon Stow, *American Mourning: Tragedy, Democracy, Resilience* (Cambridge: Cambridge University Press, 2017), 106.

7. It is worth recalling that Carl Schmitt identified this paradox at the heart of liberal democracy while observing Hitler's rise to power in the 1930s, when he wrote, "Sovereign is he who decides the exception." Carl Schmitt, *Political Theology: Four Chapters on the Concept of Sovereignty* (Chicago: University of Chicago Press, 2005), 5.

8. For a discussion of how war memorials serve to obscure the violence of sovereignty, see Jenny Edkins, *Trauma and the Memory of Politics* (Cambridge: Cambridge University Press, 2003).

9. This is nothing more than a sampling of the scholarly and diplomatic discussions between the fall of the Soviet Union and September 11, but it demonstrates that

practitioners and scholars from across the political spectrum are trying to figure out the contours and aims of American foreign policy in the absence of a clear adversary. See Francis Fukuyama, "The End of History," *National Interest* 16 (1989): 3–18; Charles Krauthammer, "The Unipolar Moment," *Foreign Affairs* 70 (1990–1991): 23–33; Samuel Huntington, "The Erosion of American National Interests," *Foreign Affairs* 76 (1997): 28–49; Madeleine Albright, "The Testing of American Foreign Policy," *Foreign Affairs* 77 (1998): 50–64; Samuel Huntington, "The Lonely Superpower," *Foreign Affairs* 78 (1999): 35–49; and Michael Mandelbaum, "The Inadequacy of American Power," *Foreign Affairs* 81 (2002): 61–73.

10. Ussama Makdisi, "'Anti-Americanism' in the Arab World: An Interpretation of a Brief History," in *History and September 11*, ed. Joanne Meyerowitz (Philadelphia: Temple University Press, 2003), 131.

11. Makdisi, "'Anti-Americanism' in the Arab World," 153.

12. See Roxanne Leslie Euben, "The New Manichaeans," *Theory and Event* 5, no. 4 (2001), https://doi.org/10.1353/tae.2001.0034.

13. Roy Harvey Pearce, *Savagism and Civilization: A Study of the Indian and the American Mind* (Baltimore: Johns Hopkins University Press, 1967).

14. Pearce, *Savagism and Civilization*, 232.

15. From a political theory perspective, three pointed articulations of this claim include Judith Shklar, *American Citizenship: The Quest for Inclusion* (Cambridge, MA: Harvard University Press, 1991); Joel Olson, *The Abolition of White Democracy* (Minneapolis: University of Minnesota Press, 1991); and Charles Mills, *The Racial Contract* (Ithaca, NY: Cornell University Press, 1999).

16. For a sampling of critical race theory that joins stories about racial identity with immigration and racialization, see Derrick Bell Jr., *And We Are Not Saved: The Elusive Quest for Racial Justice* (New York: Basic Books, 1987); Derrick Bell Jr., *Faces at the Bottom of the Well: The Permanence of Racism* (New York: Basic Books, 1992); Kimberlé Crenshaw et al., eds., *Critical Race Theory: The Key Writing That Formed the Movement* (New York: New Press, 1995); Claire Jean Kim, *Bitter Fruit: The Politics of Black-Korean Conflict in New York City* (New Haven, CT: Yale University Press, 2000); Lisa Lowe, *Immigrant Acts: On Asian American Cultural Politics* (Durham, NC: Duke University Press, 1996); Mae Ngai, *Impossible Subjects: Illegal Aliens and the Making of Modern America* (Princeton, NJ: Princeton University Press, 2005); and Patricia Williams, *The Alchemy of Race and Rights: Diary of a Law Professor* (Cambridge, MA: Harvard University Press, 1991).

17. Michael Omi and Howard Winant, *Racial Formation in the United States: From the 1960s to the 1990s*, 2nd ed. (New York: Routledge, 1994).

18. Works on whiteness that have been foundational to this view include Matthew Frye Jacobson, *Whiteness of a Different Color: European Immigrants and the Alchemy of Race* (Cambridge, MA: Harvard University Press, 1998); Ira Katznelson, *When Affirmative Action Was White: An Untold History of Racial Inequality in Twentieth-Century America* (New York: W. W. Norton, 2005); George Lipsitz, *The Possessive Investment in Whiteness: How White People Profit from Identity Politics*, rev. ed. (Philadelphia: Temple University Press, 2006); Nell Irvin Painter, *The History of White People* (New York: W. W. Norton, 2010); David Roediger, *The Wages of Whiteness: Race and the Making of the American Working Class*, rev. ed. (New York: Verso, 2007); and David Roediger, *Working toward Whiteness: How America's Immigrants Became White* (New York: Basic Books, 2005).

19. Nadine Naber, "Introduction: Arab Americans and U.S. Racial Formations," in *Race and Arab Americans before and after 9/11: From Invisible Citizens to Visible Subjects*, ed. Amaney Jamal and Nadine Naber (Syracuse, NY: Syracuse University Press, 2008), 11, referencing Junaid Rana, "Islamophobia and Racism: On the Ethnology of the Muslim," *Souls* 9, no. 2 (2007).

20. Naber, "Introduction," 14.

21. Roediger, *Working toward Whiteness*, 16.

22. Naber, "Introduction," 26.

23. Naber, "Introduction," 32.

24. Quoted in Sarah Gualtieri, "Strange Fruit? Syrian Immigrants, Extralegal Violence, and Racial Formation in the United States," in *Race and Arab Americans before and after 9/11: From Invisible Citizens to Visible Subjects*, ed. Amaney Jamal and Nadine Naber (Syracuse, NY: Syracuse University Press, 2008), 148n5. For an overview of the debate about whether Arab Americans have been subject to a discourse of racialization, see the collection of articles in Amaney Jamal and Nadine Naber, eds., *Race and Arab Americans before and after 9/11: From Invisible Citizens to Visible Subjects* (Syracuse, NY: Syracuse University Press, 2008).

25. Gualtieri, "Strange Fruit?," 147–169.

26. Louise Cainkar, "Thinking Outside the Box," in Jamal and Naber, *Race and Arab Americans before and after 9/11*, 48.

27. For a good overview of the "uneven roads" that racial and ethnic groups have traveled to increased inclusion in the United States, see Todd Cameron Shaw et al., *Uneven Roads: An Introduction to U.S. Racial and Ethnic Politics* (Thousand Oaks, CA: CQ Press, 2015).

28. Amaney Jamal, "Civil Liberties and the Otherization of Arab and Muslim Americans," in Jamal and Naber, *Race and Arab Americans before and after 9/11*, 119.

29. Sara Ahmed, "Affective Economies," *Social Text* 79 (2004): 119.

30. See Patrick Smith, "Terminal Madness: What Is Airport Security?," *Ask the Pilot* (blog), https://askthepilot.com/essaysandstories/terminal-madness/ (accessed November 8, 2020); and Patrick Smith, "News Flash: Deadly Terrorism Existed before 9/11," *Salon*, November 11, 2010, https://www.salon.com/2010/11/11/airport_security_5/.

31. Ernest May, ed., *The 9/11 Commission Report with Related Documents* (New York: Bedford/St. Martin's Press, 2007), 62.

32. May, *9/11 Commission Report*, 80; CNN Editorial Research, "1998 US Embassies in Africa Bombings Fast Facts," *CNN*, August 3, 2020, https://www.cnn.com/2013/10/06/world/africa/africa-embassy-bombings-fast-facts/index.html.

33. May, *9/11 Commission Report*, 110–111.

34. May, *9/11 Commission Report*, 65–66.

35. Schmitt, *Political Theology*, 5.

36. Jade Larissa Schiff, *Burdens of Political Responsibility: Narrative and the Cultivation of Responsiveness* (Cambridge: Cambridge University Press, 2014), 17–19.

37. Rick Bragg, "Terror in Oklahoma City: At Ground Zero; In Shock, Loathing, Denial; 'This Doesn't Happen Here,'" *New York Times*, April 20, 1995, https://nyti.ms/2uzUm02.

38. The Comprehensive Terrorism Prevention Act of 1995, S. 375, became the Antiterrorism and Effective Death Penalty Act of 1996, Pub. L. No. 104-132, 110 Stat. 1214–1319, available at https://www.govinfo.gov/app/details/PLAW-104publ132.

39. David Johnston, "Terror in Oklahoma City: The Investigation; At Least 31 Are Dead, Scores Missing after Car Bomb Attack in Oklahoma City Wrecks 9-Story Federal Building," *New York Times*, April 20, 1995, https://nyti.ms/2tYFrMD.

40. Laurie Goodstein, "Report Cites Harassment of Muslims," *Washington Post*, April 20, 1996, https://www.washingtonpost.com/archive/politics/1996/04/20/report -cites-harassment-of-muslims/63dd282e-e1db-4727-8672-b89f6f33f899.

41. Jerry Gray, "Senate Approves Anti-Terror Bill by 91-to-8 Vote," *New York Times*, June 8, 1995, p. A1.

42. While Timothy McVeigh's actions were certainly out of the norm in terms of death toll and method, mass shooters are disproportionately male. There is some debate about whether white men are overrepresented among mass shooters. See John Kruzel, "Are White Males Responsible for More Mass Shootings Than Any Other Group?," *Politi-Fact*, October 6, 2017, https://www.politifact.com/punditfact/statements/2017/oct/06/ newsweek/are-white-males-responsible-more-mass-shootings-an/.

For a more scholarly approach that subjected data about mass shootings to regression analysis, see Adam Lankford, "Race and Mass Murder in the United States: A Social and Behavioral Analysis," *Current Sociology* 64, no. 3 (2016): 470–490. Lankford's analysis determines that white men are not the primary perpetrators of mass shootings. However, white men are the primary perpetrators of public mass killings, as contrasted with mass killings in conjunction with burglary or some other crime. Lankford claims that "structural advantage and aggrieved entitlement" is the best explanation for the different kinds of killings perpetrated by white mass murderers (482).

43. Leti Volpp, "Citizen and Terrorist," in *September 11 in History: A Watershed Moment?*, ed. Mary Dudziak (Durham, NC: Duke University Press, 2003), 151.

44. Everett M. Rogers and Nancy Seidel, "Diffusion of News of the Terrorist Attacks of September 11, 2001," *Prometheus* 20 (2002): 209–219.

45. Rogers and Seidel, "Diffusion of News," 215–216.

46. Pew Research Center, "American Psyche Reeling from Terror Attacks," September 19, 2001, https://www.pewresearch.org/politics/2001/09/19/american-psy che-reeling-from-terror-attacks/.

47. Pew Research, "American Psyche," 13.

48. Edkins, *Trauma and the Memory of Politics*, 224–225.

49. Tom Junod, "The Falling Man: An Unforgettable Story," *Esquire*, September 9, 2016, https://www.esquire.com/news-politics/a48031/the-falling-man-tom-junod/. See also *The Falling Man*, directed by Henry Singer, written by Tom Junod (London: Darlow Smithson Productions, 2006).

50. Junod, "The Falling Man."

51. Jeffrey W. S. Green, "Eyewitness to History," *Uptown Chronicle*, September 8, 2011, previously available at http://theuptownchronicle.com/?p=1759. I have since located Maisel's image on a blog: "The Day the Twin Towers Fell," *Iconic Photos*, September 5, 2011, https://iconicphotos.wordpress.com/tag/todd-maisel/.

52. Junod, "The Falling Man."

53. Gérôme Truc, "Seeing Double: 9/11 and Its Mirror Image," *Books and Ideas*, September 16, 2010, https://booksandideas.net/%20spip.php?page=print&id_article=1188. Truc is reviewing Clément Chéroux, *Diplopie: L'image photographique à l'ère des médias globalisés: essai sur le 11 septembre 2001* (Cherbourg-Octeville, France: Le Point du Jour, 2009). Since I do not read French or German (Chéroux's book is available in both

languages) and *Diplopie* is not available in English, I am taking Truc's review as a good summary of Chéroux's argument.

54. Michael Idov, "Unidentified Remains," in "The Encyclopedia of 9/11," special issue, *New York Magazine*, August 27, 2011, https://nymag.com/news/9-11/10th-anniversary/unidentified-remains/.

55. Office of Chief Medical Examiner, "Update on the Results of DNA Testing of Remains Recovered at the World Trade Center Site and Surrounding Area," February 1, 2009, http://www.nyc.gov/html/ocme/downloads/pdf/public_affairs_ocme_pr_february_2009.

56. Faith Karimi, "Improved DNA Technique Used to Identify Man Killed in Sept. 11 Terror Attacks," *CNN*, July 26, 2018, https://www.cnn.com/2018/07/26/us/new-york-9-11-victim-identified/index.html.

57. Simon Stow, "Portraits 9/11/01: The *New York Times* and the Pornography of Grief," in *Literature after 9/11*, ed. Jeanne Follansbee Quinn and Ann Keniston (New York: Routledge, 2008), 235.

58. "Demographic Data on the Victims of the September 11, 2001, Terror Attack on the World Trade Center, New York City," *Population and Development Review* 28 (2002): 586–588.

59. Using census data from across the world in the early 2000s, the Migration Policy Institute defines cities as "hyperdiverse" if "1. at least 9.5 percent of the total population is foreign born; 2. no one country of origin accounts for 25 percent or more of the immigrant stock; and 3. immigrants come from all regions of the world." In the early 2000s, New York was one of these hyperdiverse cities. Marie Price and Lisa Benton-Short, "Counting Immigrants in Cities across the Globe," Migration Policy Institute, January 1, 2007, https://www.migrationpolicy.org/article/counting-immigrants-cities-across-globe.

60. George Kateb, "Is Patriotism a Mistake?," *Social Research* 67 (2000): 907.

61. Thomas Hobbes, *Leviathan* (1690; repr., Indianapolis, IN: Hackett, 1994), 127.

62. Edkins, *Trauma and the Memory of Politics*, 54.

63. Edkins, *Trauma and the Memory of Politics*, 54.

64. It is telling, of course, that these same first responders have had to beg to have their post–September 11 ailments covered by federal funds. The state was quite happy to honor their sacrifices as long as their sacrifices did not cost much. There is something about how sovereignty works in this instance, too; the sovereign gets to decide whether the first responders deserve care, while most Americans assume that care was a given.

65. Susannah Radstone, "The War of the Fathers: Trauma, Fantasy, and September 11," *Signs* 28 (2002): 458.

66. Mary Marshall Clark, "The September 11 Oral History Narrative and Memory Project," in *History and September 11*, ed. Joanne Meyerowitz (Philadelphia: Temple University Press, 2003), 120.

67. Clark, "The September 11 Oral History," 118.

68. Clark, "The September 11 Oral History," 120.

69. Carla Echevarria, personal correspondence with the author, April 12, 2011.

70. Bob Woodward, *Bush at War* (New York: Simon and Schuster, 2002), 32.

71. George Kateb, "A Life of Fear," *Social Research: An International Quarterly* 71, no. 4 (Winter 2004): 891.

72. John Hutcheson et al., "U.S. National Identity, Political Elites, and a Patriotic Press Following September 11," *Political Communication* 21 (2004): 27.

73. Hutcheson et al., "U.S. National Identity," 36.

74. Hutcheson et al., "U.S. National Identity," 37.

75. Hutcheson and colleagues define American values as "the presence of language about values and ideals commonly considered as part of the 'American' ethos, including freedom, equality, capitalism, tolerance, justice, compassion, moral courage, progress, and innovation." Hutcheson et al., "U.S. National Identity," 33. In their examination of various speakers' discussions of values, the authors coded sources as offering a negative, positive, or mixed evaluation of American values.

76. "America under Attack: Bush Holds Press Briefing," *CNN*, September 11, 2001, http://transcripts.cnn.com/TRANSCRIPTS/0109/11/bn.35.html.

77. Hutcheson et al., "National Identity," 40.

78. Hutcheson et al., "National Identity," 39–40.

79. Hutcheson et al., "National Identity," 44 (emphasis in original).

80. Elisabeth Anker, "Villains, Victim, and Heroes: Melodrama, Media, and September 11," *Journal of Communication* 55 (2005): 23. See also Elisabeth Anker, *Orgies of Feeling: Melodrama and the Politics of Freedom* (Durham, NC: Duke University Press, 2014).

81. Denise Bostdorff, "George W. Bush's Post-September 11 Rhetoric of Covenant Renewal: Upholding the Faith of the Greatest Generation," *Quarterly Journal of Speech* 89 (2003): 294.

82. Bill Carter and Felicity Barringer, "In Patriotic Time, Dissent Is Muted," *New York Times*, September 28, 2001, p. A1.

83. David Stout, "Ashcroft Defends Crackdown on Terrorism before Senate," *New York Times*, December 6, 2001, https://www.nytimes.com/2001/12/06/politics/ashcroft-defends-crackdown-on-terrorism-before-senate.html.

84. Hutcheson et al., "National Identity," 47.

85. Pew Research Center, "American Psyche," 2.

86. Pew Research Center, "American Psyche," 3.

87. Pew Research Center, "American Psyche," 14.

88. May, *9/11 Commission Report*, 65–66.

89. James Berger, "'There's No Backhand to This,'" in *Trauma at Home: After 9/11*, ed. Judith Greenberg (Lincoln: University of Nebraska Press, 2003), 54.

90. Quoted in Joan Didion, *Fixed Ideas: America since 9/11* (New York: New York Review of Books, 2003), 20.

91. Stow, *American Mourning*.

92. For two discussions of whether the events of September 11 might be understood as a crime against humanity, see Antonio Cassese, "Terrorism Is Also Disrupting Some Crucial Legal Categories of International Law," *European Journal of International Law* 12 (2001): 993–1001; and Christopher Greenwood, "International Law and the 'War Against Terrorism,'" *International Affairs* 18 (2001): 301–317.

Some scholars argue that there are conceptual difficulties to claiming that al-Qaeda's actions were an act of war; because al-Qaeda was not a state, there was no legal justification to declare war. Legally, this was an international crime rather than an act of war because the perpetrator was a nonstate actor rather than a state actor. See Jordan Paust, "War and Enemy Status after 9/11: Attacks on the Laws of War," *Yale Journal of International Law* 28 (2003): 325–335.

93. Schmitt, *Political Theology*, 5.

94. Bonnie Honig, *Emergency Politics: Paradox, Law, Democracy* (Princeton, NJ: Princeton University Press, 2009), 10.

95. Sayyid Qutb was an early member and later leader of the Muslim Brotherhood in Egypt. His views and writings deeply influenced Ayman Al-Zawahiri, who went on to become bin Laden's partner in the formation of al-Qaeda. Qutb was executed for his participation in conspiracies to overthrow the Egyptian government. See Lawrence Wright, *The Looming Tower: Al-Qaeda and the Road to 9/11* (New York: Vintage Books, 2006), 9–37.

96. Wright, *Looming Tower*, 344.

97. Judith Butler, *Precarious Life: The Powers of Mourning and Violence* (New York: Verso Books, 2004), chap. 1.

98. For a thorough discussion of the limitations of bin Laden's vision of Islam, which he terms "nihilistic," see Khaled Abou El Fadl, "9/11 and the Muslim Transformation," in *September 11 in History: A Watershed Moment?*, ed. Mary Dudziak (Durham, NC: Duke University Press, 2003), 70–111.

99. "Declarations by Usama Bin Laden," in May, *9/11 Commission Report*, 169–170.

100. Wright, *Looming Tower*, 279–280.

101. Wright, *Looming Tower*, 280.

102. Wright, *Looming Tower*, 280.

103. See, generally, Abou El Fadl, "9/11 and Muslim Transformation," for support of this claim about the long tradition of debate and the goal of reaching consensus in Islam.

104. Wright, *Looming Towers*, 280.

105. Brian Whitaker, "The Definition of Terrorism," in *History and September 11*, ed. Joanne Meyerowitz (Philadelphia: Temple University Press, 2003), 237–240.

106. Whitaker, "Definition of Terrorism," 237.

107. Whitaker, "Definition of Terrorism," 239.

108. Whitaker, "Definition of Terrorism," 240.

109. Stow, *American Mourning*, 114–115.

110. Anonymous, "I Am Part of the Resistance inside the Trump Administration," *New York Times*, September 5, 2018, https://nyti.ms/2CyF3Jh; Donald Trump, Twitter post, September 5, 2018, https://twitter.com/realDonaldTrump/status/1037464177269 514240.

111. A summary and the text of the bill, H.R. 3162, are available at https://www.congress.gov/bill/107th-congress/house-bill/3162.

112. See, for example, Kam C. Wong, "The USA Patriot Act: A Policy of Alienation," *Michigan Journal of Race and Law* 12 (2006): 161–202. See also Volpp, "Citizen and Terrorist"; and Nadine Naber, "'Look, Mohammed the Terrorist Is Coming!': Cultural Racism, Nation-Based Racism, and the Intersectionality of Oppressions after 9/11," in *Race and Arab Americans before and after 9/11: From Invisible Citizens to Visible Subjects*, ed. Amaney Jamal and Nadine Naber (Syracuse, NY: Syracuse University Press, 2008), 276–304.

113. Maja Zehfuss, "Forget September 11," *Third World Quarterly* 24 (2003): 515.

114. Zehfuss, "Forget September 11," 516.

115. Zehfuss, "Forget September 11," 517.

116. Zehfuss, "Forget September 11," 518.

117. Zehfuss, "Forget September 11," 520.

118. Stow, *American Mourning*; David McIvor, *Mourning in America: Race and the Politics of Loss* (Ithaca, NY: Cornell University Press, 2016), xii.

119. Stow, *American Mourning*, 115.

120. Edkins, *Trauma and the Memory of Politics*, 227. Edkins is referencing Giorgio Agamben's work, including *Homo Sacer: Sovereign Power and Bare Life*, trans. Daniel

Heller-Roazen (Stanford, CA: Stanford University Press, 1998), *Remnants of Auschwitz*, trans. Daniel Heller-Roazen (New York: Zone Books, 1999), and *State of Exception*, trans. Kevin Attell (Chicago: University of Chicago Press, 2005). While Agamben might seem like a natural fit for the argument I am making here, a recent paper by Inés Valdez, Mat Coleman, and Amna Akbar suggests that Agamben overgeneralizes law in ways that obscure the unevenness of state violence. While we may all possibly become bare life, Valdez and colleagues argue that Walter Benjamin's insight about the unevenness of law enforcement is a necessary correction; not all communities or individuals are policed the same. See Inés Valdez, Mat Coleman, and Amna Akbar, "Law, Police Violence, and Race: Grounding and Embodying the State of Exception," *Theory and Event* 23, no. 4 (2020): 902–934. See also Walter Benjamin, "Critique of Violence," in *Reflections: Essays, Aphorisms, Autobiographical Writings*, ed. Peter Demetz (New York: Schocken Books, 1986), 277–300; and Walter Benjamin, "Theses on the Philosophy of History," in *Illuminations*, ed. Hannah Arendt (New York: Schocken Books, 1968), 253–264.

121. Steven Johnston, "This Patriotism Which Is Not One," *Polity* 34 (2002): 289.

122. Kateb, "Life of Fear," 889–890.

123. McIvor, *Mourning in America*.

124. Stow, *American Mourning*, 61–62.

125. Sabine Sielke, "Why '9/11 Is [Not] Unique,' or Troping Trauma," *Amerikasstudien/American Studies* 55 (2010): 385–408.

126. Sielke, "Why '9/11 Is [Not] Unique,'" 388.

127. Sielke, "Why '9/11 Is [Not] Unique,'" 388.

128. Marilyn B. Young, "Ground Zero: Enduring War," in Dudziak, *September 11 in History: A Watershed Moment?*, 14.

129. Chad Lavin, *The Politics of Responsibility* (Champaign: University of Illinois Press, 2008).

130. See Rogers Smith, *Civic Ideals: Conflicting Visions of Citizenship in U.S. History* (New Haven, CT: Yale University Press, 1997), 3, 508n5.

131. Volpp, "Citizen and Terrorist," 147.

132. Volpp, "Citizen and Terrorist," 153.

133. For example, in 2006 alone, the Council on American-Islamic Relations reported 143 hate crimes related to women wearing hijab in the United States. See Council on American-Islamic Relations, "The Status of Muslim Civil Rights in the United States, 2007: Presumption of Guilt," 2007, https://www.cair.com/wp-content/uploads/2017/09/CAIR-2007-Civil-Rights-Report.pdf.

134. Lila Abu-Lughod, "Do Muslim Women Really Need Saving? Anthropological Reflections on Cultural Relativism and Its Others," *American Anthropologist* 104 (2002): 784.

135. Volpp, "Citizen and Terrorist," 154.

136. Bonnie Mann, *Sovereign Masculinity: Gender Lessons from the War on Terror* (New York: Oxford University Press, 2014).

137. Anna M. Agathangelou and L.H.M. Ling, "Power, Borders, Security, Wealth: Lessons of Violence and Desire from September 11," *International Studies Quarterly* 48 (2004): 519.

138. Agathangelou and Ling, "Power, Borders, Security, Wealth," 521.

139. Euben, "The New Manichaeans."

140. Anker, *Orgies of Feeling*, 2 (emphasis in original).

141. Richard Devetak, "The Gothic Scene of International Relations: Ghosts, Monsters, Terror and the Sublime after September 11," *Review of International Studies* 31 (2005): 640, quoting John Quincy Adams.

142. Euben, "The New Manichaeans."

CHAPTER 5

1. Juliet Hooker, "Black Protest/White Grievance: On the Problem of White Political Imaginations Not Shaped by Loss," *South Atlantic Quarterly* 116, no. 3 (2017): 483–504.

2. Baldwin writes, "This is the crime of which I accuse my country and my countrymen, and for which neither I nor time nor history will ever forgive them, that they have destroyed and are destroying hundreds of thousands of lives and do not know it and do not want to know it. . . . But it is not permissible that the authors of devastation should also be innocent. It is the innocence which constitutes the crime." James Baldwin, *The Fire Next Time* (New York: Vintage International, 1993), 5–6.

3. Keeanga-Yamahtta Taylor, *From #BlackLivesMatter to Black Liberation* (Chicago: Haymarket Books, 2016), 29.

4. Taylor, *From #BlackLivesMatter*, 51–73.

5. Taylor, *From #BlackLivesMatter*, 75–106.

6. Taylor, *From #BlackLivesMatter*, 107–133.

7. Taylor, *From #BlackLivesMatter*, 135–152.

8. Taylor, *From #BlackLivesMatter*, 138.

9. See, for example, recent scholarly work on the Tea Party, such as Leonard Zeskin, "A Nation Dispossessed: The Tea Party Movement and Race," *Critical Sociology* 38, no. 4 (2012): 495–509. See also Arlie Hochschild, *Strangers in Their Own Land: Anger and Mourning on the American Right* (New York: New Press, 2016). Hochschild's work is particularly intriguing as, having completed countless hours of interviews with conservatives in Louisiana, she narrates what she calls "the deep story" about race in America (16); there, she identifies whites losing their expected racial privilege as a key part of their anger toward the federal government (135–151).

10. Christopher Lebron, *The Making of Black Lives Matter: A Brief History of an Idea* (New York: Oxford University Press, 2017), xx–xxi.

11. Barbara Ransby, *Making All Black Lives Matter: Reimagining Freedom in the 21st Century* (Berkeley: University of California Press, 2018), ix.

12. "Timeline of Events in Trayvon Martin Case," *CNN*, April 23, 2012, https://www.cnn.com/2012/04/23/justice/florida-zimmerman-timeline/index.html.

13. Monica Potts, "Barack Obama, Trayvon Martin, and the Presidency," *Vogue*, December 22, 2016, https://www.vogue.com/article/barack-obama-trayvon-martin-presidency.

14. Erhardt Graeff, Matt Stempeck, and Ethan Zuckerman, "The Battle for 'Trayvon Martin': Mapping a Media Controversy Online and Off-line," *First Monday* 19, no. 2–3 (February 2014): 10.

15. Tamara F. Lawson, "A Fresh Cut in an Old Wound—a Critical Analysis of the Trayvon Martin Killing: The Public Outcry, the Prosecutors' Discretion, and the Stand Your Ground Law," *University of Florida Journal of Law and Public Policy* 23, no. 3 (December 2012): 271–310.

16. According to the Giffords Law Center to Prevent Gun Violence, twenty-seven states have enacted stand-your-ground laws, while another seven states have essentially

done away with the duty to retreat through court decisions. Giffords Law Center to Prevent Gun Violence, "Guns in Public: Stand Your Ground," https://lawcenter.giffords.org/gun -laws/policy-areas/guns-in-public/stand-your-ground-laws/ (accessed November 10, 2020).

17. Lawson, "Fresh Cut in an Old Wound," 296. See also Derrick A. Bell Jr., "*Brown v. Board of Education* and the Interest-Convergence Dilemma," *Harvard Law Review* 93, no. 3 (1980): 518–533.

18. See Lizette Alvarez and Cara Buckley, "Zimmerman Is Acquitted in Trayvon Martin Killing," *New York Times*, July 13, 2013, https://nyti.ms/12MKyWV. See also Carol D. Leonnig and Jenna Johnson, "Anger Flows at Acquittal of George Zimmerman in Death of Trayvon Martin," *Washington Post*, July 14, 2013, http://wapo.st/18hYbp7.

19. Jake Miller, "Obama Calls for Calm in Wake of George Zimmerman Verdict," *CBS News*, July 15, 2013, https://www.cbsnews.com/news/obama-calls-for-calm -in-wake-of-george-zimmerman-verdict/.

20. For an overview of some of these recent instances, see Antonia Noori Farzan, "BBQ Becky, Permit Patty and Cornerstore Caroline: Too 'Cutesy' for Those White Women Calling Police on Black People?," *Washington Post*, October 18, 2019, https://www.washingtonpost.com/news/morning-mix/wp/2018/10/19/bbq -becky-permit-patty-and-cornerstore-caroline-too-cutesy-for-those-white-women -calling-cops-on-blacks/.

21. Charles Mills, *The Racial Contract* (Ithaca, NY: Cornell University Press, 1998), 41–62, 81–89.

22. Many of the details in the following summary of events are taken from "Timeline of Events in Shooting of Michael Brown in Ferguson," *AP*, August 8, 2019, https:// apnews.com/9aa32033692547699a3b61da8fd1fc62; and "What Happened in Ferguson?" *New York Times*, August 10, 2015, https://www.nytimes.com/interactive/2014/08/ 13/us/ferguson-missouri-town-under-siege-after-police-shooting.html.

23. Amy Davidson Sorkin, "Michael Brown's Body," *New Yorker*, August 19, 2014, https://www.newyorker.com/news/amy-davidson/michael-browns-body.

24. Julie Bosman and Joseph Goldstein, "Timeline for a Body: 4 Hours in the Middle of a Ferguson Street," *New York Times*, August 23, 2014, https://nyti.ms/1qAFMqN.

25. "What Happened in Ferguson?"

26. Christina Carrega, "5 Years after Eric Garner's Death, a Look Back at the Case and the Movement It Sparked," *ABC News*, July 16, 2019, https://abcn.ws/2XMI82j.

27. Emily Shapiro and Alex Perez, "Former Chicago Police Officer Jason Van Dyke Sentenced to 81 Months in Prison for Laquan McDonald Murder," *ABC News*, January 18, 2019, https://abcn.ws/2FKxT4C.

28. Jason Volack, Tara Fowler, and Emily Shapiro, "Cleveland Police Officer Who Killed Tamir Rice Fired after Rule Violations," *ABC News*, May 30, 2017, http:// abcn.ws/2qwxQCN.

29. Adeel Hassan, "The Sandra Bland Video: What We Know," *New York Times*, May 7, 2019, https://nyti.ms/2Vk2You.

30. George Floyd's public execution by a white police officer in Minneapolis in the summer of 2020—days after a white woman in New York had called police to report being "assaulted" when a black man who was bird-watching asked her to follow publicly posted rules—is certainly a continuation of this trend. However, these events happened after the manuscript for this book was completed and so are not addressed here. For coverage of these two events, see, for example, Meredith Deliso, "Timeline: The Impact of George Floyd's Death in Minneapolis and Beyond," *ABC News*, June 10, 2020,

https://abcn.ws/2ZXDEWx; and Jan Ransom, "Amy Cooper Faces Charges after Calling Police on Black Bird-Watcher," *New York Times*, July 6, 2020, https://nyti.ms/38xp4ap.

31. Erin McClam, "Chief Defends Release of Robbery Surveillance Video," *NBC News*, August 15, 2014, https://www.nbcnews.com/storyline/michael-brown-shooting/chief-defends-release-robbery-surveillance-video-n181786.

32. Ransby, *Making All Black Lives Matter*, 49.

33. As noted previously, Floyd's murder and the subsequent protests occurred after this book was in production; as a result, these events are only briefly referenced.

34. Baldwin, *The Fire Next Time*, 5–6 (emphasis in original).

35. Mills, *Racial Contract*, 18.

36. Lawrie Balfour, *The Evidence of Things Not Said: James Baldwin and the Promise of American Democracy* (Ithaca, NY: Cornell University Press, 2001), esp. chap. 1 and 2. See also Lawrie Balfour, "'A Most Disagreeable Mirror': Race Consciousness as Double Consciousness," *Political Theory* 26, no. 3 (June 1998): 346–369.

37. Mills, *Racial Contract*, xiv.

38. Taylor, *From #BlackLivesMatter to Black Liberation*, 24–25.

39. For an excellent overview of the effects on the black community of not being able to own their own homes, see Clarissa Rile Hayward, *How Americans Make Race: Stories, Institutions, Spaces* (Cambridge: Cambridge University Press, 2013).

40. Pew Research Center, "The Partisan Divide on Political Values Grows Even Wider," October 5, 2017, https://www.people-press.org/2017/10/05/the-partisan-divide-on-political-values-grows-even-wider/.

41. Cheryl Harris, "Whiteness as Property," *Harvard Law Review* 106, no. 8 (1993): 1707–1791; George Lipsitz, *The Possessive Investment in Whiteness: How White People Profit from Identity Politics*, rev. ed. (Philadelphia: Temple University Press, 2006).

42. For a recent argument about how law enforcement typically targets marginalized groups first, see Inés Valdez, Mat Coleman, and Amna Akbar, "Law, Police Violence, and Race: Grounding and Embodying the State of Exception," *Theory and Event* 23, no. 4 (2020): 902–934.

43. Taylor, *From #BlackLivesMatter*, 131.

44. Nikita Carney, "All Lives Matter, but So Does Race: Black Lives Matter and the Evolving Role of Social Media," *Humanity and Society* 40, no. 2 (April 2016): 189–190.

45. Carney, "All Lives Matter, but So Does Race," 190.

46. Carney, "All Lives Matter, but So Does Race," 191.

47. Carney, "All Lives Matter, but So Does Race," 190–193.

48. Ryan J. Gallagher et al., "Divergent Discourse between Protests and Counter-protests: #BlackLivesMatter and #AllLivesMatter," *PLoS ONE* 13, no. 4 (2018), https://doi.org/10.1371/journal.pone.0195644.

49. Gallagher et al., "Divergent Discourse," 18.

50. Cheryl Harris, "Whiteness as Property"; Loïc Wacquant, "From Slavery to Mass Incarceration," *New Left Review* 13 (2002): 41–60. Taylor provides an overview of the connection between slavery and policing in *From #BlackLivesMatter*, 108–115.

51. Jonathan Easley, "Poll: 57 Percent Have Negative View of Black Lives Matter Movement," *The Hill*, August 2, 2017, https://thehill.com/homenews/campaign/344985-poll-57-percent-have-negative-view-of-black-lives-matter-movement. See also Harvard Center for American Political Studies and Harris Insights and Analytics, "Harvard Harris Poll," July 27, 2017, https://harvardharrispoll.com/wp-content/uploads/2017/07/Harvard-Harris-Poll_July_07.27.2017.pptx.

52. Easley, "Poll: 57 Percent Have Negative View."

53. Taylor, *From #BlackLivesMatter*; Ransby, *Making All Black Lives Matter*. See also Keeanga-Yamahtta Taylor, ed., *How We Get Free: Black Feminism and the Combahee River Collective* (Chicago: Haymarket Books, 2017).

54. Ransby, *Making All Black Lives Matter*, 3.

55. John Dewey, *The Public and Its Problems* (1927; repr., Athens: University of Ohio Press, 1991), 134–135, 131, 183–184, 208, respectively.

56. Dewey, *Public and Its Problems*, 208.

57. Dewey, *Public and Its Problems*, 28.

58. Melvin Rogers, "Introduction," in John Dewey, *The Public and Its Problems: An Essay in Political Inquiry*, ed. Melvin Rogers (Athens: Swallow Press, 2016), 3.

59. Dewey, *Public and Its Problems*, 31.

60. Dewey, *Public and Its Problems*, 71–72.

61. Dewey, *Public and Its Problems*, 71.

62. See Rogers, "Introduction," 2–7.

63. Rogers, "Introduction," 17.

64. Danielle Allen, *Talking to Strangers: Anxieties of Citizenship since Brown v. Board of Education* (Chicago: University of Chicago Press, 2006); Juliet Hooker, *Race and the Politics of Solidarity* (Oxford: Oxford University Press, 2009).

65. Lebron, *Making of All Black Lives Matter*, 10–13.

66. Lebron, *Making of All Black Lives Matter*, 135.

67. Lebron, *Making of All Black Lives Matter*, 158.

68. Hooker, *Race and the Politics of Solidarity*.

69. In describing why the rule of law is important for a public that has established a state, Dewey writes that "rule of law" is "the institution of conditions under which persons make their arrangements with one another. They are structures which canalize action." Dewey, *Public and Its Problems*, 54.

70. Dewey, *Public and Its Problems*, 31.

71. Ransby, *Making All Black Lives Matter*, 5.

72. Taylor offers a more traditionally Marxist interpretation of what is needed for black lives to truly matter, writing that "racism, capitalism, and class rule have always been tangled together in such a way that it is impossible to imagine one without the other. Can there be Black liberation in the United States as the country is currently constituted? No. Capitalism is contingent on the absence of freedom and liberation for Black people and anyone else who does not directly benefit from its economic disorder." Taylor, *From #BlackLivesMatter*, 216. See also 191–219, where the argument about the interrelationship between race and class is fleshed out more broadly.

Ransby writes, "I use the term *Black-led mass struggle* because it is decidedly not Black-only struggle, and it is not only for Black liberation but rather contextualizes the oppression, exploitation, and liberation of Black poor and working-class people with the simple understanding, at least in the US context, that 'once all Black people are free, all people will be free.' In other words, poor Black people are represented in all categories of the oppressed in the United States. They are poor and working class. They are disabled. They are indigenous. They are LGBTQIA. They are Latinx and Afro-Asians. They are also Muslim and other religious minorities and the list goes on. So to realize the liberation of 'all' Black people means undoing systems of injustice that impact all other oppressed groups as well." Ransby, *Making All Black Lives Matter*, 3–4.

204 / Notes to Chapter 5

Similarly, Christopher Lebron reformulates Anna Julia Cooper's famous quotation— "Only the BLACK WOMAN can say, 'when and where I enter, in the quiet, undisputed dignity of my womanhood, without violence and without suing or special patronage, then and there the whole *Negro race enters with me*'"—to reflect the foundational aspect of equality still absent from American democracy. He suggests that we might reimagine Cooper's argument as follows: "It might be time to follow Cooper's lead and get even bolder by suggesting to America: only the BLACK AMERICAN can say, 'when and where I enter, in the quiet, undisputed dignity of my personhood, without violence and without suing or special patronage, then and there the whole *of American democracy enters with me*.'" Lebron, *Making of Black Lives Matter*, 141, 143.

While all of these advocate an inclusive view, the different emphases—on how capitalism has prevented black liberation, how various identity categories have the potential to split the movement, or how democracy itself is undercut by racial exclusion—provide slightly different, though potentially complementary, road maps for political change.

73. The response of ALM, which seeks to falsely universalize the particular claim of BLM, does what Bonnie Honig critiques Judith Butler for doing: assuming the inevitability of democracy based on a shared mortality. Simon Stow sought to revise Butler's claim, arguing that we have much evidence to show that vulnerability does not automatically lead to a democratic response; it is instead an achievement that must serve as the ground of democracy. This insight helps us make sense of the pointed particularity of BLM. See Chapter 1; Judith Butler, *Undoing Gender* (New York: Routledge, 2004), 19; Judith Butler, *Precarious Life: The Powers of Mourning and Violence* (New York: Verso, 2004), 20; Bonnie Honig, *Antigone, Interrupted* (Cambridge: Cambridge University Press, 2013), 2, 17, 10, 31; and Simon Stow, *American Mourning: Tragedy, Democracy, Resilience* (Cambridge: Cambridge University Press, 2017), 101.

74. Stow, *American Mourning*, 103–148.

75. Ransby, *Making All Black Lives Matter*, 69.

76. Ransby, *Making All Black Lives Matter*, 70.

77. W.E.B. Du Bois, *Black Reconstruction in America: 1860–1880* (1935, repr., New York: Free Press, 1998).

78. Lebron, *Making of Black Lives Matter*, xxi.

79. David McIvor, *Mourning in America: Race and the Politics of Loss* (Ithaca, NY: Cornell University Press, 2016), 162.

80. McIvor, *Mourning in America*, 162.

81. McIvor, *Mourning in America*, 154.

82. McIvor, *Mourning in America*, 153.

83. McIvor, *Mourning in America*, 168.

84. Ta-Nehisi Coates, *Between the World and Me* (New York: Spiegel and Grau, 2015); Claudia Rankine, *Citizen: An American Lyric* (Minneapolis: Graywolf Press, 2014).

85. McIvor, *Mourning in America*, 177.

86. McIvor, *Mourning in America*, 178.

87. McIvor, *Mourning in America*, 179.

88. Hooker, "Black Protest, White Grievance," 484.

89. Hooker, "Black Protest, White Grievance," 485.

90. Pew Research Center, "Political Typology Reveals Deep Fissures on the Right and Left," October 24, 2017, https://www.people-press.org/wp-content/uploads/sites/4/2018/09/10-24-2017-Typology-release.pdf.

91. Hochschild, *Strangers in Their Own Land*, 230.

CONCLUSION

1. Peter J. Verovšek, "Collective Memory, Politics, and the Influence of the Past: The Politics of Memory as a Research Paradigm," *Politics, Groups, and Identities* 4, no. 3 (2016): 529–543.

2. Clarissa Rile Hayward, *How Americans Make Race: Stories, Institutions, Spaces* (Cambridge: Cambridge University Press, 2013).

3. As discussed in Chapter 1, several recent works of political theory have addressed the question of how and when we take up expanded conceptions of responsibility. See Chad Lavin, *The Politics of Responsibility* (Champaign: University of Illinois Press, 2008); Iris Marion Young, *Responsibility for Justice* (New York: Oxford University Press, 2011); Jade Larissa Schiff, *Burdens of Political Responsibility: Narrative and the Cultivation of Responsiveness* (Cambridge: Cambridge University Press, 2014); Shalini Satkunanandan, *Extraordinary Responsibility: Politics beyond the Moral Calculus* (Cambridge: Cambridge University Press, 2015); and Antonio Vázquez-Arroyo, *Political Responsibility: Responding to Predicaments of Power* (New York: Columbia University Press, 2016).

4. Stuart Scheingold, *The Politics of Rights: Lawyers, Public Policy, and Political Change*, 2nd ed. (Ann Arbor: University of Michigan Press, 2004).

5. Jane Addams, *Democracy and Social Ethics* (1902; repr., Champaign: University of Illinois Press, 2002).

6. Simon Stow, *American Mourning: Tragedy, Democracy, Resilience* (Cambridge: Cambridge University Press, 2017).

7. Bonnie Honig, *Emergency Politics: Paradox, Law, Democracy* (Princeton, NJ: Princeton University Press, 2009), 4–5.

8. Juliet Hooker, "Black Protest, White Grievance: On the Problem of White Political Imaginations Not Shaped by Loss," *South Atlantic Quarterly* 116, no. 3 (July 2017): 483–504.

9. Honig, *Emergency Politics*, 5.

10. Elisabeth Anker, *Orgies of Feeling: Melodrama and the Politics of Freedom* (Durham, NC: Duke University Press, 2014).

11. For an excellent overview of how immigrants morph into forces of nature or animals, see Otto Santa Ana, *Brown Tide Rising: Metaphors of Latinos in Contemporary American Public Discourse* (Austin: University of Texas Press, 2002).

12. Stow, *American Mourning*, chap. 3.

13. Stow, *American Mourning*, 105.

14. Eli Rosenberg, Nick Miroff, and Cleve R. Wootson, "Man Charged with Killing Mollie Tibbetts Is an Undocumented Immigrant, Authorities Say," *Washington Post*, August 21, 2018, https://wapo.st/2nSQ0ea?tid=ss_mail&utm_term=.64adae387678.

15. Amber Phillips, "'They're Rapists': President Trump's Campaign Launch Speech Two Years Later, Annotated," *Washington Post*, June 16, 2017, https://wapo.st/2rECXwr?tid=ss_mail&utm_term=.b03374294f74.

16. Jeremy W. Peters, "How Politics Took Over the Killing of Mollie Tibbetts," *New York Times*, August 23, 2018, https://nyti.ms/2BSU20j.

17. Rob Tibbetts, "From Mollie Tibbetts' Father: Don't Distort Her Death to Advance Racist Views," *Des Moines Register*, September 2, 2018, https://www.desmoinesregister.com/story/opinion/columnists/2018/09/01/mollie-tibbetts-father-common-decency-immigration-heartless-despicable-donald-trump-jr-column/1163131002.

18. Stow, *American Mourning*, chap. 2.
19. Honig, *Emergency Politics*, xvii.

AFTERWORD

1. "Coronavirus Map: Tracking the Global Outbreak," *New York Times*, April 25, 2020, updated at 8:03 A.M. and 2:07 P.M., https://www.nytimes.com/interactive/2020/world/coronavirus-maps.html.

2. "Coronavirus Map: Tracking the Global Outbreak," *New York Times*, May 3, 2020, updated at 2:14 P.M.

3. "Covid in the U.S.: Latest Map and Case Count," *New York Times*, May 3, 2020, updated at 2:14 P.M., https://nyti.ms/39jvJEY.

4. Regarding undercounted cases, see Gretchen Vogel, "Antibody Surveys Suggesting Vast Undercount of Coronavirus Infections May Be Unreliable," *Science*, April 21, 2020, https://www.sciencemag.org/news/2020/04/antibody-surveys-suggesting-vast-undercount-coronavirus-infections-may-be-unreliable. Regarding undercounted deaths, see Jin Wu et al., "28,000 Missing Deaths: Tracking the True Toll of the Coronavirus Crisis," *New York Times*, April 22, 2020, https://nyti.ms/34QerxA. See also Josh Katz, Denise Lu, and Margot Sanger-Katz, "U.S. Coronavirus Death Toll Is Far Higher Than Reported, C.D.C. Data Suggests," *New York Times*, April 28, 2020, https://nyti.ms/2ybWxtp. Regarding the unusual ways the virus kills, see Meredith Wadman et al., "How Does Coronavirus Kill? Clinicians Trace a Ferocious Rampage through the Body, from Brain to Toes," *Science*, April 17, 2020, https://www.sciencemag.org/news/2020/04/how-does-coronavirus-kill-clinicians-trace-ferocious-rampage-through-body-brain-toes.

5. For a report on Italy, see Jason Horowitz and Emma Bubola, "Italy's Coronavirus Victims Face Death Alone, with Funerals Postponed," *New York Times*, March 16, 2020, https://nyti.ms/2Wkcfwm. For New York's mass graves, see Jada Yuan, "Burials on Hart Island, Where New York's Unclaimed Lie in Mass Graves, Have Risen Fivefold," *Washington Post*, April 16, 2020, https://www.washingtonpost.com/national/hart-island-mass-graves-coronavirus-new-york/2020/04/16/a0c413ee-7f5f-11ea-a3ee-13e1ae0a3571_story.html.

6. Lance Lambert, "The Latest Round of Unemployment Claims Puts Real Jobless Rate near Great Depression Peak," *Forbes*, April 30, 2020, https://fortune.com/2020/04/30/unemployment-jobless-great-depression-30-million/.

7. Sal Gilbertie, "Will Oil Prices Go Negative Again?," *Forbes*, April 23, 2020, https://www.forbes.com/sites/salgilbertie/2020/04/23/will-oil-prices-go-negative-again/.

8. Andrew Soergel, "How Much Can America Spend on the Coronavirus Pandemic?," *U.S. News and World Report*, April 21, 2020, https://www.usnews.com/news/economy/articles/2020-04-21/how-much-can-america-spend-on-the-coronavirus-pandemic.

9. Maria Cohut, "Novel Coronavirus: Your Questions, Answered," *Medical News Today*, April 22, 2020, https://www.medicalnewstoday.com/articles/novel-coronavirus-your-questions-answered.

10. David Waldstein, "C.D.C. Releases Early Demographic Snapshot of Worst Coronavirus Cases," *New York Times*, April 8, 2020, https://nyti.ms/2xVMXdD.

11. Matt Simon, "Why the Coronavirus Hit Italy So Hard," *Wired*, March 17, 2020, https://www.wired.com/story/why-the-coronavirus-hit-italy-so-hard/.

12. Dan Diamond, "Inside America's 2-Decade Failure to Prepare for Coronavirus," *Politico*, April 11, 2020, https://politi.co/34HvUIC. Please note that there are several such news analyses. This piece is but one example.

13. "Coronavirus Map: Tracking the Global Outbreak," *New York Times*, April 26, 2020, updated at 8:06 A.M.

14. Uri Friedman, "New Zealand's Prime Minister May Be the Most Effective Leader on the Planet," *The Atlantic*, April 19, 2020, https://www.theatlantic.com/politics/archive/2020/04/jacinda-ardern-new-zealand-leadership-coronavirus/610237/. Regarding the essential elimination of the virus in New Zealand, see Anna Kam and Emma Reynolds, "New Zealand Claims 'Elimination' of Coronavirus with New Cases in Single Digits," *CNN*, April 27, 2020, https://www.cnn.com/2020/04/27/asia/new-zealand-elimination-coronavirus-jacinda-ardern-intl/index.html.

15. Waldstein, "C.D.C. Releases Early Demographic Snapshot," quoting the CDC report of April 8, 2020.

16. Eugene Scott, "4 Reasons Coronavirus Is Hitting Black Communities So Hard," *Washington Post*, April 10, 2020, https://www.washingtonpost.com/politics/2020/04/10/4-reasons-coronavirus-is-hitting-black-communities-so-hard/.

17. Kat Stafford, Meghan Hoyer, and Aaron Morrison, "Racial Toll of Virus Grows Even Starker as More Data Emerges," *AP*, April 18, 2020, https://apnews.com/8a3430dd37e7c44290c7621f5af96d6b.

18. City of Chicago, "Latest Data," April 23, 2020, https://www.chicago.gov/city/en/sites/covid-19/home/latest-data/2020-04-23.html.

19. Marshall Project, "A State-by-State Look at Coronavirus in Prisons," May 1, 2020, https://www.themarshallproject.org/2020/05/01/a-state-by-state-look-at-coronavirus-in-prisons.

20. Heather Cox Richardson, "April 19, 2020," *Letters from an American*, April 20, 2020, https://heathercoxrichardson.substack.com/p/april-19-2020.

21. Griff Witte, "As Protesters Swarm State Capitols, Much of the Coronavirus Backlash Is Coming from Within," *Washington Post*, April 23, 2020, https://www.washingtonpost.com/national/as-protesters-swarm-state-capitols-much-of-the-coronavirus-backlash-is-coming-from-within/2020/04/22/e4d7b1ee-84c8-11ea-a3eb-e9fc93160703_story.html.

22. Michael Harriot, "'Open the Economy' Is the New 'White Lives Matter,'" *The Root*, April 22, 2020, https://www.theroot.com/open-the-economy-is-the-new-white-lives-matter-1842987034.

23. Harriot, "'Open the Economy'" (emphasis in original).

24. Anthony Salvanto et al., "Americans Prioritize Staying Home and Worry Restrictions Will Lift Too Fast—CBS News Poll," *CBS News*, April 23, 2020, https://www.cbsnews.com/news/americans-prioritize-staying-home-and-worry-restrictions-will-lift-too-fast-cbs-news-poll/.

25. Will Feuer, "Coronavirus Cases Are on the Rise in Texas and Other States That Reopened Early, Former FDA Chief Says," *CNBC*, May 12, 2020, https://www.cnbc.com/2020/05/12/coronavirus-cases-are-on-the-rise-in-texas-and-other-states-that-reopened-early-former-fda-chief-says.html; Nicole Cobler, "Texas Sees Spike in Coronavirus Cases as Businesses Reopen," *Austin-American Statesman*, May 1, 2020, https://www

.statesman.com/news/20200501/texas-sees-spike-in-coronavirus-cases-as-businesses
-reopen.

26. Carl Hulse, "McConnell Says States Should Consider Bankruptcy, Rebuffing
Calls for Aid," *New York Times*, April 22, 2020, https://nyti.ms/3bxyG5F.

27. Office of Governor Jay Inslee, "Inslee Announces Colorado and Nevada Will
Join Washington, Oregon and California in Western States Pact," April 27, 2020,
https://www.governor.wa.gov/news-media/inslee-announces-colorado-nevada-will
-join-washington-oregon-california-western-states.

28. George Packer, "We Are Living in a Failed State," *The Atlantic*, June 2020,
https://www.theatlantic.com/magazine/archive/2020/06/underlying-conditions/
610261/.

29. Packer, "We Are Living in a Failed State."

Bibliography

Abou El Fadl, Khaled. "9/11 and the Muslim Transformation." In *September 11 in History: A Watershed Moment?*, edited by Mary Dudziak, 70–111. Durham, NC: Duke University Press, 2003.

Abu-Lughod, Janet. *Race, Space, and Riots in Chicago, New York, and Los Angeles*. New York: Oxford University Press, 2007.

Abu-Lughod, Lila. "Do Muslim Women Really Need Saving? Anthropological Reflections on Cultural Relativism and Its Others." *American Anthropologist* 104 (2002): 783–790.

Addams, Jane. *Democracy and Social Ethics*. 1902. Reprint, Champaign: University of Illinois Press, 2002.

Agathangelou, Anna M., and L.H.M. Ling. "Power, Borders, Security, Wealth: Lessons of Violence and Desire from September 11." *International Studies Quarterly* 48 (2004): 517–538.

Ahmed, Sara. "Affective Economies." *Social Text* 79 (2004): 117–139.

Albright, Madeleine. "The Testing of American Foreign Policy." *Foreign Affairs* 77 (1998): 50–64.

Alexander, Jeffrey C. *Trauma: A Social Theory*. Malden, MA: Polity Press, 2012.

Alexander, Jeffrey, Roy Eyerman, Bernhard Giesen, Neil Smelser, and Piotr Sztompka. *Cultural Trauma and Collective Identity*. Berkeley: University of California Press, 2004.

Allen, Danielle. *Talking to Strangers: Anxieties of Citizenship since Brown v. Board of Education*. Chicago: University of Chicago Press, 2006.

Allen, James, Hilton Als, John Lewis, and Leon Litwack. *Without Sanctuary: Lynching Photography in America*. Santa Fe: Twin Palms, 2000.

Allen, Theodore. *The Invention of the White Race*. Vol. 1, *Racial Oppression and Social Control*. New York: Verso, 1994.

Alvarez, Lizette, and Cara Buckley. "Zimmerman Is Acquitted in Trayvon Martin Killing." *New York Times*, July 13, 2013. https://nyti.ms/12MKyWV.

American Experience: The Murder of Emmett Till. Directed by Stanley Nelson. Written by Marcia Smith. Boston: WGBH Educational Foundation, 2003. DVD.

"America under Attack: Bush Holds Press Briefing." *CNN*, September 11, 2001. http://transcripts.cnn.com/TRANSCRIPTS/0109/11/bn.35.html.

Anderson, Benedict. *Imagined Communities: Reflections on the Origin and Spread of Nationalism.* Rev. ed. New York: Verso, 2003.

Anderson, Carol. *Eyes Off the Prize: The United Nations and the African American Struggle for Human Rights, 1944–1955.* New York: Cambridge University Press, 2003.

Anker, Elisabeth. *Orgies of Feeling: Melodrama and the Politics of Freedom.* Durham, NC: Duke University, 2014.

———. "Villains, Victims, and Heroes: Melodrama, Media, and September 11." *Journal of Communication* 55 (2005): 22–37.

Anonymous. "I Am Part of the Resistance inside the Trump Administration." *New York Times*, September 5, 2018. https://nyti.ms/2CyF3Jh.

Apel, Dora. *Imagery of Lynching: Black Men, White Women, and the Mob.* New Brunswick, NJ: Rutgers University Press, 2004.

Argersinger, Jo Ann. *The Triangle Fire: A Brief History with Documents.* New York: Bedford/St. Martin's Press, 2009.

Baldus, David C., George Woodworth, and Charles A. Pulaski. *Equal Justice and the Death Penalty: A Legal and Empirical Analysis.* Boston: Northeastern University Press, 1990.

Baldwin, James. *The Fire Next Time.* New York: Vintage International, 1993.

———. "My Dungeon Shook: Letter to My Nephew on the One Hundredth Anniversary of Emancipation." In *The Fire Next Time*, 1–10. New York: Vintage International, 1993.

Balfour, Lawrie. *The Evidence of Things Not Said: James Baldwin and the Promise of American Democracy.* Ithaca, NY: Cornell University Press, 2001.

———. "'A Most Disagreeable Mirror': Race Consciousness as Double Consciousness." *Political Theory* 26, no. 3 (June 1998): 346–369.

Barnard, Anne. "Beirut, Also the Site of Deadly Attacks, Feels Forgotten." *New York Times*, November 15, 2015. https://www.nytimes.com/2015/11/16/world/middleeast/beirut-lebanon-attacks-paris.html.

Belknap, Michal. *Federal Law and Southern Order: Racial Violence and Constitutional Conflict in the Post-Brown South.* Athens: University of Georgia Press, 1987.

Bell, Derrick A., Jr. *And We Are Not Saved: The Elusive Quest for Racial Justice.* New York: Basic Books, 1987.

———. "*Brown v. Board of Education* and the Interest-Convergence Dilemma." *Harvard Law Review* 93, no. 3 (1980): 518–533.

———. *Faces at the Bottom of the Well: The Permanence of Racism.* New York: Basic Books, 1992.

Benjamin, Walter. "Critique of Violence." In *Reflections: Essays, Aphorisms, Autobiographical Writings*, edited by Peter Demetz, 277–300. New York: Schocken Books, 1986.

———. "Theses on the Philosophy of History." In *Illuminations*, edited by Hannah Arendt, 253–264. New York: Schocken Books, 1968.

Berger, James. "'There's No Backhand to This.'" In *Trauma at Home: After 9/11*, edited by Judith Greenberg, 52–59. Lincoln: University of Nebraska Press, 2003.

Berger, Joseph. "100 Years Later, the Roll of the Dead in a Factory Fire Is Complete." *New York Times*, February 20, 2011. https://www.nytimes.com/2011/02/21/ny region/21triangle.html.

Birkland, Thomas. *After Disaster: Agenda Setting, Public Policy, and Focusing Events.* Washington, DC: Georgetown University Press, 1997.

———. *Lessons of Disaster: Policy Change after Catastrophic Events.* Washington, DC: Georgetown University Press, 2006.

Blight, David. *Race and Reunion: The Civil War in American Memory.* Cambridge, MA: Harvard University Press, 2001.

Bosman, Julie, and Joseph Goldstein. "Timeline for a Body: 4 Hours in the Middle of a Ferguson Street." *New York Times*, August 23, 2014. https://nyti.ms/1qAFMqN.

Bostdorff, Denise. "George W. Bush's Post-September 11 Rhetoric of Covenant Renewal: Upholding the Faith of the Greatest Generation." *Quarterly Journal of Speech* 89 (2003): 293–313.

Botelho, Grew, and Holly Yan. "George Zimmerman Found Not Guilty of Murder in Trayvon Martin's Death." *CNN*, July 13, 2013. https://edition.cnn.com/2013/07/ 13/justice/zimmerman-trial/index.html.

Brady, Tom. *Black Monday.* Winona, MS: Association of Citizens' Councils, 1955.

Bragg, Rick. "Terror in Oklahoma City: At Ground Zero; In Shock, Loathing, Denial: 'This Doesn't Happen Here.'" *New York Times*, April 20, 1995, https://nyti.ms/2uz Um02.

Brodkin, Karen. *How Jews Became White Folks and What That Says about Race in America.* New Brunswick, NJ: Rutgers University Press, 1998.

Brown, Wendy. *Walled States, Waning Sovereignty.* New York: Zone Books, 2014.

Buncombe, Andrew. "America Has No Idea How Many Innocent People It's Killing in the Middle East." *The Independent*, November 20, 2017. https://www.indepen dent.co.uk/voices/us-isis-air-strikes-civilian-deaths-syria-iraq-america-no-idea -how-many-dead-the-uncounted-a8066266.html.

Butler, Judith. *Antigone's Claim.* New York: Columbia University Press, 2002.

———. *Precarious Life: The Powers of Mourning and Violence.* New York: Verso, 2004.

———. *Undoing Gender.* New York: Routledge, 2004.

Cainkar, Louise. "Thinking Outside the Box." In *Race and Arab Americans before and after 9/11: From Invisible Citizens to Visible Subjects*, edited by Amaney Jamal and Nadine Naber, 46–80. Syracuse, NY: Syracuse University Press, 2008.

Carmines, Edward, and James Stimson. *Issue Evolution: Race and the Transformation of American Politics.* Princeton, NJ: Princeton University Press, 1989.

Carney, Nikita. "All Lives Matter, but So Does Race: Black Lives Matter and the Evolving Role of Social Media." *Humanity and Society* 40, no. 2 (April 2016): 180–199.

Carrega, Christina. "5 Years after Eric Garner's Death, a Look Back at the Case and the Movement It Sparked." *ABC News*, July 16, 2019. https://abcn.ws/2XMI82j.

Carter, Bill, and Felicity Barringer. "In Patriotic Time, Dissent Is Muted." *New York Times*, September 28, 2001, p. A1.

Cassese, Antonio. "Terrorism Is Also Disrupting Some Crucial Legal Categories of International Law." *European Journal of International Law* 12 (2001): 993–1001.

City of Chicago. "Latest Data." April 23, 2020. https://www.chicago.gov/city/en/sites/ covid-19/home/latest-data/2020-04-23.html.

Clark, Mary Marshall. "The September 11 Oral History Narrative and Memory Project." In *History and September 11*, edited by Joanne Meyerowitz, 117–130. Philadelphia: Temple University Press, 2003.

CNN Editorial Research. "1998 US Embassies in Africa Bombings Fast Facts." *CNN*, August 3, 2020. https://www.cnn.com/2013/10/06/world/africa/africa-embassy -bombings-fast-facts/index.html.

Coates, Ta-Nehisi. *Between the World and Me.* New York: Spiegel and Grau, 2015.

Cobler, Nicole. "Texas Sees Spike in Coronavirus Cases as Businesses Reopen." *Austin-American Statesman*, May 1, 2020. https://www.statesman.com/news/20200501/ texas-sees-spike-in-coronavirus-cases-as-businesses-reopen.

Cohen, Cathy. *The Boundaries of Blackness: AIDS and the Breakdown of Black Politics.* Chicago: University of Chicago Press, 1999.

Cohen, Elizabeth. *Semi-citizenship in Democratic Politics.* Cambridge: Cambridge University Press, 2008.

Cohut, Maria. "Novel Coronavirus: Your Questions, Answered." *Medical News Today*, April 22, 2020. https://www.medicalnewstoday.com/articles/novel-coronavirus -your-questions-answered.

"College Girls as Pickets in a Strike." *New York Times Magazine*, December 19, 1909, p. 5.

The Compact Edition of the Oxford English Dictionary. Vol. 1. Oxford: Oxford University Press, 1971.

Connolly, William E. *Identity\Difference: Democratic Negotiations of Political Paradox.* Expanded ed. Minneapolis: University of Minnesota Press, 2002.

"Coronavirus Map: Tracking the Global Outbreak." *New York Times*, April 25, 2020, April 26, 2020, and May 3, 2020. https://www.nytimes.com/interactive/2020/ world/coronavirus-maps.html.

Council on American-Islamic Relations. "The Status of Muslim Civil Rights in the United States, 2007: Presumption of Guilt." 2007. https://www.cair.com/wp -content/uploads/2017/09/CAIR-2007-Civil-Rights-Report.pdf.

Cover, Robert. *Narrative, Violence, and the Law: The Essays of Robert Cover.* Edited by Martha Minow, Michael Ryan, and Austin Sarat. Ann Arbor: University of Michigan Press, 1995.

"Covid in the U.S.: Latest Map and Case Count." *New York Times*, May 3, 2020. https://nyti.ms/39jvJEY.

Crawford, Neta C. "Human Cost of the Post-9/11 Wars: Lethality and the Need for Transparency." Brown University Watson Institute International and Public Affairs, November 2018. https://watson.brown.edu/costsofwar/files/cow/imce/papers/2018/ Human%20Costs%2C%20Nov%208%202018%20CoW.pdf.

Crenshaw, Kimberlé, Neil Gotanda, Gary Peller, and Kendall Thomas, eds. *Critical Race Theory: The Key Writing That Formed the Movement.* New York: New Press, 1995.

"The Day the Twin Towers Fell." *Iconic Photos* (blog), September 5, 2011. https:// iconicphotos.wordpress.com/tag/todd-maisel/.

Deliso, Meredith. "Timeline: The Impact of George Floyd's Death in Minneapolis and Beyond." *ABC News*, June 10, 2020. https://abcn.ws/2ZXDEWx.

Demby, Gene. "What We Know (and Don't Know) about 'Missing White Women Syndrome.'" *NPR*, April 13, 2017. https://www.npr.org/sections/codeswitch/2017/ 04/13/523769303/what-we-know-and-dont-know-about-missing-white-women -syndrome.

"Demographic Data on the Victims of the September 11, 2001, Terror Attack on the World Trade Center, New York City." *Population and Development Review* 28 (2002): 586–588.

Devetak, Richard. "The Gothic Scene of International Relations: Ghosts, Monsters, Terror and the Sublime after September 11." *Review of International Studies* 31 (2005): 621–643.

Dewey, John. *The Public and Its Problems.* 1927. Reprint, Athens: University of Ohio Press, 1991.

Diamond, Dan. "Inside America's 2-Decade Failure to Prepare for Coronavirus." *Politico*, April 11, 2020. https://politi.co/34HvUIC.

Didion, Joan. *Fixed Ideas: America since 9/11.* New York: New York Review of Books, 2003.

Doka, Kenneth. "Death, Loss, and Disenfranchised Grief." In *Disenfranchised Grief: Recognizing Hidden Sorrow*, edited by Kenneth Doka, 13–24. Lexington, MA: Lexington Books, 1989.

———, ed. *Disenfranchised Grief: New Directions, Challenges, and Strategies for Practice.* Champaign, IL: Research Press, 2002.

Du Bois, W.E.B. *Black Reconstruction in America: 1860–1880.* 1935. Reprint, New York: Free Press, 1998.

Dudziak, Mary L. *Cold War Civil Rights: Race and the Image of American Democracy.* Princeton, NJ: Princeton University Press, 2000.

———, ed. *September 11 in History: A Watershed Moment?* Durham, NC: Duke University Press, 2003.

Dye, Nancy Schrom. *As Equals and As Sisters: Feminism, the Labor Movement, and the Women's Trade Union League of New York.* Columbia: University of Missouri Press, 1980.

Easley, Jonathan. "Poll: 57 Percent Have Negative View of Black Lives Matter Movement." *The Hill*, August 2, 2017. https://thehill.com/homenews/campaign/344985-poll-57-percent-have-negative-view-of-black-lives-matter-movement.

Edkins, Jenny. *Trauma and the Memory of Politics.* Cambridge: Cambridge University Press, 2003.

Eisenhower, Dwight D. "Annual Message to the Congress on the State of the Union." January 5, 1956. https://www.presidency.ucsb.edu/documents/annual-message-the-congress-the-state-the-union-11.

Elliott, Robert. "Thousands at Rites for Till." *Chicago Defender*, September 10, 1955, p. 1.

Eng, David L., and David Kazanjian, eds. *Loss: The Politics of Mourning.* Berkeley: University of California Press, 2002.

Euben, Roxanne Leslie. "The New Manichaeans." *Theory and Event* 5, no. 4 (2001). https://doi.org/10.1353/tae.2001.0034.

"Exclusive Pictures of Lynch Victim's Funeral." *Chicago Defender*, May 28, 1955, p. 5.

Eyes on the Prize: America's Civil Rights Years. Episode 1, "Awakenings, 1954–1956." Directed by Judith Vecchione. Created by Henry Hampton. Los Angeles: Pacific Arts, 1992. DVD.

The Falling Man. Directed by Henry Singer. Written by Tom Junod. London: Darlow Smithson Productions, 2006.

Farzan, Antonia Noori. "BBQ Becky, Permit Patty and Cornerstore Caroline: Too 'Cutesy' for Those White Women Calling Police on Black People?" *Washington Post*, October 18, 2019. https://www.washingtonpost.com/news/morning-mix/wp/2018/10/19/bbq-becky-permit-patty-and-cornerstore-caroline-too-cutesy-for-those-white-women-calling-cops-on-blacks/.

Faust, Drew Gilpin. *This Republic of Suffering: Death and the American Civil War.* New York: Alfred A. Knopf, 2008.

Feuer, Will. "Coronavirus Cases Are on the Rise in Texas and Other States That Reopened Early, Former FDA Chief Says." *CNBC*, May 12, 2020. https://www.cnbc.com/2020/05/12/coronavirus-cases-are-on-the-rise-in-texas-and-other-states-that-reopened-early-former-fda-chief-says.html.

Frazer, Michael L. *The Enlightenment of Sympathy: Justice and the Moral Sentiments in the Eighteenth Century and Today.* New York: Oxford University Press, 2010.

Freud, Sigmund. "Mourning and Melancholia." In *On Murder, Mourning and Melancholia*, edited by Adam Phillips, translated by Shaun Whiteside, 201–219. New York: Penguin, 2005.

Friedman, Uri. "New Zealand's Prime Minister May Be the Most Effective Leader on the Planet." *The Atlantic*, April 19, 2020. https://www.theatlantic.com/politics/archive/2020/04/jacinda-ardern-new-zealand-leadership-coronavirus/610237/.

Frymer, Paul. *Uneasy Alliances: Race and Party Competition in America.* Princeton, NJ: Princeton University Press, 1999.

Fukuyama, Francis. "The End of History." *National Interest* 16 (1989): 3–18.

Galanter, Marc. "Why the 'Haves' Come Out Ahead: Speculations on the Limits of Legal Change." *Law and Society Review* 9, no. 1 (1974): 95–160.

Gallagher, Ryan J., Andrew J. Reagan, Christopher M. Danforth, and Peter Sheridan Dodds. "Divergent Discourse between Protests and Counter-protests: #BlackLivesMatter and #AllLivesMatter." *PLoS ONE* 13, no. 4 (2018). https://doi.org/10.1371/journal.pone.0195644.

Giffords Law Center to Prevent Gun Violence. "Guns in Public: Stand Your Ground." https://lawcenter.giffords.org/gun-laws/policy-areas/guns-in-public/stand-your-ground-laws/ (accessed November 10, 2020).

Gilbertie, Sal. "Will Oil Prices Go Negative Again?" *Forbes*, April 23, 2020. https://www.forbes.com/sites/salgilbertie/2020/04/23/will-oil-prices-go-negative-again/.

Gillis, John, ed. *Commemorations: The Politics of National Identity.* Princeton, NJ: Princeton University Press, 1994.

"Girl Strikers Tell the Rich Their Woes." *New York Times*, December 16, 1909, p. 3.

Goldberg, Vicki. *The Power of Photography: How Photographs Changed Our Lives.* New York: Abbeville, 1991.

Goldsby, Jacqueline. "The High and Low Tech of It: The Meaning of Lynching and the Death of Emmett Till." *Yale Journal of Criticism* 9 (1996): 245–282.

Goodstein, Laurie. "Report Cites Harassment of Muslims." *Washington Post*, April 20, 1996. https://www.washingtonpost.com/archive/politics/1996/04/20/report-cites-harassment-of-muslims/63dd282e-e1db-4727-8672-b89f6f33f899.

Graeff, Erhardt, Matt Stempeck, and Ethan Zuckerman. "The Battle for 'Trayvon Martin': Mapping a Media Controversy Online and Off-Line." *First Monday*, February 2014, pp. 1–23.

Gray, Jerry. "Senate Approves Anti-terror Bill by 91-to-8 Vote." *New York Times*, June 8, 1995, p. A1.

Green, Jeffrey W. S. "Eyewitness to History." *Uptown Chronicle*, September 8, 2011. Previously available at http://theuptownchronicle.com/?p=1759.

Greenwald, Richard. *The Triangle Fire, the Protocols of Peace, and Industrial Democracy in Progressive Era New York.* Philadelphia: Temple University Press, 2005.

Greenwood, Christopher. "International Law and the 'War against Terrorism.'" *International Affairs* 18 (2001): 301–317.

Gualtieri, Sarah. "Strange Fruit? Syrian Immigrants, Extralegal Violence, and Racial Formation in the United States." In *Race and Arab Americans before and after 9/11: From Invisible Citizens to Visible Subjects*, edited by Amaney Jamal and Nadine Naber, 147–169. Syracuse, NY: Syracuse University Press, 2008.

Gura, David. "'Lying in Repose' vs. 'Lying in State' vs. 'Lying in Honor': What's the Difference?" *NPR*, August 26, 2009. https://www.npr.org/sections/thetwo-way/200 9/08/lying_in_repose_v_lying_in_sta.html.

Guterl, Matthew. *The Color of Race in America, 1900–1940*. Cambridge, MA: Harvard University Press, 2001.

Halbwachs, Maurice. *On Collective Memory*. Chicago: University of Chicago Press, 1992.

Hampton, Henry, and Stephen Fayer. *Voices of Freedom: An Oral History of the Civil Rights Movement from the 1950s through the 1980s*. New York: Bantam Books, 1990.

Haney López, Ian. *White by Law: The Legal Construction of Race*. New York: New York University Press: 1996.

Harold, Christine, and Kevin Michael DeLuca. "Behold the Corpse: Violent Images and the Case of Emmett Till." *Rhetoric and Public Affairs* 8 (2005): 263–286.

Harriot, Michael. "'Open the Economy' Is the New 'White Lives Matter.'" *The Root*, April 22, 2020. https://www.theroot.com/open-the-economy-is-the-new-white-lives -matter-1842987034.

Harris, Cheryl. "Whiteness as Property." *Harvard Law Review* 106, no. 8 (1993): 1707–1791.

Harris, Frederick C. "It Takes a Tragedy to Arouse Them: Collective Memory and Collective Action during the Civil Rights Movement." *Social Movement Studies* 5 (2006): 19–43.

Harris-Lacewell, Melissa Victoria. *Barbershops, Bibles, and BET: Everyday Talk and Black Political Thought*. Princeton, NJ: Princeton University Press, 2004.

Harvard Center for American Political Studies and Harris Insights and Analytics. "Harvard-Harris Poll." July 27, 2017. https://harvardharrispoll.com/wp-content/ uploads/2017/07/Harvard-Harris-Poll_July_07.27.2017.pptx.

Hassan, Adeel. "The Sandra Bland Video: What We Know." *New York Times*, May 7, 2019. https://nyti.ms/2Vk2You.

Haver, William. *The Body of This Death: Historicity and Sociality in the Time of AIDS*. Stanford, CA: Stanford University Press, 1996.

Hayward, Clarissa Rile. *How Americans Make Race: Stories, Institutions, Spaces*. Cambridge: Cambridge University Press, 2013.

Hobbes, Thomas. *Leviathan*. 1651. Reprint, Indianapolis, IN: Hackett, 1994.

Hochschild, Arlie. *Strangers in Their Own Land: Anger and Mourning on the American Right*. New York: New Press, 2016.

"Homecoming of a Lynch Victim." *Life*, September 12, 1955, p. 47.

Honig, Bonnie. *Antigone, Interrupted*. Cambridge: Cambridge University Press, 2013.

———. *Emergency Politics: Paradox, Law, Democracy*. Princeton, NJ: Princeton University Press, 2009.

Hooker, Juliet. "Black Protest/White Grievance: On the Problem of White Political Imaginations Not Shaped by Loss." *South Atlantic Quarterly* 116, no. 3 (July 2017): 483–504.

———. *Race and the Politics of Solidarity*. Oxford: Oxford University Press, 2009.

Hopkins, Mary Alden. "1910 Newark Factory Fire." *McClure's Magazine*, April 1911. http://oldnewark.com/histories/factoryfirearticle.php.

Horowitz, Jason, and Emma Bubola. "Italy's Coronavirus Victims Face Death Alone, with Funerals Postponed." *New York Times*, March 16, 2020. https://nyti.ms/2W kcfwm.

Hudson-Weems, Clenora. *Emmett Till: The Sacrificial Lamb of the Civil Rights Movement*. Troy, MI: Bedford, 1994.

Huie, William Bradford. "The Shocking Story of Approved Killing in Mississippi." *Look*, January 24, 1956. https://www.pbs.org/wgbh/americanexperience/features/till-kill ers-confession/.

Hulse, Carl. "McConnell Says States Should Consider Bankruptcy, Rebuffing Calls for Aid." *New York Times*, April 22, 2020. https://nyti.ms/3bxyG5F.

"Hundreds Weep, Faint at Sight," *Chicago Defender*, September 17, 1955, p. 2.

Huntington, Samuel. "The Erosion of American National Interests." *Foreign Affairs* 76 (1997): 28–49.

———. "The Lonely Superpower," *Foreign Affairs* 78 (1999): 35–49.

Hutcheson, John, David Domke, Andre Billeaudeaux, and Philip Garland. "U.S. National Identity, Political Elites, and a Patriotic Press Following September 11." *Political Communication* 21 (2004): 27–50.

Idov, Michael. "Unidentified Remains." In "The Encyclopedia of 9/11," special issue, *New York Magazine*, August 27, 2011. https://nymag.com/news/9-11/10th-anniversary/ unidentified-remains/.

Ignatiev, Noel. *How the Irish Became White*. New York: Routledge, 2009.

"Inez Milholland Held in Strike Case," *New York Times*, January 18, 1910, p. 1.

Jackson, Donald, and James Riddlesperger Jr. "The Eisenhower Administration and the 1957 Civil Rights Act." In *Reexamining the Eisenhower Presidency*, edited by Shirley Anne Warshaw, 85–101. Westport, CT: Greenwood Press, 1993.

Jackson, Jesse. "Foreword." In *Death of Innocence: The Story of the Hate Crime That Changed America*, by Mamie Till-Mobley and Christopher Benson, xi–xiii. Newark, NJ: One World/Ballantine Books, 2003.

Jacobson, Matthew Frye. *Whiteness of a Different Color: European Immigrants and the Alchemy of Race*. Cambridge, MA: Harvard University Press, 1998.

Jamal, Amaney. "Civil Liberties and the Otherization of Arab and Muslim Americans." In *Race and Arab Americans before and after 9/11*, edited by Jamal Amaney and Nadine Naber, 114–130. Syracuse, NY: Syracuse University Press, 2008.

Jamal, Amaney, and Nadine Naber, eds. *Race and Arab Americans before and after 9/11: From Invisible Citizens to Visible Subjects*. Syracuse, NY: Syracuse University Press, 2008.

James, Joy. *Resisting State Violence: Radicalism, Gender, and Race in U.S. Culture*. Minneapolis: University of Minnesota Press, 1996.

Johnston, David. "Terror in Oklahoma City: The Investigation; At Least 31 Are Dead, Scores Missing after Car Bomb Attack in Oklahoma City Wrecks 9-Story Federal Building." *New York Times*, April 20, 1995, https://nyti.ms/2tYFrMD.

Johnston, Steven. "This Patriotism Which Is Not One." *Polity* 34 (2002): 285–312.

Junod, Tom. "The Falling Man: An Unforgettable Story." *Esquire*, September 9, 2016. https://www.esquire.com/news-politics/a48031/the-falling-man-tom-junod/.

Kam, Anna, and Emma Reynolds. "New Zealand Claims 'Elimination' of Coronavirus with New Cases in Single Digits." *CNN*, April 27, 2020. https://www.cnn.com/2020/ 04/27/asia/new-zealand-elimination-coronavirus-jacinda-ardern-intl/index.html.

Karimi, Faith. "Improved DNA Technique Used to Identify Man Killed in Sept. 11 Terror Attacks." *CNN*, July 26, 2018. https://www.cnn.com/2018/07/26/us/new-york-9-11-victim-identified/index.html.

Kateb, George. "Is Patriotism a Mistake?" *Social Research* 67 (2000): 901–924.

———. "A Life of Fear." *Social Research* 71, no. 4 (Winter 2004): 887–926.

Katz, Josh, Denise Lu, and Margot Sanger-Katz. "U.S. Coronavirus Death Toll Is Far Higher Than Reported, C.D.C. Data Suggests." *New York Times*, April 28, 2020. https://nyti.ms/2ybWxtp.

Katznelson, Ira. *When Affirmative Action Was White: An Untold History of Racial Inequality in Twentieth-Century America.* New York: W. W. Norton, 2005.

Kempton, Murray. "He Went All the Way." In *Reporting Civil Rights, Part I: American Journalism, 1941–1963*, edited by Clayborne Carson, David J. Garrow, Bill Kovach, and Carol Polsgrove, 214–216. New York: Library of America, 2003.

Kersch, Ken. "The Reconstruction of Constitutional Privacy Rights and the New American State." *Studies in American Political Development* 16 (2002): 61–87.

Kim, Claire Jean. *Bitter Fruit: The Politics of Black-Korean Conflict in New York City.* New Haven, CT: Yale University Press, 2000.

Kingdon, John. *Agendas, Alternatives, and Public Policies.* Boston: Longman, 2003.

Klein, Kerwin Lee. "On the Emergence of Memory in Historical Discourse." *Representations* 69 (2000): 127–150.

Krause, Sharon. *Civil Passions: Moral Sentiment and Democratic Deliberation.* Princeton, NJ: Princeton University Press, 2008.

Krauthammer, Charles. "The Unipolar Moment." *Foreign Affairs* 70 (1990–1991): 23–33.

Kruzel, John. "Are White Males Responsible for More Mass Shootings than Any Other Group?" *PolitiFact*, October 6, 2017. https://www.politifact.com/punditfact/statements/2017/oct/06/newsweek/are-white-males-responsible-more-mass-shootings-an/.

Kurtz, Sharon. *Workplace Justice: Organizing Multi-identity Movements.* Minneapolis: University of Minnesota Press, 2002.

Lambert, Lance. "The Latest Round of Unemployment Claims Puts Real Jobless Rate near Great Depression Peak." *Forbes*, April 30, 2020. https://fortune.com/2020/04/30/unemployment-jobless-great-depression-30-million/.

Lankford, Adam. "Race and Mass Murder in the United States: A Social and Behavioral Analysis." *Current Sociology* 64, no. 3 (2016): 470–490.

Lassiter, Matthew D. "De Jure/De Facto Segregation: The Long Shadow of a National Myth." In *The Myth of Southern Exceptionalism*, edited by Matthew D. Lassiter and Joseph Crespino, 25–48. New York: Oxford University Press, 2010.

Lassiter, Matthew D., and Joseph Crespino. "Introduction: The End of Southern History." In *The Myth of Southern Exceptionalism*, edited by Matthew D. Lassiter and Joseph Crespino, 3–22. New York: Oxford University Press, 2010.

———, eds. *The Myth of Southern Exceptionalism.* New York: Oxford University Press, 2010.

Lavin, Chad. *The Politics of Responsibility.* Champaign: University of Illinois Press, 2008.

Lawson, Tamara F. "A Fresh Cut in an Old Wound—a Critical Analysis of the Trayvon Martin Killing: The Public Outcry, the Prosecutors' Discretion, and the Stand Your Ground Law." *University of Florida Journal of Law and Public Policy* 23, no. 3 (December 2012): 271–310.

Layton, Azza Salama. *International Political and Civil Rights Policies in the United States, 1941–1960*. New York: Cambridge University Press, 2000.

Lebron, Chris. *The Making of Black Lives Matter: A Brief History of an Idea*. New York: Oxford University Press, 2017.

Lehrer, Susan. *Origins of Protective Labor Legislation for Women, 1905–1925*. Albany: State University of New York Press, 1987.

Lemlich, Clara. "Life in the Shop." *New York Evening Journal*, November 26, 1909.

Leonnig, Carol D., and Jenna Johnson. "Anger Flows at Acquittal of George Zimmerman in Death of Trayvon Martin." *Washington Post*, July 14, 2013. http://wapo.st/18hYbp7.

Lewis, George. *Massive Resistance: The White Response to the Civil Rights Movement*. New York: Hodder Arnold/Oxford, 2006.

Lipsitz, George. *The Possessive Investment in Whiteness: How White People Profit from Identity Politics*. Rev. ed. Philadelphia: Temple University Press, 2006.

Locke, John. *Second Treatise on Government*. 1690. Reprint, Indianapolis, IN: Hackett, 1980.

Lovell, George, and Michael McCann. "A Tangled Legacy: Federal Courts and Democratic Inclusion." In *The Politics of Democratic Inclusion*, edited by Christina Wolbrecht and Rodney E. Hero, 257–280. Philadelphia: Temple University Press, 2005.

Lowe, Lisa. *Immigrant Acts: On Asian American Cultural Politics*. Durham, NC: Duke University Press, 1996.

Makdisi, Ussama. "'Anti-Americanism' in the Arab World: An Interpretation of a Brief History." In *History and September 11*, edited by Joanne Meyerowitz, 131–156. Philadelphia: Temple University Press, 2003.

Mandelbaum, Michael. "The Inadequacy of American Power." *Foreign Affairs* 81 (2002): 61–73.

Mann, Bonnie. *Sovereign Masculinity: Gender Lessons from the War on Terror*. New York: Oxford University Press, 2014.

Marshall Project. "A State-by-State Look at Coronavirus in Prisons." May 1, 2020. https://www.themarshallproject.org/2020/05/01/a-state-by-state-look-at-coronavirus-in-prisons.

May, Ernest, ed. *The 9/11 Commission Report with Related Documents*. New York: Bedford/St. Martin's Press, 2007.

May, Peter. *Recovering from Catastrophes: Federal Disaster Relief Policy and Politics*. Westport, CT: Greenwood Press, 1985.

McAdam, Doug. *Political Process and the Development of Black Insurgency, 1930–1970*. 2nd ed. Chicago: University of Chicago Press, 1999.

McCann, Michael W. *Rights at Work: Pay Equity Reform and the Politics of Legal Mobilization*. Chicago: University of Chicago Press, 1994.

McClam, Erin. "Chief Defends Release of Robbery Surveillance Video." *NBC News*, August 15, 2014. https://www.nbcnews.com/storyline/michael-brown-shooting/chief-defends-release-robbery-surveillance-video-n181786.

McEvoy, Arthur. "The Triangle Shirtwaist Fire of 1911: Social Change, Industrial Accidents, and the Evolution of Common-Sense Causality." *Law and Social Inquiry* 20 (Spring 1995): 621–651.

McFarlane, Arthur. "Fire and the Skyscraper: The Problem of Protecting Workers in New York's Tower Factories." *McClure's Magazine*, September 1911, pp. 466–472.

McIvor, David. *Mourning in America: Race and the Politics of Loss*. Ithaca, NY: Cornell University Press, 2016.

Mensch, Elizabeth. "The History of Mainstream Legal Thought." In *The Politics of Law: A Progressive Critique*, 3rd ed., edited by David Kairys, 23–53. New York: Basic Books, 1998.

Metress, Christopher, ed. *The Lynching of Emmett Till: A Documentary Narrative*. Charlottesville: University of Virginia Press, 2002.

Miller, Jake. "Obama Calls for Calm in Wake of George Zimmerman Verdict." *CBS News*, July 15, 2013. https://www.cbsnews.com/news/obama-calls-for-calm-in-wake -of-george-zimmerman-verdict/.

Miller, Ruth. *Law in Crisis: The Ecstatic Subject of Natural Disaster*. Stanford, CA: Stanford University Press, 2009.

Mills, Charles. *The Racial Contract*. Ithaca, NY: Cornell University Press, 1999.

Morris, Aldon. *The Origins of the Civil Rights Movement: Black Communities Organizing for Change*. New York: Free Press, 1984.

Naber, Nadine. "Introduction: Arab Americans and U.S. Racial Formations." In *Race and Arab Americans before and after 9/11: From Invisible Citizens to Visible Subjects*, edited by Amaney Jamal and Nadine Naber, 1–45. Syracuse, NY: Syracuse University Press, 2008.

———. "'Look, Mohammed the Terrorist Is Coming!' Cultural Racism, Nation-Based Racism, and the Intersectionality of Oppressions after 9/11." In *Race and Arab Americans before and after 9/11: From Invisible Citizens to Visible Subjects*, edited by Amaney Jamal and Nadine Naber, 276–304. Syracuse, NY: Syracuse University Press, 2008.

"Nation Horrified by Murder of Kidnaped Youth." *Jet*, September 15, 1955, p. 8.

Neimeyer, Robert A., Holly Prigerson, and Betty Davies. "Mourning and Meaning." *American Behavioral Scientist* 46 (2002): 235–251.

"New Drive Set in Congress." *New York Times*, October 22, 1955, p. 40.

Ngai, Mae. *Impossible Subjects: Illegal Aliens and the Making of Modern America*. Princeton, NJ: Princeton University Press, 2005.

Nichols, David Allen. *A Matter of Justice: Eisenhower and the Beginning of the Civil Rights Revolution*. New York: Simon and Schuster, 2007.

Norton, Anne. *Reflections on Political Identity*. Baltimore: Johns Hopkins University Press, 1988.

Nussbaum, Martha. *Creating Capabilities: The Human Development Approach*. Cambridge, MA: Harvard University Press, 2013.

Oby, Michael Randolph. "Black Press Coverage of the Emmett Till Lynching as a Catalyst to the Civil Rights Movement." Master's thesis, Georgia State University, 2007.

Office of Chief Medical Examiner. "Update on the Results of DNA Testing of Remains Recovered at the World Trade Center Site and Surrounding Area." February 1, 2009. http://www.nyc.gov/html/ocme/downloads/pdf/public_affairs_ocme_pr_february _2009.pdf.

Office of Governor Jay Inslee. "Inslee Announces Colorado and Nevada Will Join Washington, Oregon and California in Western States Pact." April 27, 2020. https://www.governor.wa.gov/news-media/inslee-announces-colorado-nevada-will -join-washington-oregon-california-western-states.

Olson, Joel. *The Abolition of White Democracy*. Minneapolis: University of Minnesota Press, 2004.

Omi, Michael, and Howard Winant. *Racial Formation in the United States: From the 1960s to the 1990s*. 2nd ed. New York: Routledge, 1994.

"147 Dead, Nobody Guilty." *Literary Digest*, January 6, 1912.

"120,000 Pay Tribute to the Fire Victims." *New York Times*, April 6, 1911, p. 1.

Orleck, Annelise. *Common Sense and a Little Fire: Women and Working-Class Politics in the United States, 1900–1965*. Chapel Hill: University of North Carolina Press, 1995.

Packer, George. "We Are Living in a Failed State." *The Atlantic*, June 2020. https:// www.theatlantic.com/magazine/archive/2020/06/underlying-conditions/610261/.

Painter, Nell Irvin. *The History of White People*. New York: W. W. Norton, 2010.

"Partners' Account of the Disaster." *New York Times*, March 26, 1911.

Patterson, James. *Brown v. Board of Education: A Civil Rights Milestone and Its Troubled Legacy*. Oxford: Oxford University Press, 2001.

Paust, Jordan. "War and Enemy Status after 9/11: Attacks on the Laws of War." *Yale Journal of International Law* 28 (2003): 325–335.

Payne, Elizabeth Anne. *Reform, Labor, and Feminism: Margaret Dreier Robins and the Women's Trade Union League*. Urbana: University of Illinois Press, 1988.

Pearce, Roy Harvey. *Savagism and Civilization: A Study of the Indian and the American Mind*. Baltimore: Johns Hopkins University Press, 1967.

Perkins, Frances. Lecture at Cornell University School of Industrial and Labor Relations, September 20, 1964. https://trianglefire.ilr.cornell.edu/primary/lectures/Frances PerkinsLecture.html?CFID=5042574&CFTOKEN=23588311.

Peters, Jeremy W. "How Politics Took Over the Killing of Mollie Tibbetts." *New York Times*, August 23, 2018. https://nyti.ms/2BSU20j.

Pew Research Center. "American Psyche Reeling from Terror Attacks." September 19, 2001. https://www.pewresearch.org/politics/2001/09/19/american-psyche-reeling -from-terror-attacks/.

———. "The Partisan Divide on Political Values Grows Even Wider." October 5, 2017. https://www.people-press.org/2017/10/05/the-partisan-divide-on-political-values -grows-even-wider/.

———. "Political Typology Reveals Deep Fissures on the Right and Left." October 24, 2017. https://www.people-press.org/wp-content/uploads/sites/4/2018/09/10-24-2017 -Typology-release.pdf.

Phillips, Amber. "'They're Rapists': President Trump's Campaign Launch Speech Two Years Later, Annotated." *Washington Post*, June 16, 2017. https://wapo.st/2rECXwr ?tid=ss_mail&utm_term=.b03374294f74.

Physicians for Social Responsibility. *Body Count: Casualty Figures after 10 Years of the "War on Terror."* Washington, DC: Physicians for Social Responsibility, 2015. https://www.psr.org/wp-content/uploads/2018/05/body-count.pdf.

Polletta, Francesca. *Freedom Is an Endless Meeting: Democracy in American Social Movements*. Chicago: University of Chicago Press, 2004.

Polletta, Francesca, and James Jasper. "Collective Identity and Social Movements." *Annual Review of Sociology* 27 (2001): 283–305.

Potts, Monica. "Barack Obama, Trayvon Martin, and the Presidency." *Vogue*, December 22, 2016. https://www.vogue.com/article/barack-obama-trayvon-martin -presidency.

Price, Marie, and Lisa Benton-Short. "Counting Immigrants in Cities across the Globe." Migration Policy Institute, January 1, 2007. https://www.migrationpolicy.org/ article/counting-immigrants-cities-across-globe.

Quinlan, Casey. "Four Black Lesbians Were Killed in One Week, and the Media Still Isn't Paying Attention." *ThinkProgress*, January 10, 2018. https://archive.think progress.org/black-lesbians-murdered-393925aa7af1/.

Radstone, Susannah. "The War of the Fathers: Trauma, Fantasy, and September 11." *Signs* 28 (2002): 457–459.

Rankine, Claudia. *Citizen: An American Lyric*. Minneapolis: Graywolf Press, 2014.

Ransby, Barbara. *Making All Black Lives Matter: Reimagining Freedom in the 21st Century*. Berkeley: University of California Press, 2018.

Ransom, Jan. "Amy Cooper Faces Charges after Calling Police on Black Bird-Watcher." *New York Times*, July 6, 2020. https://nyti.ms/38xp4ap.

Richardson, Heather Cox. "April 19, 2020." *Letters from an American* (blog), April 20, 2020. https://heathercoxrichardson.substack.com/p/april-19-2020.

Roberts, Gene, and Hank Klibanoff. *The Race Beat: The Press, the Civil Rights Struggle, and the Awakening of a Nation*. New York: Alfred A. Knopf, 2006.

Roediger, David. *The Wages of Whiteness: Race and the Making of the American Working Class*. Rev. ed. New York: Verso, 2007.

———. *Working toward Whiteness: How America's Immigrants Became White*. New York: Basic Books, 2005.

Rogers, Everett M., and Nancy Seidel. "Diffusion of News of the Terrorist Attacks of September 11, 2001." *Prometheus* 20 (2002): 209–219.

Rogers, Melvin. "Introduction." In John Dewey, *The Public and Its Problems: An Essay in Political Inquiry*, edited by Melvin Rogers, 1–30. Athens: Swallow Press, 2016.

Rosenberg, Eli, Nick Miroff, and Cleve R. Wootson, "Man Charged with Killing Mollie Tibbetts Is an Undocumented Immigrant, Authorities Say." *Washington Post*, August 21, 2018. https://wapo.st/2nSQ0ea?tid=ss_mail&utm_term=.2092e022a877.

Rosenberg, Gerald. *The Hollow Hope: Can Courts Bring about Social Change?* Chicago: University of Chicago Press, 1991.

Salvanto, Anthony, Jennifer De Pinto, Fred Backus, and Kabir Khanna. "Americans Prioritize Staying Home and Worry Restrictions Will Lift Too Fast—CBS News Poll." *CBS News*, April 23, 2020. https://www.cbsnews.com/news/americans-pri oritize-staying-home-and-worry-restrictions-will-lift-too-fast-cbs-news-poll/.

Santa Ana, Otto. *Brown Tide Rising: Metaphors of Latinos in Contemporary American Public Discourse*. Austin: University of Texas Press, 2002.

Satkunanandan, Shalini. *Extraordinary Responsibility: Politics beyond the Moral Calculus*. Cambridge: Cambridge University Press, 2015.

Saxton, Alexander. *The Rise and Fall of the White Republic: Class Politics and Mass Culture in Nineteenth-Century America*. New York: Verso, 2003.

Scheingold, Stuart. *The Politics of Rights: Lawyers, Public Policy, and Political Change*. 2nd ed. Ann Arbor: University of Michigan Press, 2004.

Schiff, Jade Larissa. *Burdens of Political Responsibility: Narrative and the Cultivation of Responsiveness*. Cambridge: Cambridge University Press, 2014.

Schmitt, Carl. *Political Theology: Four Chapters on the Concept of Sovereignty*. Chicago: University of Chicago Press, 2005.

Scott, Eugene. "4 Reasons Coronavirus Is Hitting Black Communities So Hard." *Washington Post*, April 10, 2020. https://www.washingtonpost.com/politics/2020/04/10/4-reasons-coronavirus-is-hitting-black-communities-so-hard/.

Seery, John. *Political Theory for Mortals: Shades of Justice, Images of Death*. Ithaca, NY: Cornell University Press, 1996.

Sen, Amartya. *The Idea of Justice*. Cambridge, MA: Harvard University Press, 2004.

"September 11 Terror Attacks Fast Facts." *CNN*, September 18, 2020. https://www
.cnn.com/2013/07/27/us/september-11-anniversary-fast-facts/index.html.

Shapiro, Emily, and Alex Perez. "Former Chicago Police Officer Jason Van Dyke Sentenced to 81 Months in Prison for Laquan McDonald Murder." *ABC News*, January 18, 2019. https://abcn.ws/2FKxT4C.

Shaw, Todd Cameron, Louis DeSipio, Dianne M. Pinderhughes, and Toni-Michelle Travis. *Uneven Roads: An Introduction to U.S. Racial and Ethnic Politics*. Thousand Oaks, CA: CQ Press, 2015.

Shepherd, William. "Eyewitness at the Triangle." *Remembering the 1911 Triangle Fire*. http://trianglefire.ilr.cornell.edu/primary/testimonials/ootss_WilliamShepherd
.html.

Shklar, Judith. *American Citizenship: The Quest for Inclusion*. Cambridge, MA: Harvard University Press, 1991.

Sidner, Sara. "The Rise of Black Lives Matter." *CNN*, December 28, 2015. https://edition
.cnn.com/2015/12/28/us/black-lives-matter-evolution/index.html.

Sielke, Sabine. "Why '9/11 Is [Not] Unique,' or Troping Trauma." *Amerikastudien/ American Studies* 55 (2010): 385–408.

Simon, Matt. "Why the Coronavirus Hit Italy So Hard." *Wired*, March 17, 2020. https://www.wired.com/story/why-the-coronavirus-hit-italy-so-hard/.

Smith, Patrick. "News Flash: Deadly Terrorism Existed before 9/11." *Salon*, November 11, 2010. https://www.salon.com/2010/11/11/airport_security_5/.

———. "Terminal Madness: What Is Airport Security?" *Ask the Pilot* (blog). https://askthepilot.com/essaysandstories/terminal-madness/ (accessed December 14, 2020).

Smith, Rogers. *Civic Ideals: Conflicting Visions of Citizenship in U.S. History*. New Haven, CT: Yale University Press, 1997.

———. "Identities, Interests, and the Future of Political Science." *Perspectives on Politics* 2 (2004): 301–312.

Soergel, Andrew. "How Much Can America Spend on the Coronavirus Pandemic?" *U.S. News and World Report*, April 21, 2020. https://www.usnews.com/news/economy/ articles/2020-04-21/how-much-can-america-spend-on-the-coronavirus-pandemic.

Sorkin, Amy Davidson. "Michael Brown's Body." *New Yorker*, August 19, 2014. https:// www.newyorker.com/news/amy-davidson/michael-browns-body.

Stafford, Kat, Meghan Hoyer, and Aaron Morrison. "Racial Toll of Virus Grows Even Starker as More Data Emerges." *AP*, April 18, 2020. https://apnews.com/8a3430
dd37e7c44290c7621f5af96d6b.

Stein, Leon. *The Triangle Fire*. Ithaca, NY: Cornell University Press, 2001.

Stevens, Jacqueline. *States without Nations: Citizenship for Mortals*. New York: Columbia University Press, 2010.

Stout, David. "Ashcroft Defends Crackdown on Terrorism before Senate." *New York Times*, December 6, 2001. https://www.nytimes.com/2001/12/06/politics/ash
croft-defends-crackdown-on-terrorism-before-senate.html.

Stow, Simon. *American Mourning: Tragedy, Democracy, Resilience*. Cambridge: Cambridge University Press, 2017.

———. "Portraits 9/11/01: The *New York Times* and the Pornography of Grief." In *Literature after 9/11*, edited by Jeanne Follansbee Quinn and Ann Keniston, 224–241. New York: Routledge, 2008.

Strolovitch, Dara. *Affirmative Advocacy: Race, Class, and Gender in Interest Group Politics*. Chicago: University of Chicago Press, 2007.

Sturken, Marita. *Tangled Memories: The Vietnam War, the AIDS Epidemic, and the Politics of Remembering*. Berkeley: University of California Press, 1997.

Sumner, William Graham. *What Social Classes Owe Each Other*. 1883. Reprint, Caldwell, ID: Caxton Press, 1983.

"Survey Finds U.S. Hurt by Till Case." *New York Times*, October 22, 1955, p. 40.

Tax, Meredith. *The Rising of the Women: Feminist Solidarity and Class Conflict, 1880–1917*. Champaign: University of Illinois Press, 2001.

Taylor, Keeanga-Yamahtta. *From #BlackLivesMatter to Black Liberation*. Chicago: Haymarket Books, 2016.

———, ed. *How We Get Free: Black Feminism and the Combahee River Collective*. Chicago: Haymarket Books, 2017.

Tibbetts, Rob. "From Mollie Tibbetts' Father: Don't Distort Her Death to Advance Racist Views." *Des Moines Register*, September 2, 2018. https://www.desmoinesregister.com/story/opinion/columnists/2018/09/01/mollie-tibbetts-father-common-decency-immigration-heartless-despicable-donald-trump-jr-column/1163131002.

Ticktin, Miriam. "A World without Innocence," *American Ethnologist* 44, no. 4 (2017): 577–590.

Till-Mobley, Mamie, and Christopher Benson. *Death of Innocence: The Story of the Hate Crime That Changed America*. Newark, NJ: One World/Ballantine Books, 2003.

"Timeline of Events in Shooting of Michael Brown in Ferguson." *AP*, August 8, 2019. https://apnews.com/9aa32033692547699a3b61da8fd1fc62.

"Timeline of Events in Trayvon Martin case." *CNN*, April 23, 2012. https://www.cnn.com/2012/04/23/justice/florida-zimmerman-timeline/index.html.

Truc, Gérôme. "Seeing Double: 9/11 and Its Mirror Image." *Books and Ideas*, September 16, 2010. https://booksandideas.net/%20spip.php?page=print&id_article=1188.

Tushnet, Mark. *The NAACP's Legal Strategy against Segregated Education, 1925–1950*. Chapel Hill: University of North Carolina Press, 2004.

Tyson, Timothy B. *The Blood of Emmett Till*. New York: Simon and Schuster, 2017.

The Untold Story of Emmett Louis Till. Directed by Keith Beauchamp. New York: ThinkFilm, 2005. DVD.

U.S. Census Bureau. "Table 33: New York—Race and Hispanic Origin for Selected Large Cities and Other Places: Earliest Census to 1990." In "Historical Census Statistics on Population Totals by Race, 1790 to 1990, and by Hispanic Origin, 1790 to 1990, for Large Cities and Other Urban Places in the United States," by Campbell Gibson and Kay Jung, U.S. Census Bureau Working Paper no. 76, February 2005. https://www.census.gov/content/dam/Census/library/working-papers/2005/demo/POP-twps0076.pdf.

Valdez, Inés, Mat Coleman, and Amna Akbar. "Law, Police Violence, and Race: Grounding and Embodying the State of Exception." *Theory and Event* 23, no. 4 (2020): 902–934.

Vázquez-Arroyo, Antonio. *Political Responsibility: Responding to Predicaments of Power*. New York: Columbia University Press, 2016.

Verdery, Katherine. *The Political Lives of Dead Bodies: Reburial and Postsocialist Change*. New York: Columbia University Press, 1999.

Verovšek, Peter. "Collective Memory, Politics, and the Influence of the Past: The Politics of Memory as a Research Paradigm." *Politics, Groups, and Identities* 4, no. 3 (2016): 529–543.

Vogel, Gretchen. "Antibody Surveys Suggesting Vast Undercount of Coronavirus Infections May Be Unreliable." *Science*, April 21, 2020. https://www.sciencemag.org/news/2020/04/antibody-surveys-suggesting-vast-undercount-coronavirus-infections-may-be-unreliable.

Volack, Jason, Tara Fowler, and Emily Shapiro. "Cleveland Police Officer Who Killed Tamir Rice Fired after Rule Violations." *ABC News*, May 30, 2017. http://abcn.ws/2qwxQCN.

Volpp, Leti. "Citizen and Terrorist." In *September 11 in History: A Watershed Moment?*, edited by Mary Dudziak, 147–162. Durham, NC: Duke University Press, 2003.

Von Drehle, David. *Triangle: The Fire That Changed America*. New York: Atlantic Monthly Press, 2003.

Wacquant, Loïc. "From Slavery to Mass Incarceration." *New Left Review* 13 (2002): 41–60.

Wadman, Meredith, Jennifer Couzin-Frankel, Jocelyn Kaiser, and Catherine Matacic. "How Does Coronavirus Kill? Clinicians Trace a Ferocious Rampage through the Body, from Brain to Toes." *Science*, April 17, 2020. https://www.sciencemag.org/news/2020/04/how-does-coronavirus-kill-clinicians-trace-ferocious-rampage-through-body-brain-toes.

Waldstein, David. "C.D.C. Releases Early Demographic Snapshot of Worst Coronavirus Cases." *New York Times*, April 8, 2020. https://nyti.ms/2xVMXdD.

Walgrave, Stefaan, and Dieter Rucht. "Introduction." In *The World Says No to War: Demonstrations against the War in Iraq*, edited by Stefaan Walgrave and Dieter Rucht, xiii–xxvi. Minneapolis: University of Minnesota Press, 2010.

Walzer, Michael. *Spheres of Justice*. New York: Basic Books, 1983.

Welke, Barbara Young. *Law and Borders of Belonging in the Long Nineteenth-Century United States*. Cambridge: Cambridge University Press, 2008.

Wells, Ida B. *Southern Horrors and Other Writings: The Anti-lynching Campaign of Ida B. Wells, 1892–1900*. Edited by Jacqueline Jones Royster. New York: Bedford/St. Martin's Press, 1997.

"What Happened in Ferguson?" *New York Times*, August 10, 2015. https://www.nytimes.com/interactive/2014/08/13/us/ferguson-missouri-town-under-siege-after-police-shooting.html.

Whitaker, Brian. "The Definition of Terrorism." In *History and September 11*, edited by Joanne Meyerowitz, 237–240. Philadelphia: Temple University Press, 2003.

Whitaker, Hugh Stephen. "A Case Study in Southern Justice: The Emmett Till Case." Master's thesis, Florida State University, 1963.

Whitfield, Stephen. *A Death in the Delta: The Story of Emmett Till*. New York: Free Press, 1988.

Wick, Julia. "This Is How Los Angeles Buries Their Unclaimed Dead." *LAist*, December 1, 2016. http://laist.com/2016/12/01/unclaimed.php.

Williams, Patricia. *The Alchemy of Race and Rights: Diary of a Law Professor*. Cambridge, MA: Harvard University Press, 1991.

Winter, Jay. *Sites of Memory, Sites of Mourning*. Cambridge: Cambridge University Press, 2014.

Witte, Griff. "As Protesters Swarm State Capitols, Much of the Coronavirus Backlash Is Coming from Within." *Washington Post*, April 23, 2020. https://www.washington post.com/national/as-protesters-swarm-state-capitols-much-of-the-coronavirus -backlash-is-coming-from-within/2020/04/22/e4d7b1ee-84c8-11ea-a3eb-e9fc9316 0703_story.html.

Wolin, Sheldon. *Politics and Vision: Continuity and Innovation in Western Political Thought*. Expanded ed. Princeton, NJ: Princeton University Press, 2006.

"Women Socialists Rebuff Suffragists." *New York Times*, December 20, 1909, p. 5.

Wong, Kam C. "The USA Patriot Act: A Policy of Alienation." *Michigan Journal of Race and Law* 12 (2006): 161–202.

Woodward, Bob. *Bush at War*. New York: Simon and Schuster, 2002.

Wright, Lawrence. *The Looming Tower: Al-Qaeda and the Road to 9/11*. New York: Vintage Books, 2006.

Wu, Jin, Allison McCann, Josh Katz, and Elian Peltier. "28,000 Missing Deaths: Tracking the True Toll of the Coronavirus Crisis." *New York Times*, April 22, 2020. https://nyti.ms/34QerxA.

Young, Iris Marion. "Communication and the Other: Beyond Deliberative Democracy." In *Intersecting Voices: Dilemmas of Gender, Political Philosophy, and Policy*, 60–74. Princeton, NJ: Princeton University Press, 1997.

———. *Responsibility for Justice*. New York: Oxford University Press, 2011.

Young, Marilyn B. "Ground Zero: Enduring War." In *September 11 in History: A Watershed Moment?*, edited by Mary Dudziak, 10–34. Durham, NC: Duke University Press, 2003.

Yuan, Jada. "Burials on Hart Island, Where New York's Unclaimed Lie in Mass Graves, Have Risen Fivefold." *Washington Post*, April 16, 2020. https://www.washing tonpost.com/national/hart-island-mass-graves-coronavirus-new-york/2020/04/16/ a0c413ee-7f5f-11ea-a3ee-13e1ae0a3571_story.html.

Zehfuss, Maja. "Forget September 11." *Third World Quarterly* 24 (2003): 513–528.

Zeskin, Leonard. "A Nation Dispossessed: The Tea Party Movement and Race." *Critical Sociology* 38, no. 4 (2012): 495–509.

Index

Abdul-Jabbar, Kareem, 86, 189n76
Abu Ghraib, 126
Abu-Lughod, Janet, 184n88
Abu-Lughod, Lila, 125, 184n88
accountability, individual versus civiliza-
tional, 124
Addams, Jane, 60, 73, 153
"Address at Seneca Falls" (Stanton), 28–29
Aeschylus, 94–95, 106
affective economies, 80
Afghanistan, xiii, 94, 96, 111, 118–120,
124–126
AFL (American Federation of Labor), 52,
180n34
African Americans blamed for poverty, 128
After Disaster (Birkland), 24
Agamben, Giorgio, 198–199n120
Agathangelou, Anna, 125
agency, 32, 34, 40, 60–64, 109, 174n31
agonistic democratic politics, 22, 155,
172n17, 173–174n31
Ahmed, Sara, 80–81, 99
AIDS epidemic, 43
AJC (American Jewish Committee), 88
Albright, Madeleine, 96
ALEC (American Legislative Exchange
Council), 131

Alexander, Jeffrey, 23, 174n37
Ali, Muhammad, 86, 189n76
Allen, Danielle, 14, 143
ALM ("All Lives Matter"), 2, 148, 155,
204n73; analysis of tweets, 139–140;
and color blindness, 128–129, 135–140,
145; and COVID-19 pandemic, 164–165;
"Open the Economy" connection to,
164; undemocratic nature of, 153–155;
and willful racial innocence, 128, 135,
137–140, 145
al-Qaeda, 97, 117–118, 122, 197n92
Al-Zawahiri, Ayman, 198n95
"america," 146
American exceptionalism, 128
American Federation of Labor (AFL), 52,
180n34
American identity: American values, 49,
112–113, 120, 197n75; and citizenship,
26–27; and denial of responsibility, 136;
as fundamentalist, 126; and idea that
terrorism happens elsewhere, 101; post–
Cold War, 95–96; "real" Americans, 7,
28, 154, 157; and response to COVID-19
pandemic, 161–165; and September 11
sovereign anxiety, 124–125
American Jewish Committee (AJC), 88

toward NRA, 131; use of chokeholds by, 134; white trust of, 138; and Zimmerman community watch, 132. *See also* Brown, Michael (Mike)

#PoliceLivesMatter, 139. *See also* ALM

"political," defining, 21

political agency, 37, 40, 72, 87, 91, 173–174n31

political identity: borders of, 27, 36; as fluid, contested, and powerful, 30; formation of, 26, 34, 49, 68; moments of mourning and, 30, 33; and responsibility, 3, 24

Politically Incorrect (TV show), 114

political mourning, ix, 17; and acknowledging responsibility, 31; boundaries around, 11, 13; Dewey on, 19–21, 153; Emmett Till and, 91; as exposing everyday violence, 152; for good or bad ends, 95, 155–156; as leading to civil rights legislation, 71; as leading to worker protections, 49, 51; limitations of, 91, 153–157; making mourning political, 21–26, 95; mobilizing, 150; in politics, 42–43; power of, 91; processual theory of, 6–8, 33–42, 130, 151; Rogers Smith on, 33; theory and components of, 6–10, 36–39; Triangle Fire and, 65, 68; unpredictability of, 150. *See also* mourning

Political Process and the Development of Black Insurgency, 1930–1970 (McAdam), 29

political purity, calls for, 126

political responsibility, 30–31, 33, 38–39, 152

political science, 23–24, 86

Political Theology (Schmitt), 117

Political Theory for Mortals (Seery), 9

politics: end of, 126; of lamentation, 12, 21, 173–174n31; of law, 152; paradox of, 158–159; of respectability, 145

Politics and Vision (Wolin), 11

"politics beyond the polity," 120, 122

politics of memory, 176–177n74, 177n75; and memorials, 22–23; Peter Verovšek on, 12–13, 40, 151; and political mourning, 35

Polletta, Francesca, 34, 177n75

"Portraits of Grief" (*New York Times*), 107

Potts, Monica, 131

power of sudden events, 30

Powhatan, 28

Precarious Life (Butler), 118, 121, 158, 172n15, 181n57

"predicaments of power," 32

presentation, problem of, 19–20, 140–141

processual theory of political mourning, 6–8, 33–42, 151

Progressive Era New York, 55, 60, 64, 69

property and people's rights, 62–63

psychoanalytic perspective: and democratic mourning, 25; and mass trauma, 123; object relations theory, 175n47; and political identity, 26; and politics, 14, 21; subject formation, 13

The Public and Its Problems (Dewey), 19, 36, 60, 140

public response: to Emmett Till open-casket viewing, 70, 85–86, 104, 188n60; grief, 29, 42; and shifting public-private boundary, 63–64, 69; to Triangle Fire, 49, 56–60

publics, 19–20, 142–144, 152. *See also* Dewey, John

public versus private matters, 56

Qutb, Sayyid, 118, 198n95

Rabb, Maxwell, 89

Rabin, Yitzhak, 35

race: as category of exclusion, 27; construction of, 97; critical race studies, 97; institutionalized stories about, 28; partisanship in racial attitudes, 137; as political identity, 27; and religion, 97; religion as marker of, 98

Race and the Politics of Solidarity (Hooker), 143

racial coalitions, 84, 87

The Racial Contract (Mills), 132, 136

racial hierarchy, 51–52, 66–68, 179n13

racial innocence, willful, 128, 135, 137–140, 145

racialization process, 52, 69, 97–99, 123–124

racism, regional versions of, 85, 91–92

Rana, Junaid, 97

Rana Plaza fire (Bangladesh), 157

Rankine, Claudia, 148

Ransby, Barbara, 129–130, 135, 140, 144–145, 203–204n72

"real" Americans, 7, 28, 154, 157

Winant, Howard, 97, 98
Wolin, Sheldon, 6–7, 11
women: assumptions regarding Taliban
    and, 124–125; attacks on Muslim,
    124–125; birdwatcher reported by white
    woman, 201–202n30; leadership by,
    124–125; murders of, by partners, 157; as
    reformers, 53, 179n25; suffrage move-
    ment, 63; as workers, 51, 56, 62. *See also*
    Triangle Shirtwaist Factory
Woodward, Bob, 112
workplace, role of government in, 63–65,
    151; Anna Shaw on, 62; and FIC man-
    date, 63; from good to bad story of, 49,
    177–178n1; and laissez-faire policies,
    49–50, 61; and protections by race and

ethnicity, 43, 67, 69; and Triangle Fire,
    48–49, 56, 59, 61, 63, 65–67
Wright, Lawrence, 117–119
Wright, Moses, 76–78, 82–83, 187n43
WTC (World Trade Center) 1993 bombing,
    100–102, 104, 115. *See also* September 11
    attacks
WTUL (Women's Trade Union League), 47,
    52–55, 61, 67, 179n22

Yemen suicide bombing, 100
Young, Iris Marion, 31–32, 178n3

Zehfuss, Maja, 121
zero-sum thinking, 143–144
Zimmerman, George, 1, 130–132

Heather Pool is an Associate Professor of Politics and Public Affairs and the Director of the Philosophy/Politics/Economics Program at Denison University in Ohio.